D1559681

The American Father

Biocultural and Developmental Aspects

The Plenum Series in Adult Development and Aging

SERIES EDITOR:
Jack Demick, *Suffolk University, Boston, Massachusetts*

ADULT DEVELOPMENT, THERAPY, AND CULTURE
A Postmodern Synthesis
Gerald D. Young

THE AMERICAN FATHER
Biocultural and Developmental Aspects
Wade C. Mackey

HANDBOOK OF PAIN AND AGING
Edited by David I. Mostofsky and Jacob Lomranz

PSYCHOLOGICAL TREATMENT OF OLDER ADULTS
An Introductory Text
Edited by Michel Hersen and Vincent B. Van Hasselt

The American Father
Biocultural and Developmental Aspects

Wade C. Mackey

Southeastern Community College
West Burlington, Iowa

Plenum Press • New York and London

Library of Congress Cataloging-in-Publication Data

Mackey, Wade C.
    The American father : biocultural and developmental aspects / Wade
C. Mackey.
        p.   cm. -- (The Plenum series in adult development and aging)
    Includes bibliographical references and index.
    ISBN 0-306-45337-1
    1. Fathers--United States. 2. Father and child--United States.
I. Title. II. Series.
HQ756.M22 1996
306.874'2'0973--dc20   96-35570
                                                                 CIP

ISBN 0-306-45337-1

© 1996 Plenum Press, New York
A Division of Plenum Publishing Corporation
233 Spring Street, New York, N. Y. 10013

10 9 8 7 6 5 4 3 2 1

Printed in the United States of America

To Mom and Pop, whose patience with the author
could have been highly instructive to Job

Foreword

In *The American Father,* Wade C. Mackey documents a wealth of information demonstrating the vast benefits to society when its children are raised in families with fathers. The biopsychosocial approach Mackey employs is consistent with the current treatment of topics in human development. This approach—which is grounded in a variety of diverse sources—assumes that we understand little about people when we study them a bit at a time; rather, the fullness of the individual requires a fullness of examination. For example, in the cases of fathers, we note that humans do not reproduce alone; after all, we are not an asexual species. No, human reproduction and its sequelae are social, just as clearly as they are biological, and involve the whole panoply of psychic function (motivation, sociability, intelligence, and the like).

The evidence marshaled by Mackey indicates strongly that individuals and societies have an essential requirement for something more than mothering; they also need fathering.

Much of the discourse and publication on fathers during the past several decades has been posited on a "more is better" model of male parenting in which it is seldom stated who it is better for—the father, the child, the mother, the couple, or the family. Further, much of this discussion infers that fathers are merely "Mr. Moms"; yet this is not so. Fathers are not just *another* parent; they are the *other* parent. As is widely observed, fathers are seldom involved in children's routine body-focused care, such as feeding and bathing. This does not mean, however, they are not involved in their material well-being; children also need food, shelter, and protection to survive and prosper. In a parallel vein, fathers have been shown to have a distinct style of relating socio-affectively with children—a more physical, boisterous way, a way distinguished from the more gentle, quiet nurturance of mothers. The father–child relationship—different as it is—no doubt provides the child with experiences which, in combination with those provided by the mother, contribute importantly to the child's development.

The literature on mothering is replete with discussion of the *good-enough mother* (e.g., Winnicott, 1965), seeking to explicate those essential features of maternal behavior and characteristics that are essential for appropriate, if not optimal, human development. The concept of the *good-enough father* has received little, if any, explicit examination. After many years of reading, research, and collegial conversation, it appears to me that the good-enough father is *ceteris paribus,* one who is there; the good-enough father is the father who is present. The usual cautions apply, of course; mere presence is not likely to compensate for brutality or other pathological manifestations. Similarly, presence is assumed to co-occur with providing for material well-being and security. Even a superficial examination of socioeconomic conditions indicates that one of the very best predictors of poverty is being a single mother; also, destitute people are apt to live in less secure areas.

Mackey has explored the implications of fatherless families and public policies that sustain or encourage their widespread occurrence, cogently referring to the "tragedy of the commons" in his discussion. Under the vast majority of possible conditions, all involved—fathers, mothers, children, families, and societies—benefit from a child-rearing system that strongly encourages the inclusion of the father and harshly sanctions his absence. The benefits are psychological, social, material, and economic, both in the short and long term. The long-term costs for the alternative are incalculable, yet ominous.

WILLIAM T. BAILEY

Charleston, Illinois

Preface

Fathers in America is the topic of this book. Of all the subjects a behavioral scientist could study, I can think of none more interesting than fathers. They are infinitely fascinating.

Let me paint two vignettes to help introduce the main text.

Vignette 1: At an airport, a father and his young daughter, no more than two years old, were awaiting their flight's boarding call. The girl had fallen asleep on the man's lap. Like melted butter, she had fitted herself to the contours of his body. She was soundly sleeping and looked infinitely relaxed. He, too, was asleep, with his head to one side and his left hand on the small of her back. He awoke, looked down at his sleeping child, patted her back twice, gave her a little grin, and went back to sleep.

Vignette 2: A father and his young son—a Bart Simpson look-alike between the ages of three and five—were heading from the parking lot to the supermarket. For as long as I watched them, the man never looked directly at the boy. But about every 10 steps or so, the man's hand reached out to touch the boy's shoulder, perhaps to guide the child's path away from parking lot traffic. At each touch, the man softly verbalized something to his son. In the store, the boy maneuvered himself in front of the man and held up his arms. Again without direct visual contact, the father swiftly swooped the child with a giggle high into the air and gently deposited him in the shopping cart. Apparently I had just witnessed a "shipping" ritual that was performed habitually without the need for extensive communication.

Both of the scenes seem very mundane and commonplace. What could be more natural? Fathers being fathers and doing "fathering."

But the trajectory of the men of *Homo sapiens* becoming social fathers in general and how contemporary American culture treats these men in particular are anything but trivial or middling. Why are the men with their children at all? What do they get out of their efforts? What is the trade-off for their expenditure of time, energy, and resources? What

ix

incentives pull them to fathering? What disincentives push them in the opposite direction?

Our evolutionary path to social fatherhood is an intriguing story unto itself. In addition, the American father is receiving more focused analysis and rhetoric than probably any time in recorded history. For a behavioral scientist interested in fathers, this is a grand time to be alive. Large numbers of social "experiments" are being conducted both in the United States and abroad on what fathers should be and how to make sure they end up that prescribed way. Given that the various paternal expectations are often antithetical to one other, some formulas will be more successful than others. The results will not be known for many years, but I hope it will not take decades. The trick for the scientist is to be around for the results.

It is my aim in this book to share with the reader a perspective on fathers that may help analyze the sure-to-come onslaught of claims and testimonies on "dads and what to do with them." The book is arranged according to the following topics.

- The new phenomenon of American children being systematically separated from their fathers (Chapter 1).
- Why American men would want to become a social father (Chapter 2).
- How fathering behaviors are generated and how they may be studied (Chapters 3–5).
- Public images of the American father until the 1970s (Chapter 6) and from the 1970s to the 1990s (Chapter 7).
- American fathers in the current and turbulent U.S. megatribe (Chapters 8, 10).
  - American fathers compared to other non-American fathers (Chapter 9).
- American fathers in the context of American mothers (Chapter 11).
- What might be expected of American fathers in the near and not-so-near future (Chapters 12 to 14).

The goal of the book is to make three points: First, that there is an adult male-to-child bond that is independent of the man-to-woman bond and the adult female-to-child bond. That is, fathering is an inherent facet of the male's developmental track. The notion is offered that Margaret Mead was simply wrong: "Fathers are *not* a social invention" or, as some would have it, "a social accident." Fathering for men is viewed as a behavioral imperative and is as biocultural as is language acquisition or interpreting facial expressions or falling in love. Second, while the "bio" part of the biocultural phenomenon known as fathering creates themes of behavioral tendencies, the "cultural" part creates variations around those themes. Therefore, if we can understand both the bio and cultural parts of paternalistic behavior, then we can understand fathering. Third, the United States is an interesting place in which to live, to observe, and—on a good day—to analyze. We are an irascible, hurly-burly, restive collection of subtribes that represent a megatribe of some potency. Many of these subtribes collide with each other to validate the "proper" role of a proper father. As we shall see later, any common ground that simultaneously allows for both agreement and comity among these factions is scarce and slippery. If the reader leaves the book with new thoughts or questions, or new perspectives on U.S. dads, then the author will consider the book a rousing success and will raise a pint to scholarship. If the reader leaves the book reinforcing only his or her prior opinions, then I shall resort to the noble, honorable recourse and blame the editor.

But first we need to determine the demographics of U.S. fathering. And the most salient point to current trends is that U.S. fathers are being systematically abraded from their role of father. Chapter 1 delineates what is happening to fathers and attempts to grasp why they are becoming separated from their children.

Acknowledgments

The following persons and institutions are gratefully acknowledged and thanked for their input. The National Science Foundation and the Harry Frank Guggenheim Foundation provided funding. Lionel Tiger is an explorer who developed pathways which, once provided, allowed even the greenest of navigators fruitful passage. Forest Morrisett and Shari Smith salvaged mangled prose and made it fit enough for human consumption. Plenum's senior editor Eliot Werner made an idea with no home reside comfortably upon ivory leaves.

Contents

CHAPTER 1

The Abrading of the American Father

In the long course of my legal profession, I have met with several sons who had, in circumstance of difficulty, abandoned their fathers; but never did I meet with a father that would not cheerfully part with his last shilling to save or bless his son.

DAVID DAGGERT

It is a wise father that knows his own child.

WILLIAM SHAKESPEARE

A necessary, if not sufficient, precondition for successful fathering to occur, by virtually any definition, is the sheer physical ongoing presence of the man with his child. A number of social vectors have recently occurred in the United States that militate against the joint association between the father and his child. If a man is systematically precluded from being with his child or children, then it is hard to imagine that the man will become an effective social father. He has to *be* there.

To develop a context for these vectors, let's examine cross-cultural trends. The first of these is marriage. Marriage is a cross-cultural universal (Brown, 1991; Levinson & Malone, 1980; Stephens, 1963; Van den Berghe, 1979). A general consensus on the universality of marriage is its function to legitimize the wife's children. As Hartley (1975) wrote: "With hundreds of societies in the world having varied beliefs and customs, different environmental problems, and differences in group size and organization, the principle of legitimacy comes as near as any social rule to being truly universal." One of the founding graybeard fathers of anthropology, Bronislaw Malinowski (1927), believed that "the principle of legitimacy" was one of the pillars upon which the organization of the family was built. He stated that "the most important moral and legal rule concerning the physiological side of kinship is that no child should be brought into the world without a man—and one man at that—assuming the role of sociological father, that is, guardian and protector, the male link between the child and the rest of the community." That is, once legitimacy between a man—now a father— and a child has been publicly acknowledged, then that man is strongly pressured to provision and protect *his* children. The children become *his* children by a ritual of marriage (Stephens, 1963; Van den Berghe, 1979); that is, marriage is *for* children. McCary (1975, p. 289) framed the case well in noting that having children has traditionally been regarded as "the fulfillment of a marriage, if not the primary reason for marriage." The marriage aligns the child, as well as the mother, with a particular man—now a father—who has particular responsibility to ensure that the child, as well as the mother, has adequate provisions and protection. Provisioning or access to resources that would be available to the mother–child dyad is not a trivial matter and the promise of resources is an important consideration in a prospective groom being accepted as a husband. If the promise of resources is not forthcoming after a marriage, then a divorce is often a consequence of the unfulfilled expectations. This dynamic is widely in evidence from such diverse places as Amazonia (Chagnon, 1977; Stearman, 1989), Tibet (Ekvall, 1968), among the Australian Aborigines (Hart & Pilling, 1960), and the Dani of New Guinea (Heider, 1979), India (Maclachlan, 1983), Turkey (Pierce, 1964), Japan (Norbeck, 1976), and China (Chance, 1984).

In a small minority of cultures (about 12%), it is the mother's brother, the *avunculus,* who is the male figure which is, the proximate man to his sister's children (Schlegel, 1972). Nonetheless, the sister is expected to be married and the child is expected to be "legitimate."

Although a majority of cultures has a marriage system that allows for polygyny (one man, plural wives), relatively few men can afford additional wives (back to resources, again). Thus the majority of men within a polygynous society are monogamous (one wife, one husband). Across the globe, the trend toward socially imposed de jure monogamy for all men seems to be replacing a de facto monogamy for most men. In addition, while the percentage of known *cultures* which mandate monogamy is low (about 15%), in terms of numbers or percentage of people in the contemporary world, socially imposed monogamy is a clear winner. Because of the low incidence of cultures—less than 1%— which allow polyandry (one wife and plural husbands), a woman who is married is undoubtedly in a monogamous union.

The United States is a modern industrialized society, and is no exception to the catholic trend, and has a de jure monogamous marriage system. And until the 1960s, out-of-wedlock (also known as single-parent) births were a low proportion of official statistics (e.g., 5% in the 1950s). When the 1960s began, as has been voluminously reported in both the civilian and professional literature, the number and proportion of single-parent births versus biparent births has been consistently increasing so that by 1991 over a quarter of all births (30%) were to unwed mothers (U.S. Bureau of the Census, 1994).

So most families across our planet have one husband and one wife as a core. A woman becomes a mother by having her husband's children, and the husband thereby becomes a "social father." As soon as the status of social father is achieved, the father is strongly prescribed to provide singular attention to his children. Failure to nurture his children with goods and services is a source of informal social pressure against the man. Societywide expectations regarding children he has sired but not "legitimized" do not usually include a similar level of nurturance from the man when compared to his legitimate children.

But, as was just mentioned, the United States has experienced a rapid increase in out-of-wedlock births. The United States is bucking a trend both in terms of other countries and its own history. The question then becomes: What has happened to result in such a reversal? I proffer that part of the answer to the question resides in a very human tendency: If people have the chance to maximize their own freedom, they will avail themselves of that opportunity. This observation that people will enhance their own freedom if given the opportunity is not a new revelation and serves to buttress the notion that *a simple reminder can trump inspiration.* I suggest that, relative to single-parent births, this human tendency to embrace more freedom takes two forms: (1) freedom to control one's reproductive history and (2) freedom to maximize autonomy. First, let's look at the freedom to control one's reproductive history.

FATHERS' OR WOMEN'S EQUITY: A MATTER OF CHOICE?

Both within the United States and across some other countries, there has been a recent tendency toward increased and unfettered access by women to economic and political power structures, that is, increased freedom for women. This tendency has been viewed as an appropriate and positive event. Within the United States, there has also been a tendency toward increased numbers and percentages of single-parent births. This tendency has been viewed as an inappropriate and negative event. While the two social values—maximal individual freedom and the presence of a social father—may have adherents and neither may have many detractors, a problem emerges in which a priority must be determined or adjustments made in the structuring of the society. It is, at least, arguable that the two phenomena, at base, are incompatible. That is, a systematic increase in the level of one is associated with a systematic decrease in the level of the other. Given appropriate data, this putative negative association between legitimacy and freedom can be tested across cultures. Such a test is presented below.

METHOD

Definitions

Women's Freedom and Women's Equity. A working definition of individual freedom would include some reference to money and to political freedom. Women's relative access to economic and political power can be indexed by their increased participation in education beyond high school and secondary education and by their success in reaching parity with men in income.

Presence of a Social Father. A woman can give birth with or without the existence of a social father. Thus the opportunity of children being born with or without a social father is a variable that can range from 0% to 100.0%

PROCEDURE

Data from the United Nations (International Labour Office, 1986 to 1991; Smith-Morris, 1990; United Nations, 1985)[1] were surveyed to locate those countries which had information regarding the three social indixes germane to this argument: (1) Percentage of women, rather than men, who were enrolled in institutions of higher education, that is, enrolled at a tertiary level, (2) the ratio of women's wages or earnings (compared with men's),[2] and (3) the percentage of births to unmarried women.[3]

---

[1]The data presented are from the most recent year available at that time. Nearly all of the figures were from the 1975–1985 interval.

[2]Note that these incomes were from earnings and wages only. Income from investments, stocks, bonds, etc. were not included in the analysis.

[3]The definition by the United Nations for legitimacy includes the following: "Legitimate refers to persons born of parents who were married at the time of birth in accordance with the laws of the country or area. Illegitimate refers to children of parents who according to national law were not married at the time of birth, regardless of whether these children have been recognized or legitimized after birth" (United Nations, 1992, p. 104).

RESULTS

There were 49 countries located that had both the percentage of women in tertiary education *and* the percentage of births to unwed mothers (see Table 1.1). The relationship between the two indices was

Table 1.1. Values for the Three Social Indices

Country	Percentage of single-parent births	Percentage of female tertiary students	Ratio of female to male earnings
Australia	15.5	49	1.00
Belgium	5.7	47	.62
Denmark	43.0	50	.84
France	19.6	51	.81
West Germany	9.4	41	.73
Iceland	47.1	54	.90
Japan	1.0	37	.52
Luxembourg	8.7	34	.66
Netherlands	8.7	34	.52
New Zealand	24.9	48	.77
Switzerland	5.6	32	.67
United Kingdom	19.2	46	.695
United States	*21.0*	*53*	*.68*
Czechoslovakia	6.8	42	.68
Hong Kong	5.5	35	.77
South Korea	0.5	35	.48
Sri Lanka	5.4	41	.71
Cyprus	0.4	49	.585
Egypt	—	33	.68
Kenya	—	26	.85
Costa Rica	37.2	—	.72
Paraguay	33.3	—	.88
Austria	22.4	46	—
Finland	16.4	50	—
Greece	1.8	49	—
Ireland	7.8	43	—
Italy	4.4	47	—
Norway	25.8	51	—
Portugal	12.4	54	—
Spain	3.9	50	—
Sweden	46.4	53	—
Bulgaria	11.4	56	—
East Germany	33.8	52	—
Hungary	9.2	53	—
Poland	5.0	56	—
Brunei	0.4	51	—
Fiji	17.3	35	—
Philippines	6.1	54	—

(*continued*)

Table 1.1. (*Continued*)

Country	Percentage of single-parent births	Percentage of female tertiary students	Ratio of female to male earnings
Mauritius	26.0	36	—
Israel	1.0	46	—
Malta	1.2	36	—
Tunisia	0.3	37	—
Argentina	32.5	53	—
Bahamas	62.1	70	—
Barbados	73.1	49	—
Bermuda	31.2	51	—
Chile	31.8	44	—
El Salvador	67.4	43	—
Mexico	27.5	36	—
Panama	71.9	58	—
Peru	42.6	35	—
Puerto Rico	26.5	60	—
Venezuela	53.9	47	—

Source: Smith-Morris, 1990; United Nations, 1985–1992.

significant ($r_p = .367$; $p < .05$; two-tailed); as the proportion of women in tertiary education increased so did the proportion of out-of-wedlock births. Approximately 13% ($.367^2 = .134 = 13\%$) of the variability in single-parent births can be attributed to changes in the level of female participation in tertiary education (see Table 1.2).

Table 1.2. Relationships among the Three Social Indices

Compared indices			r_p	R
Percent of births out-of-wedlock N = 49 Mean = 20.84% s = 20.22%	vs.	Percent of female tertiary students N = 49 Mean = 46.6% s = 8.22%	.367[a]	
Percent of births out-of-wedlock N = 20 Mean = 15.91% s = 14.43%	vs.	Ratio of female to earnings N = 20 Mean = .724% s = .125%	.649[b]	
Percent of births out-of-wedlock N = 18 Mean = 13.76% s = 13.55%	vs. Percent of female tertiary students N = 18 Mean = 43.39% s = 7.41%	& Ratio of female to male earnings N = 18 Mean = .716% s = .127%		.758[c]

[a]$p < .05$, two-tailed.
[b]$p < .01$, two-tailed.
[c]$p < .01$.

There were 20 countries in which both the ratio of women's income to that of men *and* the percentage of out-of-wedlock births were available. The relationship between the two indices was significant (r_p = .649; p < .01; two-tailed): as the ratio approached unity the proportion of single-parent births increased. Nearly 42% ($.649^2$ = .421 = 42%) of the differences in the level of out-of-wedlock births can be attributed to changes in the income ratio (see Table 1.2).

There were 18 countries that reported all three indices. The relationship between the percentage of single-parent births and the two indices of women's equity (proportion of women in tertiary institutions and the ratio of women's earnings to that of men's) acting in tandem was significant (R = .758, F(2,15) = 8.61; p < .01). Over half $.758^2$ = .575 = 57.5%) of the variance in single parents can be attributed to changes in the other two variables.

DISCUSSION

At first blush, as well as at second blush, there seems to be a collision of the two positively valued items: individual freedom and the optimum development of children. The one dimension operates at loggerheads with the other. However, before the results are further discussed, a few caveats or qualifications need to be addressed.

1. Of the nearly 180 countries that were available to be surveyed, only 18 had all three indices reported to the satisfaction of the United Nations. The degree of representativeness that these 18 countries—the sample—represent in terms of the other countries is, of course, unknown.

2. The countries surveyed by the United Nations and analyzed in this chapter are, by any definition, a heterogeneous collection. Therefore, the relative degree of efficiency in data gathering and organizing, hence accuracy of the data, is undoubtedly not homogeneous. However, because neither the United Nations nor the individual countries were aware of the hypotheses being tested (a de facto double-blind procedure) any slippage or randomization of the data's accuracy, across countries, would tend to reduce the absolute value of the computed statistics rather than to be neutral or to inflate the figures, (see Bateson, 1972, pp. 3–8 for a discussion on this dynamic).

3. A woman in one index, for example, single mother, may or may not be included in one or more of the other two indexes. Accordingly, the unit of analysis is the society or country rather than

the individuals, each person taken one at a time, within the countries.
4. Lastly, the definition of equity via education and earnings is somewhat arbitrary. Other barometers of freedom and liberty might be successfully used by alternate authors.

With these precautions as a background an interesting result emerged in the foreground. Across the sample of countries, as the access for women to economic and political domains increased, the preclusion of men from the role of social father also increased. This association was robust for the behavioral sciences. To the extent that social fathers optimize the normative and healthy development of their children, the increased access for women to more freedom and autonomy is aligned with deficits for children. Here is a situation worthy of Solomon, if not Hardin (1968). It should be noted that the correlations give no hint as to the relative contribution in shifting the indices back and forth, to and fro, made by volition versus happenstance, or by men versus women, or by the increase of incentives versus the decrease of disincentives, or the existence of more government assistance versus less government associance, etc. Finally, while the chestnut "correlation does not prove causality" is always in force, it would be disingenuous to assume that an increase in someone's independence is unrelated to that person's level of dependence.

Given the universal attitude of the preference for a social father (Barry & Paxson, 1971; Hewlett, 1992; Levinson & Malone, 1980; Stephens, 1963; Van Den Berghe, 1979), it seems counterintuitive that such a wide variability in illegitimacy would exist. It seems more appropriate that the magnitude of differences hovers around the level of error variance. However, a mean percentage of children born out of wedlock, which is 20.84%, with a standard deviation of 22.2%, points in the direction that some social forces are tamping down rates of illegitimacy, while other forces are raising the prevalence of incidence of illegitimacy.

As was mentioned earlier, a strong cross-cultural consistency is the requirement that a prospective groom be able to provide resources for any prospective bride before a marriage is to occur. Once married, the husband is expected to provide resources for the wife, and the father is expected to provide resources for his children. A failure to harbinger resources leaves men celibate (see Buss, 1989, 1994). Failure to provide resources leaves husbands divorced. Seen from the other side of the coin, women tend to sequester a man's (read husband's) resources through marriage prior to becoming a mother. If the above is more true than not, then any process that removes the linkage between access to resources and marriage will affect rates of illegitimacy. Marriage, for some women, will become superfluous.

In the main, two major sources of direct income for any mother-to-be will include those from a husband and those she earned for herself. Accordingly, if she, rather than the male, could generate needed resources, then the male would become more supernumerary. Illegitimacy rates would increase, and as the data indicate, such is the case. Across cultures, as the ratio of female-to-male wages increases, so does the percentage of illegitimate births. Conversely, as the percentage of female-to-male wages decreases, the percentage of illegitimate births also decreases.

A third, more indirect, route to financial independence is higher levels of education. Accordingly, if women enter tertiary or college institutions on a par with men, then their expectations for financial independence are on a par with men. Again, if there is a disruption with the linkage between marriage and access to resources, the rates of illegitimacy would increase. And this description appears to be the case. As the percentage of female tertiary and college students increased, the proportion of all out-of-wedlock births increased.

It is with some personal relief to note that behavioral scientists are more charged with the task of pointing out phenomena than with solving or resolving conflicts. To wit: the two positively valued items (individual freedom and optimal childhood) appear to be on a collision course. In the 1990s, any advocacy for the constraint of freedom is difficult to promulgate, just as it is awkward to champion successfully any deficits in childhood. To the extent that this limited sample of countries both (a) accurately reflects a larger referent group and (b) portends future trends, the more difficult it is for spokespersons to avoid setting priorities.

REPRODUCTIVE HISTORY AND FREEDOM

Background

For any tribe, whether very small or very large, sheer survival is a very basic issue for both the larger social group across generations, as well as for its individual members who prefer more rather than less longevity. The current existence of any group of people that shares a common political and economic heritage, that is, a tribe, is prima facie evidence that the cultural traditions of that tribe illustrate successful solutions to problems emanating from the ecology in which the tribe has been enmeshed (Harris 1974a, 1979). For example, for any group to be ongoing, it must be able to procure reliable sources of nutrients. A source of potable water must be maintained. The birth and effective socialization of children must be actualized. Fragmentation of the commonweal caused by (especially) young men's violence must be prevented. Marauding young men from competing tribes must be prevented from attacking one's own tribe, or if they are already attacking, they must be successfully repulsed (recent examples include Rwanda, Bosnia, and Chesnya; less recent examples include Cambodia, World War II, Vietnam, World War I, etc.). Anything that systematically precludes the successful achievement of these necessary but not sufficient conditions from occurring directly threatens the existence of the tribe. The *World Ethnographic Sample* (Murdock, 1957) and the *Ethnographic Atlas* (Murdock, 1967) contain numerous examples of extinct groups. The ongoing loss of South American tribes represent current examples. An additional necessary but not sufficient prerequisite for ongoing societal continuity is a continuous supply of children who will serve as descendants to replace their mortal parents.

Sometimes it is useful to state the blatantly obvious. Children, also known as the next generation, are only going to exist if women get pregnant and carry a conceptus to term. Adults spend enormous amounts of time and treasure in nurturing that child to independence. Any questions?

I argue here that shared cultural attitudes regarding children (i.e., fertility) are directly related to underlying patterns of economic or ecological infrastructures. The United States can serve as an example. On the one hand, the public posture of adults toward children is supposed to be prosocial and one of positive emotions: children are to be seen as lovable and entities that generate emotional pleasure (Hoffman & Manis, 1979; cf Landers, 1976; Mackey, White & Day, 1992; Neal, Groat, & Wicks, 1989; Patterson, 1980; Rohner & Rohner, 1982; Turnbull, 1972). Children are to be loved and cared for because they are human, cute, sweet, and "ours." Note the public outrage at the Susan Smith case in South Carolina in which Ms. Smith was convicted of drowning her two young sons. On the other hand, the United States has been below replacement level (2.1 children per female) since 1972. Accordingly, as reviewed below, reasons to have children predicated only upon emotional rationales may not be competitive with societies that use both nonemotional and emotional reasons to have children and to have more than *two* children.

From a perspective over and beyond the emotional, children represent not only an irrational commitment but also a rational, economic utility. See Aghajanian (1979, 1988) for examples. As with any other variable, the degree of cultural utility can range from *low* to *high* depending upon the characteristics of any given society. The question then becomes: What is the degree of utility or liability that children represent to a culture and thereby reflect parental attitudes and parental behaviors?

The utility of children may be categorized in the following four ways:

1. Children can represent a latent social security system. That is, a society may expect aging parents to be taken care of by their own grown children, who, in turn, will expect to be cared for during their own period of advanced years and increasing infirmity. The United States is not such a tribe.
2. Children can become a source of cheap labor, performing labor intensive and extensive tasks that help the economy and the family, especially where agrarian subsistence is prevalent (Arnold et al., 1975; Bradley, 1984; Nag, White, & Peet, 1978). With our child labor laws and mandatory school attendance, the United States is not such a tribe.
3. The value of children, especially daughters, in creating marriage/alliance, for example dowries, and cross-cousin marriages, has been documented in a number or societies (Chagnon, 1977; cf Dickemann, 1979; Levi-Strauss, 1963; Stephens, 1963). For example, families will send their daughters as brides to alternate clans, lineages, or families to validate alliances between them. Dowries and bride-prices (i.e., money) often lubrigate the transaction. These dynamics were exemplified by the royal families of Victorian Europe. The United States is clearly not such a tribe.
4. Children may generate minimal or low economic benefits or even net costs to their parents or guardians (see Zelizer, 1985). In service-oriented technological societies, children are very expensive and, in many cases, severe economic liabilities (cf Garbarino, 1986; Huber, 1980). Such circumstances are further exacerbated by 16 plus years of formal education and its attendant costs. The United States *is* such a tribe.

BIRTHRATES AND ECONOMICS

If children can be variably utile in the economic domain, then is there a relationship between levels of fertility and economic value of children? This is a testable hypothesis.

In small-scale farms, children are traditionally used as a source of labor. Therefore, the relationship was examined between the percentage of the labor force engaged in agriculture (per country) and the level of fertility in that country. A large percentage of the labor force engaged in agriculture is a marker for small scale, that is, peasant farming. A small percentage engaged in agriculture is a marker for fewer, more mechanized farms with a large proportion of the labor forced engaged in industry and services. Data on both birthrates and percentage of the labor force employed in agriculture for 150 countries are available from the *United Nations Demographic Yearbook* (United Nations, 1992).

The hypothesis that a relationship existed between the worth ($$$$) of children and their existence was supported by the data. There was a positive relationship between crude birth rates (the number of birth rates per year per 1,000 population) and the percentage of the labor force engaged in agriculture ($r_p = .803$; $p < .001$; two tailed; 64.5% [$r_p = .803^2$] of the variance/differences in differential birthrates can be attributed to the percentage of the labor force engaged in agriculture). Presented a little differently, where children are valuable, they appear. Where children are costs, they disappear. See Bulato, Lee, Hollerbach, and Bongaarts (1983); Easterlin and Crimmins (1985); and Handwerker (1986) for discussions.

Freedom and Economics

If (a) people will gravitate toward more freedom rather than less, and (b) the "family farm" is a small proportion of a country's economic base, with few families dependent upon the farm for a livelihood, then it would be expected that increased divorce rates (freedom to dissolve or leave the family) will be associated with lower levels of family farms. This, too, becomes a testable hypothesis.

The relationship between the divorce rate (per country) and the percentage of the labor force engaged in agriculture in that country was examined. A total of 80 countries had the relevant data (United Nations, 1992).

The relationship was significant (r_p -.414; $p < .01$ [two-tailed]; 17.1% [$r_p = .414^2$]) of the variance or differences in divorce rates can be attributed to differences in the percentage of the labor force engaged in agriculture). That is, as the prevalence of family farms decreased the tendency to divorce also increased.

Discussion

There are two forces in evidence operating across cultures that separate men from children: (1) an increased equity for women tends to increase single-parent births with no social father and (2) a lessening of the family as a small-scale farming business tends to increase the separation of husband and wife through divorce and therefore separates the children from one of the parents. To the extent that the parent is the father, the divorce separates the father from his children. See Luepnitz (1982) for a historical perspective on adult custody of the child following divorce. These two trends are cross cultural. Now let's see how they reflect the U.S. megatribe.

U.S. WOMEN'S EQUITY; U.S. WOMEN'S FREEDOM

Fifty-three percent of the individuals in tertiary education were women. This percentage of women is a little above the cross-cultural average of 45.9%. The proportion of income for that of U.S. women compared with U.S. men was 68%. This figure is slightly below the cross-cultural average of 72.8%.

The U.S. level of out-of-wedlock births at that time frame was 21%. This was essentially the same as the cross-cultural average of 21.4%.

I suggest that, if the access to resources by women is a benchmark to evaluate men in becoming a husband and father and if that increased access to resources by women, due to her own efforts, elevates the woman's freedom quotient, then it is reasonable to infer that state entitlements ought to increase women's freedom and thereby lower indixes of social fathering. In other words, state entitlements compete successfully with the traditional role of the social father as a primary provider.

Let's see how this dynamic works.

Major categories of state aid through entitlement programs include cash (Aid to Families with Dependent Children [AFDC]), food (food stamps; Women, Infants, and Children [WIC] benefits; and free-lunch and free-breakfast programs in schools), medical care (Medicaid), fuel (fuel allowances, education [Head Start, Pell grants]), and housing (public housing). According to average figures from national data for the model year 1987, a person who qualifies for all these entitlements receives cash, goods, and services worth from $10,227 to $14,613. Note that none of these benefits is taxable. Also note that state and local programs, which are *not* included in this analysis, account for 67% of that provided by federal programs (in 1987). See Table 1.3 and Table 1.4.

However, if a man's earning capacity is used to develop a benchmark for comparison with the value of government entitlements, a different mosaic emerges. The range computed above (from $10,227 to $14,613) represents disposable income. Employees must pay Social

Table 1.3. Yearly Entitlement Benefits Available from Federal Programs, 1987

Category	National average ($)
Aid to Families with Dependent Children (AFDC)	4,380.00
Food stamps	549.00
Medicaid (AFDC)	740.00
Housing	3,627.00
School breakfast	124.00
School lunch	117.00
Fuel	307.00
Women, infants, and children program (WIC)	383.00
Base subtotal	10,227.00
Social Security on $10,227 at 7.15%	731.00
Total	10,958.00

Source: U.S. Bureau of the Census, 1989–1990.

Table 1.4. Yearly Entitlement Benefits Available from Federal Programs, Including Head Start and One Pell Grant, Separately, and Head Start and One Pell Grant Together, 1987

Category		National average ($)
Base subtotal from Table 1.3		10,227.00
With Head Start at $3,082.00		3,082.00
	Subtotal	13,309.00
Social Security at 7.15%		952.00
	Subtotal	14,261.00
Taxable at 15% (tax exempt)*		219.00
Total		14,480.00
Base subtotal from Table 1.3		10,227.00
With one Pell Grant at $1,304.00		1,304.00
	Subtotal	11,531.00
Social Security at 7.15%		824.00
Total		12,355.00
Base subtotal from Table 1.3		10,227.00
With Head Start at $3,082.00 plus		4,386.00
one Pell Grant at $1,304.00	Subtotal	14,613.00
Social Security at 7.15%		1,045.00
	Subtotal	15,658.00
Taxable 15% (tax exempt: $12,800)*		429.00
Total		16,087.00

aFour exemptions, standard deductions.
Source: U.S. Bureau of the Census (1989–1990).

Security and federal taxes (plus state and local taxes, depending on the locale).

If the federal taxes plus Social Security are added to the base salary, then a man has to earn between $10,958 and $16,087 in salary to match the state's programs (see Table 1.4). If he works at minimum wage ($3.35 per hour in 1987) for 52 weeks at 40 hours per week, a man will earn only $6,968 and so will not come close to matching the benefits available though entitlement programs. The salary required to match benefits through state programs exceeds the income of at least 12% to 23% of family households in 1987, and it exceeds the income of 17% to 30% of single men in 1987. Since single men are eligible to marry single women, the 17% to 30% of all single men whose incomes are below the level required to match state entitlement benefits are those who feel most acutely the effects of trying to compete as a provider with the state.

In terms of freedom for the woman, the state has two advantages compared with the male:

1. The state is remarkably reliable in its payments. The state cannot be laid off or fired. The state will not quite work. The state has excellent credit, and vendors are profoundly confident that the goods and services rendered will be reimbursed. Women are acutely aware of the greater reliability of the state versus the husband and father. Men are equally aware that the women are acutely aware.
2. The state does not require negotiations on the dispersal and allocation of available funds. The state does not sit down with the woman to prioritize a budget. Husbands and fathers are much more involved in the fate of disposable income. Informal folklore and formal marriage and family courses and textbooks are replete with the problems, friction, and frustrations of husbands and wives in prioritizing family finances.

Within this crucible of potential dissension between men and women, one can imagine the added parameter of a working class man who generates low income and, because he is poorly educated, semiskilled, and marginally employed, his future prospects for increased access to resources are dim. The man simply is not going to be able to provide for his children at the level of resources that the state can and will provide in his absence. The man knows this. The woman knows this. The man knows that the woman knows this.

In the calculus of human relationships, the possibilities for reliable resources without dependence upon and negotiations with a man create incentives for a woman to preclude legal entanglements with a significant other. That is, she is less likely to get married. If she does decide to get married, the same potentials of low levels of resources from the husband or father serve as incentives to jettison the father of her children. With one husband jettisoned, the probabilities of the woman remarrying are low. Women who receive entitlement packages from the state have disproportionately lower rates of remarriage (McLanahan & Booth, 1989).

A real asymmetry arises at this point. If a single man and a single woman become intimate and create a baby, then the option of parenthood resides solely with the woman. She can decide to carry the child to term or not. The man has no such option. Thus the woman can decide whether the man will become a biological father (genitor). The man has no such reciprocal option. The woman can also decide whether the man will become a social father. If she marries the man, he then becomes a social father. If she decides to remain single, she then can simultaneously preclude the man from the status of social father. If a man decides to get married and the woman does not, then there will be no marriage. Thus she can determine his status of social father or not. He cannot affect her status of mother. This asymmetry on the final arbiter of parenthood will be examined again in Chapter 8.

This generalized social dynamic of decision making has a negative feed-back loop. Entitlements tend to have a one-way ratchet: programs are easier to initiate and augment than to terminate or constrict. Accordingly, with a mythological middle-class childhood as a benchmark, the state will always be under social and political pressures to "up the ante" or raise the threshold of an appropriate, if suboptimal, set of entitlements. To fund the incremental entitlements, the state will have to raise taxes. Increased taxation on wages and salaries, but not on entitlements, systematically adds to the proportion of men who are not economically competitive with state programs as providers for their children.

U.S. AUTONOMY AND THE NUCLEAR FAMILY

A grim focus on the dismal science of economics might give a myopic view on the course of fathering in the United States. Within the world's community of countries, America is a comparatively prosperous megatribe. What about the majority of families that are not defined as living in poverty? Indeed, these families do not experience the sting of poverty and those economic forces that abrade the man from the father role. However, another social factor has emerged which, independent of income, can systematically peel the father from his children, and here too he is virtually powerless to do anything to counter that factor. That factor, of course, is "no-fault" divorce.

Although there are minor variations on the themes across the 50 states, the base theme in no-fault divorce is thus: if either the husband or the wife wants a divorce, the divorce happens. If the husband wants a divorce but the wife does not, the divorce happens. If the wife wants a divorce but the husband does not, the divorce happens. There is a ring of common sense and humanity to this arrangement. No adult should be forced to live with another adult that he or she does not want to live with. However, when minor children are involved, the rationale for the marital dissolution becomes more complicated.

Let's follow a normative scenario of a no-fault divorce petition that involves minor children. Because most petitions are filed by the wife (Mackey, 1993; U.S. Bureau of the Census, 1989), the scenario will be viewed from her perspective.

1. The wife files a petition at the local courthouse. This means that the divorce will happen.
2. In the majority of cases—up to 90%—the court will award custody of the minor children to the wife (Sitarz, 1990; Sack, 1987).
3. She and she alone will then have the power to make decisions for the children until they are 18 years of age. The father may have the opportunity to consult, but he cannot make divisions.
4. A formula calculated by the government will determine child support payments that the father must make. The child support can be up to 50% of his disposable income. Any failure on his part to pay punctually may result in a fine or time spent in jail or both. Again, the father need not have done anything wrong to have those payments mandated.
5. Visitation times are controlled by the ex-wife.
6. The father is not provided access to his children's home.

In other words, a parent—generally the father—having committed no transgression or having done nothing amiss, can be systematically denied association with his children and must pay a large portion of his income (through the state) to the ex wife. Framed a little differently, the nonpetitioning parent, generally the father, *without committing any offense,* can have his children taken away by the state and he has absolutely no recourse.

Thus there are two tines to the father-abrasion machine that systematically precludes fathers from being with their children: (1) single-parent births and (2) no-fault divorce. And in both tines, the father has zero legal standing to stop or refract the process.

Garfinkel and McLanahan (1986) have estimated that less than half of all children born in the United States will live with their biological mothers *and* biological fathers from birth to adulthood (18 years of age). The thundering majority of the remaining children will be separated from their fathers sometime between their birth and adulthood. There are three components to the level of separation:

1. women who have eschewed the role of wife and thereby preclude the biological father from the role of social father.
2. women who are displeased with the role of wife, jettison their husbands, and lose their status as wives. For the children involved, the woman tends to keep her role as ongoing mother, yet the role of ongoing father is simply dissolved.
3. Biological fathers who refuse to get married, or, if married, petition for divorce and leave the children with the mother.

In 1995, it is difficult to pinpoint the relative frequency of these three impediments. About 30% of the births are to single women. How this "singleness" or lack of marriage comes to be is difficult to adjudge; maybe women are driving the figure, maybe men are driving the figure, maybe it is about evenly split between the two genders. When minor children are involved in the divorce, about 65% of the petitioners are the mothers and 28% are the fathers. The remaining 7% are both parents or others. Mothers, therefore, are more than twice as likely to initiate proceedings to separate children from a parent than are the fathers.

Given that there are some men who do avoid or castoff the father role, there are others who do not. They become social fathers and stay in that role. Why would they choose to stay in that role? Chapter 2 looks at the motivational hierarchy that serves as an incentive for men to enter the role of father and, perhaps, to stay there.

Rationales for Entering into the U.S. Fathering Role

Men's Divulgences, Women's Perceptions

By profession I am a soldier and take pride in the fact, but I am prouder—infinitely prouder—to be a father. A soldier destroys in order to build; the father only builds never destroys. The one has the potentiality of death; the other embodies creation and life. And while the hordes of death are mighty, the battalions of life are mightier still. It is my hope that my son, when I am gone, will remember me not from the battle but in the home repeating with him our simple daily prayer.

DOUGLAS MACARTHUR

My son is 7 years old. I am 54. It has taken me a great many years to reach that age. I am more respected in the community, I am stronger. I am more intelligent, and I think I am better than he is. I don't want to be a pal, I want to be a father.

CLIFTON FADIMAN

It is the purpose of this chapter to explore why adult males in the United States would want to enter into the fathering role. Two perspectives are developed to help analyze male motivational hierarchies: (1) men are surveyed to profile their priorities and (2) women are surveyed to find out if they can accurately predict the men's responses. That is, could the women successfully "read" the men with whom they share the same overall culture.

It is self-evident that any tribe, mega or micro, has an absolute need to replenish the population with their own children who will grow to adulthood and carry on the traditions of their parents and their parent's tribe. For the millennia, it is the smaller unit, the family, which has served as the vehicle for the continuity for the larger unit, the tribe. Children, therefore, serve the function of perpetuity for the commonweal. The purposes or functions that children can serve for the individual nurturing adults are more multidimensional. Children may serve various types and degrees of psychological needs, social needs, and economic needs of the care-giving adults of the family. The U.S. adult-child dyad is neither an exception nor can it be considered transcendent.

CROSS-CULTURAL CONTEXT
OF FATHERING

Across cultures, several patterns are in evidence that provide a context which, in turn, surrounds and immerses the U.S. man-child dyad:

1. Across cultures women are the primary child caretakers. Usually it is the mother who fulfills that role. If it is not the mother, older female kin fill that role, for example, older sister, grandmother, maternal aunt (Barry, Josephson, Lauer, & Marshall, 1977; Barry & Paxson, 1971; Hames, 1988; Hewlett, 1992; Tronick, Morelli, & Winn, 1987; Weisner & Gallimore, 1977).
2. Across cultures, men are systematically given access to children and the men avail themselves of that opportunity. Generally the man is the father (biological, social, genitor), but, as was mentioned earlier, occasionally it is the mother's brother (*avunculus*) who fills that role (Mackey, 1985, 1986, 1988; Schlegel, 1972).
3. Although the U.S. culture promulgates public, overt posture of adult affiliation toward children (e.g., Garbarino, 1986; Luepnitz, 1982; Zelizer, 1985), this cultural vector is not universally shared. Other cultures exhibit more indifferent or even antagonistic relationships from adults toward their children, for example, the Alorese (natives of Alor Island, east of Java) (Rohner, 1975; Rohner & Rohner, 1982) and the Ik (a tribe from Africa) (Turnbull, 1972). In other words, adult-to-child acceptance or rejection lies on a continuum and parental doting upon their children cannot be considered as a given.
4. As was discussed in Chapter 1, where children are economically valuable, for example, rural, small-farm agriculture, they appear in larger numbers. That is, when children can be net economic benefits, birthrates are high. Conversely, when children are net economic costs, the birthrates drop. Children disappear.

5. Women, if given control of their own reproductive histories, and, if allowed access to paid employment outside of the domicile, will limit their births and avail themselves of the cash economy (Bulatao et al., 1983; Caldwell, 1982; Easterlin & Crimmins, 1985; Fawcett, 1983; cf. Handwerker, 1986).

VALUE OF CHILDREN SURVEYS

Earlier surveys, primarily with women and mothers suggested that where children do provide labor and earning to the family economy, the perceived advantages or value of additional children are focused on the economic domain. In contrast, when children contribute only minimally or are net economic costs to the family's microeconomy, the perceived value of children is voiced more in terms of noneconomic qualities, for example, psychological and social dimensions (Caldwell, 1982; Hoffman & Manis, 1979; Neal, Groat, & Wicks, 1989). See Table 2.1.

The data gathered in these earlier surveys were constructed using a checklist format such that a value attributed to having children was scored if that facet was mentioned. Means of separating the less important from the more important were unavailable. Accordingly, it is difficult to determine the prepotency of any of the various attributes.

Table 2.1. Cross-Cultural Comparison of Value of Children: Economic Value versus Noneconomic Value

	Percentage of women who viewed the advantages of children in terms of:					
	Economic value					Noneconomic value
Country	Household help	Labor	Financial help	Help in old age	Total	
Philippines	34	5	11	43	93	75
Turkey	8	0	5	35	48	82
Indonesia	32	21	16	58	127	67
Thailand	9	8	1	28	46	38
Korea	2	0	0	21	23	96
Taiwan	4	3	3	29	39	96
Singapore	9	0	1	39	49	98
United States	3	0	0	7	10	99
Iran (rural)	26	21	45	15	107	37
Iran (urban)	4	0	23	11	38	67

Source: Adapted from Aghajanian (1988).

It is the purpose of Chapter 2 to delineate both (1) what U.S. men will divulge as reasons for entering fatherhood and (2) what may be the more powerful motivations for them to become a father. Similarly, women will be independently surveyed to investigate their relative ability to anticipate or read what the men will divulge by having the women predict the results of the men's survey.

METHOD

Sample

Subjects were recruited as a convenience sample from the evening classes in a community college. Ninety men and 136 women participated in the survey. A community college locale was selected because these institutions tend to draw from a wide swathe or cross section of Americana including age differentials, ethnic differentials, and parenting differentials. Essentially, the upwardly mobile working class—Joe and Josephine Six Pack—is well represented in these individuals (cf. Rubin, 1976).

Procedure

To create an atmosphere as innocuous as possible in what is a sensitive terrain, a gameboard format was devised to survey the subjects. On the gameboard were 10 items that referred to possible reasons men would enter into the fathering role. Because humans respond to three interdependent levels of incentives—the psychological, the social, and the economic—all three of these motivational candidates were represented on the gameboard. See Figure 2.1 at the end of this chapter. The two psychological categories of motivation were *men have children because the children (1) bring love and emotional satisfaction to the family and (2) are fun to be with.* The three social categories of motivation were *men have children because the children (1) are expected by parents, (2) are expected by friends and society, and (3) are wanted by the wife.* The two economic categories were *men have children because the children (1) help parents in their old age and retirement and (2) are expected by parents to earn income for the family and help with the chores.* A category serving a psychosocial motivation was *men have children because the children carry on the name or bloodline.* An additional category that indicates a low level of paternalistic motivation was *men have children because the children were accidents: just happened.* A final category was simply entitled *Other.*

For one-half of the subjects, the order of the reasons were reversed to counter any order effect (except for *other*), which remained in the bottom right corner. The items were pretested for readability and clarity.

Each subject was tested in his or her classroom in a group. Each subject was given 10 tokens, a gameboard, and the following instructions: "Here are ten tokens. Please distribute the tokens among the reasons that you think men enter into fathering or become fathers. That is, distribute the tokens in proportion to the importance of the category. The more important the reason, the more tokens would be placed on that reason. The less important the reason, the fewer the tokens. You may leave as many reasons blank as you want. There are no right or wrong answers. . . . you have as much time as you want."

Once the final arrangement of tokens was complete, the subjects wrote down the number of tokens for each reason in the slots provided on the gameboard and handed the gameboard face down to the surveyor. The ethnicity, age, and parental status of each subject was also coded. See Figure 2.1.

It is important to note that both men and women were to respond to the men's hierarchy of motivations.

RESULTS

Men

For men, the distribution of the tokens was not random ($X^2 = 642.99$; $p < .001$; $df = 9$, $C = 0.646$ (see Table 2.2). The choice *bring love and emotional satisfaction to the family* was the most preferred and received nearly a third (31.4%) of the tokens. The two psychological reasons, *love and satisfaction* plus *are fun to be with* together received a plurality of the tokens (44.8%). Social reasons, *wanted by the wife* plus *expected by parents* plus *expected by friends and society* received approximately a fifth of the tokens (19.4%). *Continue the bloodline/name* was the second most used reason (17.5%). *Accidents/just happened* ranked fourth and received approximately a tenth of the tokens (9.8%), which was nearly twice as many as the economic reasons (5.4%) *earn income for the family/help the family with chores* (2.9%) plus *help parents with their old age and retirement* (2.5%). *Other* received 3.2% of the tokens. See Table 2.3 for the percentage of men that mentioned each of the categories.

The generalized pattern described above held across the two ethnic groups tested (Hispanic [$n = 51$] versus White [$n = 39$]). The correla-

Table 2.2. Hierarchy of Men's Motivations to Become Fathers

Motivation category: "Children . . ."	Number of tokens	Expected frequency	Rank	Percent of total
Bring love and emotional satisfaction	281	90	1	31.2
Carry on name or bloodline	158	90	2	17.5
Are fun	121	90	3	13.4
Are accidents, just happened	88	90	4	9.8
Are wanted by the wife	72	90	5	8.0
Are expected by parents	59	90	6	6.6
Are expected by friends	43	90	7	4.8
Other	29	90	8	3.2
Earn money for the family or do chores	26	90	9	2.9
Help parents in their retirement	23	90	10	2.6
Total				100.0

tion between these two ethnic groups across the 10 motivational reasons was significant, whether ranks were analyzed ($r_s = 0.879$; $p < .01$; 2-tailed) or percentage of allocated tokens were analyzed ($r_p = 0.961$; $p < .001$; 2-tailed). Similarly computed data indicated that neither age of man (28-years or less ($n = 55$) versus 29-years or more ($n = 35$; $r_s = 0.751$; $p < .05$; 2-tailed; $r_p = .882$; $p < .001$; 2-tailed) nor parental status (no children, $n = 59$) versus one or more children ($n = 31$; $r_s = 0.903$; $p < .01$; 2-tailed; $r_p = 0.912$; $p < .001$; 2-tailed] changed the hierarchy of priorities.

Table 2.3. Percentage of Men (n = 90) and Women (n = 136) Who Mentioned Each Motivation to Become a Father

Motivation category: "Children . . ."	Men		Women			
	%	Rank	%	Rank	Z score	$p <$ [a]
Bring love and emotional satisfaction	89.2	1	81.1	1	1.639	ns
Carry on name or bloodline	83.8	2	71.3	2	2.162	.05
Are fun	64.9	3	43.4	6	3.167	.01
Are wanted by the wife	54.1	4	62.5	3	1.257	ns
Are expected by friends	35.1	5	32.4	7	0.421	ns
Are expected by parents	29.7	6	48.5	5	2.813	.01
Are accidents, just happened	27.0	7	55.1	4	4.166	.001
Other	18.9	8	8.8	8	2.223	.05
Earn money for the family or do chores	10.8	9	5.9	10	1.340	ns
Help parents in their retirement	8.1	10	8.1	9	0.000	ns

[a]All p values were 2-tailed .

Women

The women's predictions of the men's ranking (see Table 2.4) and the men's actual ranking were accurate whether analyzed by rank ($r_s = .927$; $p < .001$; 2-tailed) or analyzed by percentage of token allocation ($r_p = .918$; $p < .001$; 2-tailed). See Table 2.3 for the percentage of women that mentioned each of the categories.

In addition, an item by item analysis across the ten reasons showed that the proportion of the tokens given to each reason by women versus men was not different (Z-scores from 0.058 to 1.217, n.s.) See Table 2.4.

As was the case with the men, neither ethnicity (Hispanic, $n = 95$; versus White, $n = 41$; $r_s = .952$; $p < .001$; 2-tailed; $r_p = .929$; $p < .001$; 2-tailed) nor age (28-years or younger, $n = 91$; versus 29-years or more, $n = 42$; $r_s = .952$; $p < .001$; 2-tailed; $r_p = .920$; $p < .001$; 2-tailed) nor parental status (parent of one or more children ($n = 59$) versus childless ($n = 77$), [$r_s = .888$; $p < .01$; 2-tailed; $r_p = .941$; $p < .001$; 2-tailed) affected the women's predictions of the men's hierarchy.

DISCUSSION

Two points are clear from these results: (1) The U.S. men indicated that they enter the father role for emotional reasons based on psychological, and to a much lesser extent, social rewards generated by the personhood or personality qualities of the child. The economic return from the child is peripheralized as irrelevant. (2) The U.S. women who

Table 2.4. Women's Perceptions of the Hierarchy of Men's Motivations to Become Fathers

Motivation category: "Children . . ."	Number of tokens	Expected frequency	Rank	Percent of total
Bring love and emotional satisfaction	357	135.9[a]	1	26.3
Carry on name or bloodline	242	135.9	2	17.8
Are fun	125	135.9	5	9.2
Are accidents, just happened	205	135.9	3	15.1
Are wanted by the wife	179	135.9	4	13.2
Are expected by parents	116	135.9	6	8.5
Are expected by friends	84	135.9	7	6.2
Other	16	135.9	9	1.2
Earn money for the family or do chores	15	135.9	10	1.1
Help parents in their retirement	20	135.9	8	1.5
Total				100.0

[a]One woman was rather determined to allocate only nine tokens.

Table 2.5. Comparison of Men's Divulgences and Women's Perceptions
Based on the Percentage of Tokens Allocated to Each Motivation

Motivation category: "Children . . ."	Men's divulgences (%)	Women's perceptions (%)	Z score[a]
Bring love and emotional satisfaction	31.2	26.3	0.833
Carry on name or bloodline	17.5	17.8	0.058
Are fun	13.4	9.2	0.993
Are accidents, just happened	9.8	15.1	1.160
Are wanted by the wife	8.0	13.2	1.217
Are expected by parents	6.6	8.5	0.552
Are expected by friends	4.8	6.2	0.446
Other	3.2	1.2	1.052
Earn money for the family or do chores	2.9	1.1	0.992
Help parents in their retirement	2.6	1.5	0.539
Total	100.0	100.0	

[a]All "ps" were not significant.

were sampled either through (a) projection or (b) an incisive, singular reading of their men or (c) a correct generalized reading of a cultural theme, accurately predicted the men's responses. With apologizes to Deborah Tannen, they *do* understand.

A CHINESE AND CHINESE
AMERICAN SAMPLE

The potential genesis of the men's motivational hierarchy will be examined in Chapter 5. However, the generalizability of the results is an interesting route to pursue. To that end, a cohort of Chinese and Chinese Americans were recruited and surveyed by Nancy S. Coney. The subjects all belonged to social clubs and organizations in a metropolitan area and varied from nationalized Americans to Chinese nationals working in the United States.

The procedure for surveying these subjects was the same as with the previous group with two exceptions. The social categories of *expected by parents* and *expected by friends, and others* were collapsed into one category, *expected by parents and friends*. Hence, nine, not ten, categories were available to be evaluated. Secondly, the instructions and the gameboards were translated into Chinese and the subject had the option to use the English or the Chinese format. The subjects were either surveyed individually or in small groups by a Chinese American woman. Seventeen men and 21 women were surveyed.

Results

Chinese and Chinese American Men. The allocation of the tokens by these men was not random (X^2 [8, N = 17] = 93.56; $p < .01$; C = .597). The top three priorities were *love and emotional satisfaction* (26.0% of the tokens), *continue the name and bloodline* (18.9%), and *children are fun* (17.2%). Again, the psychological dimension dominated. Social expectations and economic benefits that could accrue from having children received only marginal support (see Table 2.6).

The Chinese and Chinese American men were then compared to the men from the early sample (Whites and Hispanics), henceforth the Men's Core Sample. The Men's Core Sample was predictive of the Chinese and Chinese American men's motivational hierarchy, both by rank (r_s = .767, $p < .05$; 2-tailed) and by percentage of token allocation (r_p = .903; $p < .01$; 2-tailed). See Table 2.7.

The Chinese and Chinese American women were predictive of their Chinese and Chinese American men's hierarchy of motivation both by rank (r_s = .883; $p < .001$; 2-tailed) and by percentage of token allocation (r_p = .949; $p < .01$; 2-tailed). And, as expected by the parallels between the hierarchy of the Men's Core Sample and the hierarchy of the Chinese and Chinese American men, the Chinese and Chinese American women were predictive of the Men's Core Sample both by rank (r_s = .817; $p < .817$; 2-tailed) and by percentage of token allocation (r_p = .943; $p < .01$; 2-tailed). See Table 2.7.

Finally, the women from the earlier sample (Whites and Hispanics), henceforth the Women's Core Sample, was predictive of the Chi-

Table 2.6. Evaluations (by Rank and by Percentages of Tokens) of Reasons Men Have Children: by Gender of Chinese and Chinese Americans

	Men (n = 17)		Women (n = 21)	
Motivation category: "Children . . ."	Rank	%	Rank	%
Bring love and emotional satisfaction	1	26.0	1	28.7
Carry on name or bloodline	2	18.9	2	17.2
Are fun	3	17.2	3	15.3
Expected by others	4	14.2	4	13.4
Are accidents, just happened	8	3.6	6	7.2
Are wanted by the wife	7	4.7	7	5.7
Other	6	5.9	9	1.0
Earn money for the family or do chores	9	3.0	8	2.4
Help parents in their retirement	5	6.5	5	9.1
Total		100.0		100.0

Table 2.7. Correlations between Genders and between the
Chinese and Chinese Americans and Core Sample in the
Analysis of Why Men Would Enter the Role of Social Father[a]

| Ethnic affiliation and gender | Chinese and Chinese American | | Core sample male |
	Male	Female	
Chinese and Chinese American female			
r_s	.883**		
r_p	.949**		
Core sample male			
r_s	.767*	.817*	
r_p	.903**	.943**	
Core sample female			
r_s	.617	.767*	.833*
r_p	.721*	.814**	.909**

[a]r_s = ranking of motivation category; r_p = percentage of token allocation.
* = $p < .05$ (2-tailed); ** = $p < .01$ (2-tailed).

nese and Chinese American men, but only by percentage of token allocation (r_p = .721; $p < .05$; 2-tailed) and not by rank (r_s = .617; n.s.).
See Table 2.6.

Thus, for white, Hispanic, and Chinese and Chinese American men,
psychological dimensions were clearly prepotent in their views on why
their men would enter the father role. Furthermore, the women of all
three groups were accurate in predicting not only how the men of their
own ethnic group respond, but also how the other two groups respond.

AN AFRICAN AMERICAN SAMPLE

Coney recruited two subsamples of African Americans. One sample was from an inner city community organization and one was from a
rural church organization: 31 men and 48 women were surveyed. At
their discretion, these subjects were surveyed either individually or in
small groups by an African American woman.

The gameboard and procedure was the same as the one used with
the Chinese and Chinese American sample.

Results

African American Men. The allocation of tokens by African
American men was not random (X^2 [8, $N = 31$] = 162; $p < .001$). The

top three priorities were *wanted by wife* (31.6% of the tokens), *love and emotional satisfaction* (15.2%), and *accidents* (12.6%). The prepotency of the social category *wanted by wife* seemed clear. See Table 2.8.

None of the other four samples (Men's Core Sample, Women's Core Sample, Chinese and Chinese American Men and Chinese and Chinese American Women) was predictive of nor predicted by either the African American men's rankings or their percentage of token allocations (see Table 2.9).

African American Women.   The allocation of tokens was not random (X^2 [8, $N = 48$] $= 314.43$; $p < .001$; $C = .629$). The top three priorities were *accidents* (29.0% of the tokens), *continue the bloodline and name* (24.4%), and *expected by parents or friends* (11.4%). Of interest, the category of *love and emotional satisfaction* received only 10.4% of the tokens and ranked only 4th. See Table 2.7.

The African American women's predictions of the African American men's hierarchy were not accurate either by rankings or by percentage of token allocation, nor was the African American women's profile predictive either of the Chinese or Chinese American sample (men or women). The African American women were predictive of the Core Sample (men and women) but only by rank ($r_s = .683$; $p < .05$; 2-tailed; and $r_s = .817$; $p < .05$; 2-tailed respectively), not by percentage of token allocation ($r_p = .360$; n.s. and $r_p = .607$ n.s., respectively). See Table 2.8.

The African American sample represents an anomaly. This anomaly will be revisited in Chapter 10.

Three of the four ethnicities (White, Hispanic, and Chinese and

Table 2.8. Evaluations, by Rank and Percentage of Tokens, of Reasons Men Have Children, by Gender of African Americans

Motivation category: "Children . . ."	Men ($n = 31$)		Women ($n = 48$)	
	Rank	%	Rank	%
Bring love and emotional satisfaction	2	15.2	4	10.4
Carry on name or bloodline	6	7.1	2	24.4
Are fun	4.5	9.7	6	7.1
Expected by others	4.5	9.7	3	11.4
Are accidents, just happened	3	12.6	1	29.0
Are wanted by the wife	1	31.6	5	9.6
Other	8.5	4.5	8	3.1
Earn money for the family or do chores	7	5.1	7	3.5
Help parents in their retirement	8.5	4.5	9	1.5
Total		100.0		100.0

Table 2.9. Relationships between Genders and among Ethnic Groups
in the Analysis of Why Men Would Enter the Role of Social Father[a]

Ethnic affiliation and gender	African American		Chinese and Chinese American		Core sample male
	Male	Female	Male	Female	
African American female					
r_s	.625				
r_p	.164				
Chinese and Chinese American male					
r_s	−.142	.200			
r_p	−.022	.147			
Chinese and Chinese American female					
r_s	.350	.450	.883**		
r_p	.092	.238	.949**		
Core sample male					
r_s	.567	.683*	.767*	.817*	
r_p	.233	.360	.903**	.943**	
Core sample female					
r_s	.650	.817*	.617	.767*	.833*
r_p	.457	.607	.721*	.814**	.909**

[a]r_s = ranking of motivation category; r_p = percentage of token allocation.
* = $p < .05$ (2-tailed); ** = $p < .01$ (2-tailed)

Chinese American), however, were virtually interchangeable. These
men strongly indicate that men enter into the father role for psychological reasons: they like kids and kids are fun. Social reasons are clearly
secondary, and economic reasons are largely irrelevant. Their women
seem to be fully cognizant of their priorities.

DISCUSSION

While it seems reasonable that the motivational hierarchies surveyed indicate some facet of reality for the White, Hispanic, and Chinese and Chinese American men (and women), which facet, image, or
behavior is more problematic? It is arguable that the hierarchy only
delineates the motivation to enter parenthood. The hierarchy may not
tap whether the expectations were actually fulfilled. That is, children
may be expected to bring love and emotional satisfaction into the familial domain, but there is no indication, from the data gathered, whether
the children, in fact, do, or whether they, in fact, do not.

Framed differently, does the pancultural value of love and emotional satisfaction (plus fun), which is pervasive across a wide swathe of categories, accurately depict the realities of that microecology known as the "family"? Are the children net emotional benefits to the parents or guardians or caregivers? This is a very delicate question that is at least as equally difficult to access or perhaps even to generate funding to be able to access. It is hard to interpret the sources of gaps in the literature.

A more inferential, still useful, route to follow to inquire into the relationship between (a) the rationale for entering into fatherhood for self-satisfaction and (b) the realization of that rationale is birthrates. That is, do fathers tend to have another child or additional children after experiencing parenthood? Or are we witnessing a variation on the theme of "once a philosopher, twice a pervert?"

Three interrelated points seem reasonable:

1. The rationales men have prioritized to enter fatherhood include the self-satisfaction they receive via love and emotional benefits.
2. Such emotions are positive items that are enjoyed and sought rather than endured or avoided.
3. It is their children who, in fact, are instrumental in creating a coveted emotional milieu for the fathers.

If the above three points are more true than not, then additional children would be expected to be forthcoming, i.e. born, to maintain the men's pleasure as the first child leaves childhood. Framed differently, a rewarding first child should harbinger a rewarding second child who precedes a joyful third child and so on. A quick scan of the U.S. fertility rates (measured here in mean number of lifetime births per woman) indicates problems with this scenario. Historically, there has been centuries-long downward pressure in birthrates in Europe and its extensions, for example, U.S. Australia, Canada (Goode, 1970; Ross & Harris, 1987; Wattenberg, 1987). After the Aberrant post-World War II baby boom, the U.S. birthrates continued their decline until, in 1972, the United States dropped below replacement value to 2.1 children per woman; and has stayed below replacement value (U.S. Dept. of Census, 1994).

Aligned with (a) the clear preference for *love, emotional satisfaction, and fun* as more prepotent motives for fatherhood and (b) the subreplacement level fertility rates are two overlapping interpretations: (1) one or two children can easily fill the parental love quotients. Cups runneth over. Additional children are overkill with a diminishing re-

turn quickly setting in. (2) The alternative is that the highly promul-
gated cultural value is simply off target, a miss: children create at least
as much psychological distress as they do psychological satisfaction.
Because other sources of psychological satisfaction are available that
are much less demanding and their use is much more discretionary in
terms of time, intensity, and frequency, these alternate sources compete
successfully with children for adult attention and resources, for example, spouse, friends, recreation, and occupations (cf Bryson & Bryson,
1978; Bulatao et al., 1983; White & Kim, 1987).

The oft heard explanation that available resources preclude additional offspring might well have a hefty dollop of the disingenuous. For
a relatively affluent nation to have a folklore that (a) is replete with
admonitions such as "for the love of money is the root of all evil" and
"money cannot buy happiness" and "I cannot afford to waste my time
making money", and (b) solidly advocates love and emotional satisfaction as a priority reason (at the expense of economic reasons) to have
children, then the explanation that a paucity of money precludes an
additional child is one of questionable validity, if not tortuous reason-
ing (cf. Harris [1974a] for examples of critiques on the credibility of any
cultural maxim).

Accordingly, let's examine the more indelicate alternative that
children are emotionally equivocal. Other studies that focus on the
topic of the net psychological value of children that are in situ are
remarkably difficult to ferret out. Again, whether the sparseness is because funding agencies are chary, or editors and publishers are reluctant, or referees are hypercritical, or researchers are unimaginative is
difficult to determine. Review processes are understandably private
endeavors. Nonetheless, literature on the relative balance of emotional
costs-to-benefits of children is scarce. This scarcity in and of itself
might be informative.

DISINCENTIVES OF PARENTING

There are, however, five pieces of disparate evidence that suggests
being a parent, that is, being a father, may not generate anything like
perpetual bliss:

1. Birth rates in the United States
2. Ann Landers
3. Surveyed spouses
4. Surveyed fathers
5. From Patterson (1980), aversive events from normal children

Birthrates

As birth control technology has increased and as the proportion of the population living on family farms had dwindled to single digits, birthrates in the United States have consistently dropped. Since 1972, the U.S. birthrates as measured by the number of children per woman has been below the replacement value of 2.1 (U.S. Bureau of the Census, 1993). When men and women have a chance to have fewer children they accept the opportunity.

A subdiscipline of psychology, learning theory, has solidified its niche in academia by noting that people repeat those behaviors that give them satisfaction and pleasure and avoid those behaviors that cause them discomfort or distress. The decrease in birthrates, that is, the fewer number of children per family, is offered as prima facie evidence that rearing children is problematic in generating net psychological rewards. If children were, on balance, more positive than otherwise, stopping at two or less seems at odds with classic learning theory.

Ann Landers

In 1975, the definitive populist Ann Landers (1976) polled her readers to learn whether those who had become parents would be parents again—if they could do their lives over again. Seventy percent (of 10,000 responses) wrote back "NO." The majority of the parents indicated a strong dissatisfaction with their parenting experiences. Despite sampling problems of the highest order, the results are intriguing, worthy of exploration, and a splendid pilot study. There has been no follow-up survey with more rigorous sampling techniques.

Surveyed Spouses

A number of studies on marital happiness, for example, Heaton (1990); Neal, Groat, & Hicks (1989); Rankin & Maneker (1985); Suiter (1991); and Waite, Haggstrom, & Kanouse (1985) converge on the notion that those years of marriage that include young children are the least happy for the spouses. The syllogism is rarely finished: it is the children who are creating the extra stress in a marriage. The work by Renne (1976) is illustrative. Renne surveyed 2,480 married couples and examined the health and well-being of the couples. Her conclusions include the following:

1. Parenthood detracts from the physical and psychological health of husbands and wives, particularly among younger couples,
2. Rates of joint marital satisfaction also were lower for active parents than for former parents and for childless couples (Independent of the duration of the marriage and the wife's age and employment status),
3. Parenthood may be detrimental to both health and martial satisfaction. This conclusion is suggested by the fact that former parents were better off than active parents (on both indixes); although not as well off as the childless couples.

Surveyed Fathers

As part of their larger survey *National Survey of Family and Households,* Bumpass and Sweet (1986) found that, as the number of children increased in a family, the youngest child was consistently evaluated by the father as less appealing when compared to the evaluations by the father of the child's older siblings.

Aversive Events from Children

In his undercited monograph *Mothers: The Unacknowledged Victims,* Patterson (1980) recorded normal children's behavior as they behaved in normal families. The sampling problems in Ann Landers' situation were not repeated in Patterson's study. Patterson's work was well within the guidelines of the scientific enterprise. He found that these children created "aversive events" for the mother at a rate of 20 per hour, and the typical mother was suffering from dysphoria. Hyperactive children or those who were, in some manner, behavioral problems escalated the density of aversive events and the level of dysphoria. The earlier question can then be repeated: "Why would a man want to enter or to remain in the father role?" Neither aversive events nor dysphoria seem particularly appealing incentives.

Patterson's conclusions (1980, pp. 45–49) included:

> Rearing normal children provides the mother with high rates of aversive events. Observations in both the home and laboratory settings showed minor aversive events may occur as often as once every 3 minutes when the mother is dealing with preschoolers. 'Major' conflicts between mothers and I may occur as often as three per hour. . . . Normal child rearing may be accompanied by dysphoria for mother. . . . At the very least, young would-be parents should be taught reasonable expectations for the flood of aversive

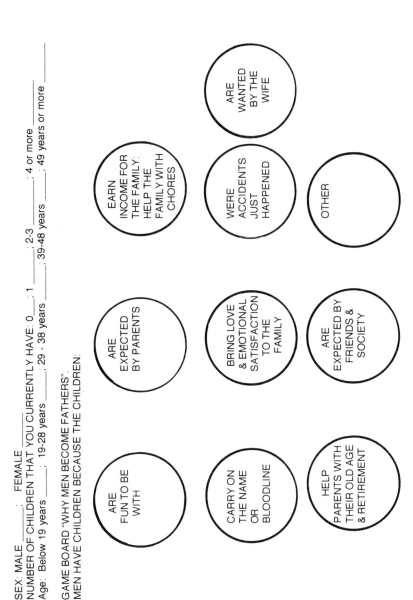

SEX: MALE _____; FEMALE _____
NUMBER OF CHILDREN THAT YOU CURRENTLY HAVE: 0 _____; 1 _____; 2-3 _____; 4 or more _____
Age: Below 19 years _____; 19-28 years _____; 29 - 38 years _____; 39-48 years _____; 49 years or more _____

GAME BOARD "WHY MEN BECOME FATHERS".
MEN HAVE CHILDREN BECAUSE THE CHILDREN:

ARE
FUN TO BE
WITH

ARE
EXPECTED
BY PARENTS

EARN
INCOME FOR
THE FAMILY;
HELP THE
FAMILY WITH
CHORES

ARE
WANTED
BY THE
WIFE

CARRY ON
THE NAME
OR
BLOODLINE

BRING LOVE
& EMOTIONAL
SATISFACTION
TO THE
FAMILY

WERE
ACCIDENTS
JUST
HAPPENED

HELP
PARENTS WITH
THEIR OLD AGE
& RETIREMENT

ARE
EXPECTED BY
FRIENDS &
SOCIETY

OTHER

Figure 2.1.   Gameboard containing the categories of "motivations to become a father."

events which normally accompany the role of parent. It also seems a pro-
pitious time to reconsider the traditional cultural roles for mother and for
father.

As they stand, the findings also suggest the need for a discussion of just
what is involved in the role of parent, of mother. . . . Various themes emerge
from the published literature suggesting that even under normal circumstances being a mother can be very painful. . . . At the very least, it would
seem necessary to accurately describe to the expectant parents just what
kind and level of pain can be expected. . . . At present, each young woman
makes this discovery in the bewildering context of trying to socialize an
infant. . . . As things now stand, the problem goes unnoticed. Even normally skilled mothers raising normal infants are likely to find themselves
often feeling overwhelmed, angry, and depressed without quite understanding its cause.

Virtually no other research offered refutation or replication or con-
firmation following the publication of Patterson's work. Why such an
academic taboo was seemingly violated is beyond the scope of this
book to explore. Suffice it to notice that the linkage between scientific
inquiry and sociopolitical realities ($$$$) surrounding that inquiry is
not the null set.

We will return to the United States as a special focus momentarily.
But first, a sojourn into the knotty nature–nurture versus nurture only
quagmire is needed. The argument will be made that an independent
man-to-child bond exists. That is, men have been selected over the
millennia to "like" their children; men are biologically built to nurture
their children.

CHAPTER 3

Looking for a Man-to-Child Bond

Setting Up the Fieldwork

Blood is thicker than water.

PROVERB

Like father, like son.

PROVERB

The base question being asked in this chapter is, "Why would a man, any man, *want* to be a father?" A secondary question becomes, "What is the genesis of that *want?* Why is *want* there at all? A tertiary question becomes, "How would someone investigate that *want* or inclination?

To set up an experiment or survey, a series of choice points are inevitable, and, as soon as a choice is made, the alternatives are eliminated. There is that gnawing feeling of finality with the possibility of a poorly made choice. For any investigation of any human behavior, five immediate and crucial decisions or choices have to be made:

1. Whom are you going to study? Who will be your subjects?
2. Where are you going to study your subjects?
3. Is your method of research influencing the character of the data being collected on your subjects, in this instance fathering? Framed in a different way, are you viewing behavior reflecting your subjects' own priorities, agenda, and decisions or are you viewing behavior that is reacting to your scientific intrusion?
4. What actual behaviors are to be coded? Behavior is ongoing and continuous. Codings have to be discrete with a beginning and an end and sometimes with a vexing middle.
5. From what perspective or vantage point—paradigm or model— will the data be organized and interpreted?

With a seemingly infinite number of options available for choice, the following decisions—for ill or will—were made early in this project's inception. Each selection made simultaneously voided the benefits and unique opportunities to be gained from the rejected options. However, no study has an infinite number of variables with an infinite number of subjects with unlimited time and funds. Accordingly, decisions that reject some options and thereby make that information unavailable are not merely inconvenient, they are necessary and inevitable.

SUBJECT SELECTION

The people to be surveyed include men and children: these are the irreducible components of fathering. Women are also studied. Well, why the women? What does fathering have to do with women? Why study the woman-child relationship if the man-child bond is the real focus of interest? The response to this question is in two parts.

1. There was, and still is, good reason to believe that child rearing and child caretaking are vital and irreplaceable facets of the social structure of a viable society. Living, socially competent children are a sine qua non of a culture, any culture, be that culture a tribe, a village, or a nation-state.

The form, rhythm, and character of child rearing are sensitive to a large array of variables impacting "all-at-once-ness" on the overall functioning of any society (Hewlett, 1992; Levinson & Malone, 1980, pp. 185–228; Ross & Harris, 1987; Van den Berghe, 1979). Consequently, there will be a mosaic of culturally unique prescriptions and proscriptions, the do's and the don'ts, orchestrating and perturbating the behavior of men (and women) toward their children. In other words, the man-child bond of any society is enmeshed in and operating within the context of the cultural traditions and prerogatives of that society (Rohner, 1975; Whiting & Whiting, 1975). Knowledge of this within-culture context becomes an integral part of an analysis of the man-child bond. Different cultures may have different starting places or givens in the realm of interpersonal behavior. For example, touching, holding, or hugging may be more appropriate within one culture than another. The minimum amount of interpersonal distance felt to be comfortable may be quite small in one society, while much larger in an alternative society (Hall, 1969, 1973). Any list of the covert, tacit behavioral rules in a cultural infrastructure can be extensive indeed. Touching, eye contact, facial expression, speaking voice, terms of address, posture, and so on, are subtly and effectively regulated by the expectations of others around a referent individual, that is, our culture affects nearly everything that we do in our social world.

A problem faced with this project—which was going to be cross-cultural if nothing else—was the same problem faced by every other cross-culture survey. The problem was to find a baseline or common denominator against which the man-child relationship could be compared *within* each surveyed culture and then compared with some sense of legitimacy *across* cultural boundaries (see Moore [1961] and Rohner et al. [1978] for discussions.) Fortunately, every society recognizes gender as a real construct and uses gender differentials to assemble its social structure (Levinson & Malone, 1980, pp. 267–278; Murdock, 1937; Murdock & Provost, 1973; Stewart, 1977). It is the woman, the mother, which thereby becomes the baseline or benchmark to evaluate and give context to the father-child interaction. Within each society, the level and type of activity between men and children is compared with the levels and types of activity between women and children.

Men and women within any culture or tribe do not experience that culture or tribe identically or even equivalently. In the sense that cultures can and do expect distinct responses from the two genders, men and women, fathers and mothers, do not experience congruent cultures. On the other hand, the culture which the men and fathers experience is the same culture viewed by the women and mothers. And, conversely, the culture experience by the women is the same culture viewed by the men. In the sense that one gender is the actor and the other gender is the potential spectator, the two genders are from the same culture. There is a symmetry in the two asymmetries. It is this sense of greater similarity of shared overview *within* any one culture—versus differences in worldviews between cultures—which serves as the buttress underpinning this conceptualization of the project.

Once an ordinal relationship (more than or less than or equal to) was established that index fathering behaviors compared with mothering behaviors *within* a culture, the ordinal relationships can be compared directly with each other *across* cultures. Using this technique, the problems inherent in cultural relativity (Levinson & Malone, 1980; Moore, 1961), that is, the judging of a society on its own terms, and of highly variegated cultural bases were lessened, if not completely countered. Framed a little differently, the ordinal data allowed apples to be compared with apples and oranges to be compared with oranges. Different soils, rainfalls, and temperatures may influence the growth of the fruit, but cannot change an apple to an orange or an orange to an apple.

2. The second part of the decision to survey women in a project that targeted a man-child relationship is as follows. Family life and familial dynamics tend to be integrated, interactive sets of activities. Fathers and mothers and their children will triangulate their own behaviors off feedback mechanisms and the expectations that each offers

the other two. Not only does the macroaspects of a culture, for example the subsistence technique, kinship systems, and political structure, affect the man-child relationship, but also the simple micro aspect of having a mother present or not may affect how a father responds to a child. As the pilot study strongly indicated, it did, indeed, matter if a mother was present or absent from a father-child dyad. Patterns of the man-child relationships were different when a woman was present versus when there was no woman present.

To encapsulate the rhyme and reason for studying women in a project about fathers and children to avoid tapping purely idiosyncratic socialization traditions (of Western Europe and United States), cross-cultural data are essential. To minimize the inherent problems of different cultural bases, comparable units of analysis were constructed *within* each society of the man-child relationship compared with the woman-child relationship. The ordinal relationship developed *within* a society can then be compared *across* societies. Because of potential interpersonal dynamics operating within a father and mother and child triad, the recording of the woman-child interaction was mandated to make available for analysis any influence that the presence of a woman had on a man–child dyad.

WHERE TO STUDY SUBJECTS

The options for places to investigate fathering include three prototypes: the laboratory, the home, and the public domain.

The advantages of the laboratory, nestled safely and snugly in an academic environs, are profound. The control of the variables (the always chaotic environment) is most available in the scientist's laboratory. Because the isolation of important versus trivial variables is the very goal that the scientist seeks, a laboratory environment with its control of those messy extraneous variables, becomes a valuable research tool. The laboratory setting is well tailored for finding the capacity or limits of subjects' sensorimotor skills or for divining the relative prepotency or penetration of the variables selected prior to the study. In addition, and not inconsequentially, the lab is the scientist's home turf with the attendant emotional security and confidence of the familiar. The subjects enter into a strange, often peculiar, and intimidating place, not unlike a dentist's office or the loan manager's sanctum on the third story of the bank, and then are to follow instructions that often include "just act natural and be yourself."

The disadvantages of a laboratory regimen are primarily that the subjects *are* in an alien place. They know full well they are under scrutiny and thereby may act unnaturally (Rosnow, 1974; Rubin, 1974).

Neither TV cameras and microphones nor the laboratory setting are well met to profile the subjects' own priorities and agenda as the subjects themselves choose to exercise them.

The home of the subjects, as a place for investigating the subjects' behavior patterns, gives the home turf or home team advantage to the subjects and allows their typical habits to unfold and be recorded. However, it is problematic whether their knowledge of the presence of an observer or recording device is massively affecting the normal range and central tendencies of their behavior patterns. It is certainly possible that, in this instance, the means of gathering data can fundamentally affect the character of the data itself. The physicists have the Heisenberg uncertainty principle. Behavioral scientists can point to TV cameras in the courtroom during the O.J. trial.

The last option, that of observing behaviors in public places, is the mirror image of the laboratory milieu. Whereas the laboratory setting minimizes spontaneous, "feral" behavior of individuals who are interacting ad lib and maximizes control of variables or immediate input that the subjects receive, an alternate study based on merely observing behavior in a public place maximizes the naturalness or spontaneity of the subject's behavior and minimizes any control that the experimenter may wish to exercise.

The aims of this project were to seek what fathers actually do and then make a stab at conjuring why they do what they do. Consequently, the lure of the laboratory was rejected for the great outdoors where humidity, rain, dust, mud, lack of shade, and mind-numbing boredom can all avail themselves. All observations were made during (1) daylight hours (2) in public places that had (3) equal access by gender. The project might retain the prerogative of selecting which public places with equal access for males and for females would become the observations sites, but, after that decision was made, the subjects selected themselves. Once they selected themselves, they then could behave in any manner or means that struck their fancy. They would come when they wanted. They would leave when they wanted. They would behave as they so chose at the speed, amplitude, and direction they chose. The fieldworker was to be an uninvited and very quiet guest in their lifespace.

Once the type of observation locus was decided, the next problem was where to distribute those loci. A cross-cultural study, by its very name, should include a number of different cultures, but which ones? Several immediate filters limited the potential pool of cultures as exemplified by the *World Ethnographic Sample, Ethnographic Atlas,* or the *Human Relations Area Files.* Not unlike the stars and the species of flora and fauna, cultures too seem to have a life cycle. They are born. They flourish. They die. Large numbers of cultures from antiquity such as the Aztecs, the Incas, the Maya, Pharaoh's Egypt, Socrates' Greece, Caesar's Rome, the Vikings, and Babylon are no more. In addition, large numbers of preliterate societies are likewise permanently unavailable. Tasmanians, the Kiowa, the Cheyenne, the Caribs, the Yahgan, and the Ona are simply gone.

Political considerations and health considerations further winnowed down the field. Not every government is unabashedly enthusiastic to have behavioral scientists (especially Western behavioral scientists) scrambling among its peasantry and doing any number of things, from censuses on the number and timing of menstrual cycles to consciousness raising. In addition, a number of areas of the globe are clearly dangerous to life and limb—and thereby become good places in which to lose a fieldworker, even if he or she could gain access. For example, neither Bosnia nor Rwanda nor Sri Lanka nor Chechnya seem inviting areas in which to leisurely survey the normal rhythms of daily family life.

Geographically, the five major continents were represented: North America, South America, Europe, Africa, Asia. In addition, urban and rural sites were represented, plus places with ethnically homogeneous and heterogeneous populations. Within the limitations of funding and personnel, there was an attempt to maximize cultural variability.

Fieldwork proceeded in two stages. Four cultures were surveyed to develop a baseline: The United States (sampled by Virginia, El Paso, Texas, and southeast Iowa) and Coahuila, Mexico (North America); Spain (Europe), and Lima, Peru (South America). Eighteen additional cultures were surveyed to test more fine-grained hypotheses: Reykjavik, Iceland; Ireland (Europe); Israeli kibbutzim; India; rural Taiwan; Sri Lanka; Japan; Hong Kong (Asia); Morocco; Ivory Coast; the Senufo of the Ivory Coast (Africa); the Karaja of Brazil; rural Brazil and urban Brazil (South America); Kenya; London (Great Britain); Paris (France); and Austria. In a bit of serendipity, a parallel project by Jankowiak (1992) made available some comparable data from China. A search of the literature in the United States found useful data from California (Hoffman & Teyber, 1985) and from an odd combination of California and Kansas (Amato, 1989) plus Kentucky (Sigelmann & Adams, 1990).

Please note that the data from these cultures are not meant to be exhaustive ethnographic amounts of the referent cultures. That is, the data from India are not intended in any way to profile the huge kaleidoscope of India's great diversity of peoples, customs, and lifestyles. The data should be viewed as data from India. Similarly, the data from the Israeli kibbutzim were not developed to reflect all of the various subcultures in Israel. These data are most diagnostically useful when interpreted as data from the Israeli kibbutzim.

If it can be agreed that India is distinct from Ireland, which is distinct from Israel, which is distinct from Virginia, which is distinct from China and so on, then the data sets drawn from within these distinct cultures can be conceptualized as representing different cultural bases. It is distinct cultural bases that establish the aim of the project, not any detailed ethnography. It is the various magnitudes of similarity and dissimilarity of fathering behavior found among these (agreed upon) distinct cultures that become the profound interest of this project.

METHOD OF STUDYING

All observations were conducted as anonymously as feasible. The influence of the observer upon the responses of the observed was ideally to be restricted to only the influence of the observer's sedentary, physical presence within the vicinity. In larger areas—playgrounds or parks in large urban areas—anonymity was easy to adopt. Sunglasses, tourist guidebooks, and newspapers hid eye direction and recording notebooks effectively. For small villages or towns effective anonymity of the fieldworkers was more of a challenge and the fieldworkers exercised their skills in creativity and interpersonal relations in appearing benign, nonthreatening, and unobtrusive. The infusion of cash into the local economy for bread and board of course helped, but engaging personalities probably aided the most. In any event, anonymity of the fieldworker and his or her observing duties were key elements in the study and were, from all accounts, maintained effectively. The gathered data reflect men and women and children allocating their preferences and their priorities and their choices as they, themselves, decided. It became the requirements of this study to reflect accurately what were the behavioral results of those decisions made by the subjects: that is, by the men and women and children.

There were no questionnaires, no interviews, no intrusion into the private space and time of the observed subjects. With such a restrictive decision, much information of great value becomes unavailable. However, the importance of anonymity generated benefits judged to be at least equivalent to the heavy costs incurred.

BEHAVIOR TO BE CODED

A cross-cultural project such as this one require comparable units of analysis. That is, whatever behaviors were coded in one culture had to be comparable or equivalent to the kinds of behavior coded in alternative cultures. To achieve comparability, the level of behavior coded was generalized enough or abstract enough for all the cultures surveyed. Vocabulary, for example, would be far too specific across societies for any kind of useful comparison. The heart pumping blood or the direction of peristalsis would be equivalent across societies, but too obvious to be interesting.

This project was built to find evidence—if such evidence existed—which indicated an independent man-to-child bond. From Tiger and Fox (1977, p. 58) a "bond" will be defined as a "major regularity in the social behavior of a species." If such a bond existed, then the right regularities or patterns had to be anticipated and actually observed in diverse cultures. The cultural meaning of the putative regularities did not have to be equivalent. The sheer existence of the similarities across divergent cultural boundaries was crucial.

After a good deal of trial and error—mostly error—four basic behaviors were selected from the pilot studies for coding across cultural boundaries. The four dimensions (from Hall, 1961) were:

1. A person could be present with or absent from another person.
2. A person could be touching or not touching someone else.
3. A person could be near or far from someone else.
4. A person could be looking at or not looking at someone else.

A more detailed and technical description of the coding categories is presented below in the Procedure section.

It may be useful to note that verbalization (talk—not talk) was a major disappointment as a candidate for inclusion in the study. The logistics of determining whether someone has spoken or not were invincible. Smell and taste were additional candidates for coding categories, but only for a very short time. However, many of the names for the proposed scales were innovative.

For each coded group including at least one adult and at least one child, the following variables were coded:

- Number of individuals in the group.
- Gender of each person in the group.
- Developmental status (age) of each person in the group.
- The behavioral indices from the adult(s) to the child or children.

THEORETICAL PERSPECTIVE

In what amounts to a totally arbitrary decision, the emergence or development of human social behavior is seen as a triune phenomenon—three major forces acting simultaneously on the actual emitted response. It is possible that another theoretician might be more comfortable with two forces; still others may find four, five or seven forces more diagnostic. For this project, however, three is a manageable, useful number and faithful to the notion of an epigenetic unfolding of the human condition. The three forces or tiers of analysis include:

1. The symbolic tier.
2. The cultural or socialization tradition tier.
3. The biological or phylogenetic tier.

What is being suggested here is that behavioral development and variance can be conceptualized as emerging from two (main effect) variables (genotypic information and cultural information) plus a multitude of interaction effects (Jensen, 1972; Plomin, 1990; Rowe, 1994; Scarr & McCartney, 1983). Because of the interdependence and short-term and long-term feedback loops that exist among these three tiers, any dissection of ongoing human social behavior will always have elements of the artificial and the arbitrary. Within the context of these final interpretations, tempered by this caveat, the threefold analysis can be accepted as diagnostically useful.

The Symbolic Tier

The universal proclivity by humans to symbolize and to form metaphor and simile has been richly documented by ethnographers for decades (e.g., Benedict, 1959; Douglas, 1978; Geertz, 1974; cf Jung, 1969; Leach, 1982; Levi-Strauss, 1963,1979; Turner, 1969). It is self-evident that analyses by symbolic anthropologists have constituted a broadly useful and informative discipline. However, a systematic relationship between symbols as a class of events and the referent behaviors is very difficult to ascertain (Harris, 1974a; 1974b; for examples see Arens [1979] on cannibalism and Freeman [1983] on Margaret Mead). Symbols can reinforce and parallel behavior tendencies, but they can also camouflage or obfuscate the accurate perception of empirical behavioral patterns. The symbol, in the form of an image or rule or a spoken phrase that attempts to profile "the way things are," may be actualized more in the breach than in the observance. In addition, contrasting symbols or images can reflect the same trait. The following maxims serve as nice examples: "fools rush in where angels fear to tread," yet we should "strike while the iron is hot"; however, "haste makes waste," but "time and tide wait for no man"; on the other hand, "he sows hurry and reaps indigestion"; then again, "hoist your sail when the wind is fair"; nonetheless, "wisely and slow, they stumble that run fast"; in addition, consider "make hay while the sun shines," while tempered by "marry in haste and repent in leisure"; and finally, compare "opportunity seldom knocks twice." These symbols of Western folklore give no real aid on how to manage one's time.

Because of the equivocal consonance between symbols, including verbal reports from informants and the referent behaviors, this chapter will concentrate on the cultural and biological tiers. This present concentration can in no way be construed to suggest that work within the symbolic or verbal domain is not important. Emic analyses are of course necessary for a more complete understanding to the problem of what it means to be human. Nevertheless, the current lack of a paradigm, which allows the matching of empirically normative behavior across cultures with parallel imagery or symbols across cultures, severely limits and constrains simultaneously the utility of a symbolic analysis toward the *validation* of causal agents generating the emergence of human social behavior. Of course, when we begin to focus on the analysis of the United States father (Chapter 6) image, if not everything as the sports icon argues, is certainly important.

The Socialization Tradition Tier

In a rare display of consensus among behavioral and social scientists, the notion has been accepted that socialization or enculturation of traditions that surround and immerse each citizen of a society influence the form and intensity of the individual's behavior. There is virtually no theorist who discounts the impact on a culture's citizenry of their assimilation of that culture. The importance of norms, expectations, and worldviews of each culture on its populace is agreed to be broad, deep, and pervasive.

To accede to the strength of cultural prerogatives on the ontogenetic (individual) development of human behavior, however, by no means disavows or argues against an additional (causal) influence on human behavior by biological processes that are under (partial) genetic control. Moreover, an acceptance of the power of social processes to affect behavior does not also necessitate a further acceptance of idiosyncrasy or total arbitrariness of each culture. Regardless of any proposed genotypic penetrance into behavior (both central tendency and variance), the notion that cultural elements often follow regular, predictable relationships with each other has been well documented (White, Burton, & Brudner, 1977; White, Burton, & Dow, 1981; Whiting, 1964; cf. Divale & Harris, 1976).

For this project, it is also accepted that a culture and human phylogny track each other (i.e., coevolution), and the feedback loops align the biological substrate of *Homo* with the cultural manifestations that emanate from that substrate (Barkow, 1980, 1989; Boyd & Richerson, 1985; Durham, 1979, 1990). Said a little differently, the genotype held in common by our genus *Homo* generates thematic modes of behaviors, whereas the cultural circumstances generate variants of that theme.

Personality type and subsistence technique are good examples of a systematic linkage between theme and variations: (1) the acquisition of a personality is panhuman, and (2) the various facets of the personality are differentially emphasized or deemphasized as a function of a culture's mode of procuring food from the environment (Barry, Bacon, & Child, 1957; Barry, Child, & Bacon, 1959). The ability to generate grammar (theme) and the myriad languages and dialects (variations) is an example of a linkage which, at present, points to no scaled relationship.

The Phylogenetic Tier

This project accepts the proposition that the development of human behavior, in addition to human morphology or anatomy and physiology, can be biased and canalized by genotypic information mediated by the two motivational systems: the neural and endocrine systems. The central nervous system in particular is viewed here as not only processing information originating from the external and internal environments but also as autogenetically creating motivational states. (Lorenz, 1958, 1965; Tinbergen, 1951). These motivational states are then available for selection, both phylogenetically and ontogenetically, from a wide range of other potential motivations to be actualized into overt behaviors and finally to be directed and molded by the culturally idiosyncratic milieu in which the individuals happen to reside.

PROCEDURE

This project used naturalistic observation as the means to gather data. All observations were conducted during daylight hours at sites that were places of public access with equal access for both males and females. There was strict anonymity concerning the project. Observers were not to interact with the people being observed in any manner over and beyond whatever impact the observer's physical presence had upon the people within the surrounding vicinity. The potential of the method of observation to influence the results of observation was very real, therefore, the anonymity of the observers and of the project was essential to minimize such influence. Of utmost importance were the time intervals used for observation. Observations were coded in one of two categories: observations occurred in time intervals in which adult males were normally expected to be precluded from association with children because of cultural norms, for example, tilling fields, tending herds, being at work, and attending special ritual events. The code for this time interval was Male Precluded (MP).

Observations also occurred in time intervals when males were available to children: for example, sabbaths, festival days, after-work hours, weekends, and holidays. The code for this time interval was Males Not Precluded (MNP). The MNP time tended to be *free* time for men when they had numerous alternatives for their time and presence. These men could have been with their children, but they were not forced or coerced to be with them. That is, a *not precluded* interval was not the same as either a *men-are-present* interval or a *men-must-be-present* interval. The individual times for the MP and MNP intervals varied considerably within the same culture at different communities as well as between cultures. The boundaries separating MP from MNP intervals were developed by the judgment of each field researcher at each site.

For any given culture, if the total percentage of adult male-child association was significantly different between the MP and MNP intervals, thereby indicating two populations, the *diagnostic intervals for subsequent analysis would be only the MNP intervals.* (The MP figures generated the expected frequencies.) If the percentage of adult male-child association was *not* significantly different between the MNP and MP intervals, thus indicating one population, then the diagnostic intervals for the subsequent analysis were the totals (MP plus MNP intervals). A lack of difference in adult male-child association between MP and MNP intervals did not occur for any of the surveyed cultures.

Group Size and Composition

The joint association of two or more people with at least one adult and at least one child was defined as a "group." As well as recording the age bracket of each child, the composition of each group was recorded by the number of individuals, gender of each individual, and adult-child status. See Appendix 3.1 for definitions and reliability measures for the fieldworkers.

Note that a child was coded in one of three types of adult groups: (1) a men-only group, (2) a women-only group, or (3) a men-and-women group.

1. A men-only group was composed of at least one child and at least one man, with no women present.
2. A women-only group was composed of at least one child and at least one woman, with no men present.
3. A men-and-women group was composed of at least one child and at least one man, and at least one woman.

Note that this project was *not* designed to collect or study kinship or consanguinity data. Thus, societal norms for kinship status–role complexes were not available for analysis. The questioning of paternity of strange men in a strange land by a stranger is indelicate at best. What is available is a view of how societies allocate and distribute men and children with each other. Because of the lack of kinship data, terms such as "paternalistic," "adult male," "man," and "father figure" are probably more technically accurate than "father" or "genitor". On the other hand, no theory that I know of predicts appreciable numbers of nonkin men who associate with children in public places. In a similar vein, it is logically possible that much older siblings were baby-sitting their much younger brothers or sisters. However, due to the public locale of the sets of observations, baby-sitting episodes were undoubtedly negligible. To the extent the baby-sitting was captured by this project, that type of data—baby-sitter and child dyads—argues against a man-(to)-child bond. The reason for this counterforce is that baby-sitting is, cross-culturally, a uniformly female event (Barry & Paxson, 1971; Hewlett, 1992; Weisner & Gallimore, 1977). Thus as the proportion of baby-sitting episodes increases, the proportion of man-child dyads necessarily decreases.

Proxemic Indices

Tactile Contact. As soon as the group composition was determined, a 30-second observation interval was begun. Within the 30 seconds, the most active physical contiguity from the adult's hands to the child was recorded. See Appendix 3.2 for the coding system: adult-to-child tactile contact.

For the tactile contact scale and the following two scales, adult males in men-only groups were compared exclusively with adult female in women-only groups.

Personal Distance. With the adult's head and trunk as the frame of reference, the closest in terms of (spatial) distance that the adult came to the child, within the 30-second observation limit, was recorded. See Appendix 3.2 for the coding system of adult-to-child personal distance.

Visual Orientation. The immediate visual field was considered to be directly in front of any individual's eyes plus segments to the left and right of the center. The coding interval for visual orientation was the last 5 seconds of the 30-second observation interval. If, during the full 5 seconds the child was never in the visual scan of the adult, then the child was recorded as being out of the adult's visual field (coded NONSEE). If, during any portion of the 5-second interval the child was within the visual scan of the adult, then the child was recorded as being in the adult's visual field (coded SEE). See Appendix 3.2 for the coding system of visual orientation—adult to child.

Selection of Communities within Each Culture

The selection of communities within each culture depended in part on logistical accessibility, geographic dispersion, and the type of culture being researched. For example, rural Taiwan dictated communities that were agrarian based and within ready traveling distance of one another. Urbanized Iceland was restricted to Reykjavik. See Table 3.1 for the communities surveyed per culture.

Selection of Observation Sites per Community

A minimum of four observation sites per community were used. One site was where the children were playing. A second site was a place of commerce. Subsequent sites were developed by the fieldworkers as circumstances dictated.

Length of Fieldwork

Fieldwork varied in time from two weeks (Lima, Peru) to approximately 24 weeks (the Karaja of Brazil). Urban sites quickly generated a large number of dyads. An appropriate number of dyads was slower to develop at rural sites. Consequently, seven weeks for observations was the modal duration in rural cultures, while four weeks of observation was the modal duration in urban cultures. To date everyone has returned from the field reasonably happy and reasonably healthy. The caveats of "watch what you eat and watch what you drink" still seem to be worthwhile to remember and to repeat.

Table 3.1. Communities in Which Observations Took Place in the 23
Cultures and the Number of Children Observed Associating with
Adults during Discretionary Times for Men[a]

Culture[b]	Number of children	Communities
United States	*14,692*	Kentucky (309), Texas (873), Virginia (8,953), Iowa (639), California (1,357), Nebraska-California (2,561).
Mexico	1,355	Saltillo, Sabinas, Piedras Negras, Allende, Morelos
Spain	1,058	Madrid, Guadalajara, Lerida, Zuera
Ireland	1,852	Dublin, Tralee, Cashel, Athlone, Sligo
Karaja (Brazil)	399	Villages of Sao Felix, Fontoura, Tapirape Macauba
Ivory Coast	1,642	Korhogo, Bouke, Dimbokro, Ferkesedougou, Abidjan
Morocco	1,398	Marrakech, Ouirgane, Casablanca, Azrou, Fes
Lima, Peru	490	Greater Lima area
Iceland	1,694	Greater Reykjavik area
Japan	1,336	Okayama, Ogi-Megi, Seto, Takamatsu, Nagoya
India	1,104	New Delhi, Madras, Khajuraho, Allahabad, Bombay
Hong Kong	164	Hong Kong Island
Israel (kibbutzim)	2,139	Givat Brenner, K'far Monash, K'far Blum, Givat Hay'yin, Sde Nitzan, Moshen Tsofet
Sri Lanka	1,973	Colombo, Kandy, Nagambo, Rathapura, Hatton, Polanurawa, Chilow
Taiwan	2,790	Lu Kang, Ma Kung, Da Yan, Lung Tan, Chu Nan, Tung Hsiao, Ching Shui
Senufo (Ivory Coast)	1,132	Ferkessedougou, Dabakala, Gbon, Boundial, Siempurgo, Kikogougou
Brazil (rural)	549	Bom Jardin, Silvania, Vianopolis
Brazil (urban)	542	Monte Mor
London, U.K.	397	London
Paris, France	485	Paris suburb
Kenya	748	Ifiolo, Gilgil, Maralal, Nyeri, Nanuk, Njumbi
Austria	132	Greiz and Vienna
China	2,162	Huhhot (Inner Mongolia)
Total	40,233	

[a]Males Not Precluded (MNP) intervals.
[b]This survey is designed only to record the regularities of how *different* cultures allocate men and men
and children in their associations with each other. The unique properties of each culture is *not*
intended to be surveyed, nor are the individualized traditions of each culture available for comparisons. It is the intent of this survey to survey different cultures, but not to delinate a full ethnographic
account of any one or more cultures.

APPENDIX 3.1: CODING SPECIFICATIONS
OF THE SAMPLES

It should be made clear that these cultures are not completely
separate, independent entities. Accordingly, "Galton's Problems," the
term given to the dilemma of divining independent invention (func-

tional relationships) from cultural diffusion (historical relationships) becomes not problematic but is a guarantee. As a result of Galton's intrusion with his problem, interpretations are based more on the weight and direction of the data than on any one decisive litmus test or Newtonian proof. See Ford (1961) for a discussion.

Child and Adult

The meanings of the terms "child" and "adult" vary enormously across cultures and often vary between genders within the same culture. To facilitate cross-cultural comparability, anyone of either gender was arbitrarily defined as a child if that individual was not well into or through biological puberty as determined by physically observable secondary sex characteristics. A child was defined as a prepubescent. An adult was arbitrarily defined as anyone of either gender who was either well into puberty or had finished puberty. Adults were defined as pubescents and postpubescents. Given that an adult was defined as a pubescent or a postpubescent and a child was defined as a prepubescent, a logical category existed of an association between a person who had just become a pubescent (e.g., 15 years), and a person who was late in childhood and still a prepubescent (e.g., 13 years). This association is nominally one of peers, not one of a caretaking dimension. To avoid the distortion of counting peer groups as caretaking groups, the judgments of the fieldworkers were the best barometers. A perceived gap of at least eight years between the postpubescent and the prepubescent was available to demarcate an adult-child dyad from a child-child dyad or an adult-adult dyad. However, the judgment of the fieldworker at the site was relied upon to make the distinction between a play or peer group and a caretaking group.

Observation Sites

For each subculture, there were at least four sites for observing adults and children interacting with each other. One site was a place where children were playing. One site was a place of commerce. At least two additional and separate sites were selected by the fieldworker ad lib.

All observation sites were in public places with equal access for both males and females. All observations were during daylight hours. Strict anonymity of the fieldworker and his or her errand was attempted to minimize the influence of the coder on the coded. Ideally, the only influence that the coder had on the adults and children was the affect of a sedentary stranger on the groups of individuals in public places.

Coded Items

Fieldworkers coded the gender composition of each adult–child group, the developmental status per person, and the number of children and adults per group. Any one group of adults and children was coded only once per day per site.

Unique Characteristics

The Kentucky sample (Sigelman & Adams, 1990) was restricted to public parks. Adult–child groups were excluded from analysis if the group included an adult who was less than 18 years of age or more than 40 years older than the oldest child in the group, or if the group had more than three children, or if there was a child over 12 years of age. The Nebraska–California sample (Amato, 1989) coded only children who appeared to be five years or younger. The California sample (Hoffman & Teyber, 1985) represented adults with children only if the adults appeared to be 21 years or older.

APPENDIX 3.2: CODING SYSTEM

Tactile Contact: Adult to Child

As soon as the group composition is determined, a 30-second observation interval is begun. Within the 30 seconds, the *most* active physical contiguity from the adult's hands to the child is recorded. See below for the coding system for "tactile contact: adult to child."

0. Caressing and holding (most active tactile contact)
1. Feeling or caressing
2. Extended or prolonged holding (holding for the entire 30-second interval)
3. Holding (holding for a portion of the 30-second interval)
4. Spot touching (e.g., a hand peck)
5. Accidental touching (e.g., brushing)
6. No contact whatsoever (least active tactile contact)

Statistical instrument: Chi-square extension of the median test.

Personal Distance: Adult to Child

With the adult's head and trunk as the locus, the closest in terms of (spatial) distance that the adult comes to the child, within the 30-second observation limit, is recorded. See below for the coding system of "personal distance: adult to child".

     11.   Touching with head or trunk (closest distance)
    101. Just outside body contact
     12.   Touching with forearms, elbows, or knees
    102. Within forearm distance, but not touching
     13.   Touching with arms fully extended
    103. Within arm reach, but not touching
     14.   Touching with arm extended and body leaning
    104. Within reach if body is leaning and arm is extended
     55.   Outside the system; applicable only with extensions (farthest distance)

Statistical instrument: Chi-square extension of the median test.

Visual Orientation: Adult to Child

The immediate visual field is considered to be directly in front of any individual's eyes plus segments to the left and right of center. The coding interval for visual orientation is the *last* 5 seconds of the 30-second observation interval. If, during the full 5 seconds, the child is never in the visual scan of the adult, the child is recorded as being out of the adult's visual field (coded *nonsee*). If during any portion of the 5-second interval, the child *is* within the adult's visual field (coded *see*). Figure 3.1 illustrates the coding system of visual orientation: adult to child.

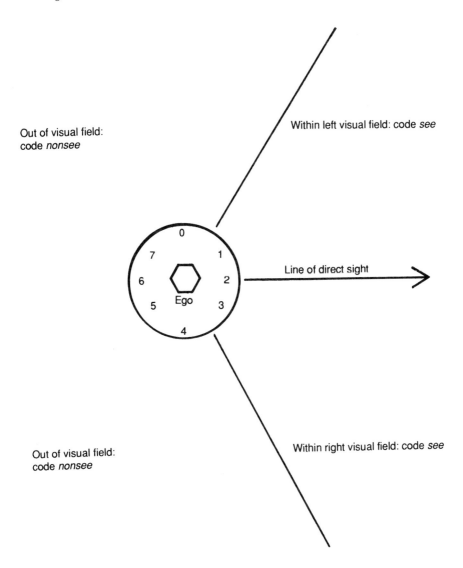

Out of visual field:
code *nonsee*

Within left visual field: code *see*

Line of direct sight

Out of visual field:
code *nonsee*

Within right visual field: code *see*

0
7   1
6   2
5   3
Ego
4

Statistical instrument: chi-square

Figure 3.1.   Coding system for visual orientation—adult to child.

CHAPTER 4

Results of the Fieldwork
The Joys and Tedium of Promiscuous Empiricism

> *There was an old woman who lived in a shoe*
> *She had so many children*
> *She didn't know what to do.*
>
> NURSERY RHYME

> *The four eaglets are my four sons*
> *who cease not to persecute me*
> *even into death.*
>
> WILLIAM SHAKESPEARE, *Henry II*

Fieldworkers traveled out to their destinations. The fieldworkers surveyed and coded adults and children. Fieldworkers came home. The following is what they found.

ASSOCIATIONS BY AGE AND GENDER AND NUMBER

A total of 59,182 children associated with adults were surveyed: 18,949 when men were generally precluded from easy access to their children (MP intervals) and 40,233 when there were no culturally normative impediments to the joint association of fathers and children (MNP intervals). Twenty-three cultures had available data in the MNP intervals. Nearly a fifth (20.9%; sd = 5.8%) of the children were with men-only groups. Another third (34.7%; sd = 14.5%) were with men when women were also present (men and women groups). See Table 4.1.

Said a little differently, if a child were with one or more adults, the

Table 4.1. Associations in Percentages among All Children and Adult Groups in 23 Cultures[a]

Culture	Adult group			
	Men-only (%)	Women-only (%)	Men and women (%)	Total percentage of children
Israel	31.9	53.5	14.6	100.0
Iceland	29.0	39.6	31.4	100.0
Morocco	28.5	56.8	14.7	100.0
India	28.5	43.0	28.5	100.0
Brazil (urban)	24.4	46.4	29.2	100.0
Taiwan	23.8	56.8	19.4	100.0
Ireland	22.9	36.5	40.6	100.0
Japan	22.9	38.3	38.8	100.0
Brazil (rural)	22.8	54.3	22.9	100.0
Kenya	21.9	49.2	28.9	100.0
China	21.3	20.2	58.5	100.0
Senufo	21.0	41.5	37.5	100.0
Hong Kong	20.7	32.3	47.0	100.0
Austria	20.5	37.1	42.4	100.0
Sri Lanka	20.5	64.7	14.8	100.0
United States	*20.5*	*43.65*	*35.85*	*100.0*
Virginia	17.5	43.5	39.0	100.0
Iowa	18.6	46.6	34.8	100.0
El Paso, Texas	21.8	44.3	33.9	100.0
Kentucky	30.7	44.7	24.6	100.0
Nebraska and California	18.8	33.2	48.0	100.0
California	15.6	49.6	34.8	100.0
Ivory Coast	17.4	67.4	15.2	100.0
London, United Kingdom	17.4	42.3	40.3	100.0
Lima, Peru	17.4	52.2	30.4	100.0
Spain	16.8	31.5	51.7	100.0
Mexico	14.2	50.2	35.6	100.0
Paris, France	8.7	22.9	68.4	100.0
Karaja	8.3	40.8	50.9	100.0
Mean =	20.9	44.4	34.7	100.0
s =	5.81	11.90	14.53	

[a]Males not precluded intervals only.

odds were that the child was in the presence of a caretaking man, undoubtedly the child's father. Seventeen of the cultures had data gathered in both MP and MNP intervals. (MP data were not coded in Austria, Paris, Hong Kong, Brazil [urban], China, and London). When men's presence was compared between MP and MNP, all 17 cultures showed an increase in the men's association with their children (X^2; $p < .01$ per culture). The average increase from the benchmark of the MP interval was 22.0% ($sd = 12.8$). The men-only group revealed an average gain of 8.5% and the men-and-women groups averaged a gain of 13.5% ($sd = 11.6\%$). Hence, men are found with children in substantial proportions (compared to women) *when and where they do not have to be.* Of particular interest is the men-only group during the MNP interval wherein 20.9% of the children were with men away from the domicile, but no women were present. The average increase from MP to MNP intervals was substantial (8.5%).

Boys Only

More than a quarter (27.3%; $sd = 8.74$) of the boys were in men-only groups. About a third (33.8%; $sd = 14.75$) of the boys were in men and women groups. See Table 4.2.

Girls Only

The percentage of girls in men-only groups was 17.62% ($sd = 6.51$). More than 30% (31.23%; $sd = 13.60$) of the surveyed girls were in men and women groups. See Table 4.3.

Given both the ethnographic literature on power by gender (Whyte, 1978; Levinson & Malone, 1980) and the cottage industry of the popularized polemics on power by gender, adult males are conceded the power position in any culture one wishes to examine. Accordingly, the surveyed men had ample opportunity to be someplace else with someone else. Yet over 20% of the children were with men (no mother present) in public places. These fathers and children were together because the fathers were able and willing to do so. Consequently, it seems eminently reasonable to conclude that when men can be with their children, they choose to do so. Another 34.7% of the children were with men and the women were also present. It is difficult to imagine what forces might override any putative reluctance on the part of the men who refused to join their women and children. A light use of Occam's razor, suggests that the men are there because they want to be.

An unexpected relationship emerged across the cultures between the percentages of children in men-only groups and the percentages of children in men-and-women groups. As the percentage of children in men and women groups decreased, the percentage of children in men-only groups *increased* ($rp = -.611$; $p < .01$; 2-tailed). A respectable

Table 4.2. Associations in Percentages among Boys-Only and Adult Groups in 22 Cultures[a]

Culture	Adult group			Total percentage of boys
	Men-only (%)	Women-only (%)	Men and women (%)	
Israel	40.7	43.8	15.5	100.0
Iceland	40.1	33.5	26.4	100.0
Morocco	37.5	48.9	13.6	100.0
Ivory Coast	36.3	48.0	15.7	100.0
Brazil (urban)	35.9	38.7	25.4	100.0
India	34.2	34.7	31.1	100.0
Brazil (rural)	32.7	41.7	25.6	100.0
Taiwan	31.4	50.2	18.4	100.0
Kenya	30.8	42.3	26.9	100.0
Senufo	28.6	34.8	36.6	100.0
Ireland	28.4	26.9	44.7	100.0
Sri Lanka	27.3	57.3	15.4	100.0
United States[b]	*24.7*	*41.1*	*34.2*	*100.0*
Virginia	20.9	38.9	40.2	100.0
Iowa	23.2	44.3	32.5	100.0
El Paso, Texas	28.7	36.6	34.7	100.0
Kentucky	30.2	43.3	26.5	100.0
California	20.5	42.6	36.9	100.0
London, United Kingdom	23.4	36.3	40.3	100.0
Lima, Peru	23.1	46.2	40.3	100.0
Mexico	22.6	41.0	36.4	100.0
Austria	22.4	34.5	43.2	100.0
Hong Kong	21.5	30.8	47.7	100.0
Spain	20.0	31.6	48.4	100.0
Japan	19.7	42.6	37.7	100.0
Paris, France	11.3	21.3	67.4	100.0
Karaja	7.1	29.9	63.0	100.0
Mean =	27.3	38.9	33.8	100.0
s =	8.74	8.49	14.75	

[a]Males not precluded intervals only.
[b]Gender × adult group was not available for the Nebraska and California sample.

37.3% ($.611^2$) of the variance in differences in men-only groups' levels of association can be attributed to changes in the level of men-and-women groups.

In other words, if, for whatever reason, when a society maximized division of labor by gender and proscribed the joint association between women-and-men (hence men-and-women groups would be re-

Table 4.3. Associations (in Percentages) among Girls-Only and Adult Groups in 22 Cultures[a]

Culture	Adult group			Total percentage of girls
	Men-only (%)	Women-only (%)	Men and women (%)	
Israel	28.2	58.6	13.2	100.0
Japan	27.9	35.8	36.3	100.0
India	26.6	47.9	25.5	100.0
Hong Kong	25.4	34.3	40.3	100.0
Iceland	24.3	46.0	29.7	100.0
Taiwan	22.0	60.4	17.6	100.0
Ireland	21.9	42.1	36.0	100.0
Austria	21.7	38.3	40.0	100.0
Kenya	18.7	55.0	26.3	100.0
Morocco	18.2	69.1	12.7	100.0
United States[b]	18.1	50.3	31.6	100.0
Virginia	15.1	48.5	36.4	100.0
Iowa	15.8	50.0	34.2	100.0
El Paso, Texas	17.4	50.8	31.8	100.0
Kentucky	31.3	46.3	22.4	100.0
California	11.1	55.9	33.0	100.0
Spain	17.7	31.7	50.6	100.0
Senufo	15.6	45.9	38.5	100.0
Sri Lanka	13.9	73.4	12.7	100.0
London, United Kingdom	13.9	54.3	31.8	100.0
Lima, Peru	13.3	57.5	29.2	100.0
Brazil (rural)	12.9	65.8	21.3	100.0
Brazil (urban)	12.9	56.6	30.5	100.0
Ivory Coast	10.6	73.9	15.5	100.0
Mexico	9.3	56.9	33.8	100.0
Karaja	8.6	46.8	44.6	100.0
Paris, France	6.0	24.6	69.4	100.0
Mean =	17.6	51.2	31.2	100.0
s =	6.51	13.37	13.60	

[a]Males not precluded intervals only.
[b]Gender × adult group was not available for the Nebraska-California sample.

stricted), the percentage of children with men (men-only group) systematically increased.

For boys only, the correlation between their association with men-only groups and men-and-women groups was $(r_p =) -.861; p < .01;$ 2-tailed). A respectable 74.1% ($.861^2$) of the variance in the percentage of boys in men-only groups can be attributed to changes in the percentage of boys in men-and-women groups.

For girls only, the correlation was not significantly related to the percentage of girls in men-and-women groups (r_p = .2752; n.s.). At first blush, there seems to be no cross-cultural pattern in the association between men and girls. Again, however, the biocultural character of humans becomes apparent.

Part of any culture is its view of gender. Some cultures have stronger division by gender than others. If cultural norms restrict association between males and females, then there ought to be decreased association between men and women in the diagnostic times (during daylight hours) and diagnostic public places (public places with equal access by gender) of this project. Conversely, if there were minimal division of labor by gender in a culture, then the number of men-and-women groups in that culture ought to be relatively large. In addition, if division of labor by gender is strong within a society, then associations between men and girls (compared to men and boys) ought to be comparatively low. Therefore, the following statistic was computed. The ratio of girls to boys in men-only groups for each culture was determined. This ratio (girls/boys) was then compared to the percentage of children that were in men-and-women groups. The relationship was significant: r_p = .500; p < .05; 2-tailed. As the number of children in men-and-women groups increased (thus signaling *less* division of labor by gender), the ratio of girls/boys increased, that is, the proportion of girls with men-only groups became higher. See Table 4.4.

Thus the man–girl relationship *is* patterned across cultures. When channels are opened via cultural expectations for men to be with their daughters, the men systematically avail themselves of that opportunity.

Synopsis

Thus there seems to be a threshold of father–child association that societies sustain. If some conduits of father–child associations are constrained, others emerge to allow the easy flow of children to be with their fathers. The men, although quite capable of staunching the flow, seem to be willing participants.

Below, MNP data (only) will be analyzed by the germane demographics.

Gender

Did the gender of the child affect the chances of being with a father?

Because we are dealing with the human condition and all of its complexity, the answer is both "Yes" and "No."

Table 4.4. The Relationship between the Ratio (of Girls to Boys) in Men-Only Groups per Culture to the Percentage of (All) Children in Men and Women Groups per Culture[a]

Culture	Ratio of girls to boys	Percentage of children in men & women groups
Israel	.667	14.6
Japan	.678	38.8
India	.651	28.5
Hong Kong	1.214	47.0
Iceland	.535	31.4
Taiwan	.572	19.4
Ireland	.761	40.6
Austria	.500	42.4
Kenya	.713	28.9
Morocco	.394	14.7
United States[a]	.701	33.3
Virginia	.698	39.0
Iowa	.642	34.8
California	.582	34.8
Kentucky	1.065	24.6
El Paso	.516	33.4
Spain	.977	51.7
Senufo	.500	37.5
Sri Lanka	.429	14.8
London, United Kingdom	.725	40.3
Lima, Peru	.596	30.4
Brazil (rural)	.368	22.9
Brazil (urban)	.294	29.2
Ivory Coast	.292	15.2
Mexico	.434	35.6
Karaja	2.111	50.9
Paris, France	.577	68.4

[a]n = 22

The "Yes" Part

In 11 cultures, women, in women-only groups, were biased toward daughters (X^2; $p < .05$; two-tailed $df = 1$; per culture). In 11 societies, children of both genders were equally represented in women-only groups. (Note that gender of child was not coded in the China sample.) In 14 societies, men, in men-only groups, were biased toward their sons (X^2; $p < .05$; 2-tailed $df = 1$; per culture). However, in 8 societies, boys and girls were equally represented. When adult groups (men-only groups vs. women-only groups) were tested for independence in relationship to gender of child (boys versus girl), 16 societies revealed a bias: men more toward boys (away from girls); women toward girls (away from boys). X^2, $df = 1$; $p < .05$; 2-tailed.

The "No" Part

In 19 cultures, there was *no* gender bias or preference in the men-and-women groups: boys and girls were equally represented. A bias emerged in only three cultures (X^2; df = 1; $p < .05$; 2-tailed): Ireland, India, and Sri Lanka had a bias toward boys.

Age and Developmental Status

Men-Only Groups: Boys. Younger boys were overrepresented in 18 cultures (birth to 4 or 5 to 7 years; census data generated expected frequencies; X^2 $df = 2$; $p < .05$, per culture). In 3 cultures, levels of association and census data were the same. On one (Sri Lanka), older boys (8 years to puberty) were overrepresented ($X^2 = 61.18$, $p < .05$; $df = 2$). The children in the Chinese sample were not coded by age.

Men-Only Groups: Girls. In 19 cultures, younger girls (birth to 4 or 5 to 7 years) were overrepresented (X^2; $df = 2$; $p < .05$). In 3 cultures, Mexico, Peru and Paris, the level of association was not different from the census data.

Women-Only: Boys and Girls. Of the 44 comparisons (22 cultures and 2 genders) 43 had younger children overrepresented (X^2, $p < .05$, $df = 2$). Only the level of association between women-only groups and girls in Peru was not different from census data.

Men-and-Women Groups: Boys and Girls. For all 44 comparisons (22 cultures and 2 genders), younger children were overrepresented (X^2; $p < .05$, $df = 2$ [census data generated the expected frequencies]).

Synopsis. In the main, men and women, either in single gender groups or with the *other* gender, biased their association toward younger children. Along this dimension, it is difficult to separate out fathering behaviors from mothering behaviors. There are, however, two exceptions: infants and older boys.

Infants. Men associated at a *lower* percentage with infants (5.4%; $sd = 5.4\%$ of all children associating with men-only groups) than did women (14.0%; sd = 8.4 of all children associating with women-only groups; t = 3.85, p < .01; 2-tailed; df = 20). However, if women join the man–child dyad (to form a men-and-women group), then the percentage of infants involved was not different from the women-only group (t = 0.25; n.s.)

Older Boys. A higher percentage of older boys were more likely to be in men-only groups (rather than in women-only groups; Signs test, p < .05; 2-tailed). In 18 cultures, the highest percentage of older boys was found in men-only groups. In four cultures, the men-and-women groups had the highest percentage of older boys. In no culture was the highest percentage of older boys found in women-only groups. Men-only groups bias toward older boys was not paralleled with a symmetrical bias of women-only groups toward older girls (Signs test, n.s.). In five cultures, the highest percentage of older girls was in the men-and-women groups. In seven cultures, the highest percentage of older girls was in the men-only groups. In nine cultures, the highest percentage of older girls was in the women-only group. There was one tie.

Number of Adults per Group

The average number of women in women-only groups (mean = 1.368; sd = .275) was not greater than the average number of men in men-only groups (mean = 1.222; sd .336; t = n.s.). However, in 19 cultures, surveyed one at a time, the mean number of women per women-only group was greater than the mean number of men per men-only group (Signs test, p < .05). In three cultures, the mean number of men in men-only group exceeded that mean number of women in women-only group. Of interest is that the modal number of adults for both the single gender adult groups (across the 22 culture sample) was one.

Number of Children per Adult Group

Men-Only Groups versus Women-Only Groups. Across the 22 culture sample, the mean number of children in men-only groups (1.442, sd = .239) was not less than the mean number of children in women-only groups (1.564, sd. = .225; t = 0.50, n.s.).

However, in 18 cultures, the average number of children in women-only groups exceeded those in men-only groups (Signs test, p < .05, 2-tailed).

In four cultures, the average number of children in men-only groups exceeded those of women-only groups.

Men and Women Groups versus Women-Only Groups.   The average number of children in men-and-women groups (1.768, $sd = .249$) was greater than that of the women-only groups (1.442, $sd = .239$; t = 4.33, $df = 20$; $p < .05$; 2-tailed).

In 19 cultures, the average number of children in men-and-women groups exceeded those in women-only groups (Signs test, $p < .05$ 2-tailed).

In two cultures, the average number of children in women-only groups exceeded those in men-and-women groups.

In one culture, the average number of children in women-only groups was the same as that in the men-and-women group.

Men and Women Groups versus Men-Only Groups.   The average number of children in men-and-women (1.768, $sd = .249$) groups exceeded those in men-only groups (1.442, $sd = .239$; $t = 4.33$, $df = 20$; $p < .05$ 2-tailed).

In 21 cultures the mean number of children in men-and-women groups exceeded those in men-only groups (Signs test; $p < .05$ 2-tailed).

In one culture, the average number of children in men-only groups exceeded those in men-and-women groups.

SUMMARY

What do all these figures indicate?

1. Societies systematically open up conduits for men to be with their children (in public areas with equal access by gender during daylight hours). When the conduits are opened, men systematically increase their association with their children: both with women present and with no women present.
2. If, for whatever reason, a society restricts the joint association of men and women (and by extension daughters and infants), men systematically increase their association with children with no women present.
3. Men, similar to women, associate with younger children more so than with older children. In the absence of a spouse, men, similar to women, bias toward children of their own gender.
4. In the presence of a spouse, men, similar to women, were with boys and girls equally.
5. Men, dissimilar to women, are rarely with infants with no wom-

an present. But, if the women *are* present, then men are with infants in comparatively high numbers.

6. Men, with no woman present, have a uniquely high level of association with older boys.

7. A man with his child is less likely to be joined by another man than is a woman with her children is likely to be joined with another woman.

8. Men, in the absence of a woman, were with fewer children than were women (in the absence of a man).

9. However, when men are with women, the number of children exceeds that of both single gender adult groups.

INTERACTION FROM ADULTS
TO CHILDREN

It should be noted that men in men-only groups were compared exclusively to women in women-only groups and that men in men-and-women groups were compared exclusively to women in men-and-women groups. For the two interaction indices—Tactile Contact and Personal Distance—the statistical instrument used was the X^2—extension of the median test. For the Visual Orientation index, the only two codes were *see* and *nonsee*, and a X^2 analysis was then performed on the data.

Men-Only Groups versus Women-Only Groups

There were 54 comparisons available to compare men (no women present) versus women (no men present) and their level of interaction to their children (3 interaction categories $\times$ 18 cultures = 54) (London, Austria, Kenya, China, and Paris were not coded for interaction indices.) Forty of the comparisons (74.0%) indicated no differences in activity.

In 10 cultures, men were more active (4 Tactile Contact + 2 Personal + 4 Visual Orientation = 10). In four instances, women were more active (1 Tactile + 3 Personal Distance = 4). (Signs test 10 versus 4; n.s.)

Men in Men and Women Groups versus Women in Men and Women Groups

In 54 comparisons (3 interactions indices $\times$ 18 cultures = 54), 36 cultures (66.7%) indicated neither gender was more active in interacting with their children.

- In 16 cultures, women were more active than men (6 Tactile + 5 Personal Distance + 5 Visual Orientation = 16).
- In two cultures, the men were more active than the woman (1 Tactile Contact + 1 Visual Orientation = 2).
- For the 18 cases (16 + 2 = 18) involving a gender differential, it was the woman who was the more active gender (Signs test; $p <$ .01; 2-tailed).

Note that there is a significant relationship between the type of adult (single gender versus two gender) and the gender (man, woman) of the *more* active adult (X^2 = 12.22 df = 1, n = 32; $p <$ .01; 2-tailed).

Interaction and Gender of the Child: Men in Men-Only Groups versus Women in Women-Only Groups

There are 105 comparisons available for analysis (3 interaction indixes × 2 genders of child × 18 cultures − 3 [men in men-only groups in the Karaja had too few cases for analysis] = 105).

Of the 105 comparisons, 85 (81.0%) indicated no differences between men and women. In 17 cases, men were more active than were women (4 with boys [1 Tactile Contact, 2 Personal Distance, and 1 Visual Orientation]; 13 with girls [4 Tactile Contact, 5 Personal Distance, and 4 Visual Orientation]).

In three cases, women were more active than men (all 3 were with boys [2 Tactile Contact and 1 Visual Orientation]).

Interaction and Gender of the Child: Men in Men-and-Women Groups versus Women in Men-and-Women Groups

Of the 108 comparisons (3 interaction indices × 2 genders of child × 18 cultures = 108), 86 (79.6%) indicated no differences between men and women.

In 15 cases, women were more active (12 with girls [2 Tactile Contact + 5 Personal Distance + 5 Visual Orientation] and 3 with boys [3 Visual Orientation]).

In 7 cases, men were more active (6 with boys [3 Tactile Contact + 2 Personal Distance + 1 Visual Orientation] and 1 with girls [1 Visual Orientation]).

Again, there is a significant relationship between the type of group (single gender versus two-gender) and the gender of the *more* active adult (man versus woman; X^2 = 12.1; $p <$ .05; df = 1). Men were relatively more active in single-gender groups and women were more active in the two-gender groups.

Interaction and Gender of the Child: Men and Women Analyzed Separately

Men-Only Groups.   There were 51 comparisons available (3 interactions indices × 17 cultures [the Karaja men in their men-only group had too few cases for analysis] = 51).

- In 45 comparisons (88.2%) men had the same level of activity toward their sons and their daughters.
- In 6 cases, the girls received more active interaction (4 Tactile Contact = 2, Personal Distance = 6).
- In no case did the boys receive more active interaction.

Women-Only Groups.   There were 54 comparisons available for analysis (3 interaction indices × 18 cultures = 54).

- In 49 cases (90.7%), the women had the same level of activity toward their sons and their daughters.
- In 5 cases, boys received more active interaction (3 Personal Distance + 2 Visual Orientation = 5).
- In no case did the girls receive more active interaction.

Men in Men-and-Women Groups.   There were 54 comparisons available for analysis (3 interaction indices × 18 cultures = 54).

- In 46 cases (85.2%), the men had the same level of activity toward their sons and their daughters.
- In 1 case, girls received more active interaction (1 Visual Orientation).
- In 7 cases, boys received the more active interaction (2 Tactile contact + 4 Personal Distance + 1 Visual Orientation = 7).

Women in Men-and-Women Groups.   There were 54 comparisons available for analysis (3 interaction indices × 18 cultures = 54).

- In 50 cases (92.6%), the women had the same level of activity toward their sons and their daughters.
- In four cases, the girls received more active interaction (1 Tactile Contact + 3 Personal Distance = 4).
- In no case did the boys receive more active interaction.

AGE/DEVELOPMENTAL STATUS
AND LEVEL OF INTERACTION

Tactile Contact

Men in Men-Only Groups.   In 16 cultures (both the Karaja and Hong Kong had too few children to be analyzed), men interacted at a more active level with younger children (both genders combined) than with older children.

Women in Women-Only Groups.   In 16 of 17 cultures (Hong Kong had too few cases for analysis), women interacted at a more active level with younger children (both genders combined) than with older children. In one culture, there was no relationship between age and level of interaction.

Men in Men-and-Women Groups.   In 16 of 17 cultures (Hong Kong had too few cases for analysis), men interacted with young children (both genders combined) than with older children. In one culture, there was no relationship between age and level of interaction.

Women in Men-and-Women Groups.   In 14 of 17 cultures, women interacted more actively with younger children (both genders combined) than with older children. In three cultures, there was no relationship between age and level of interaction.
Thus in 62 of 67 comparisons (92.5%) in the four categories (2 genders × 2 adult groups [single gender, two-gender]), younger children received more active interaction from the adults than did older children. Men and women did not interact differently to the children (Sign's test, n.s.).

Personal Distance

Men in Men-Only Groups.   In 13 of 16 cultures, men stayed closer to younger children than older children.
In 3 cultures, there was no relationship between age of the child and interpersonal distance from the man.

Women in Women-Only Groups.   In 13 of 17 cultures, women were closer to younger children than older children.
In 3 cultures, there was no relationship between age of the child and interpersonal distance from the woman.

In one culture, women were closer to older children than to younger children.

Men in Men-and-Women Groups. In 10 cultures, men were closer to younger children than to older children.

In seven cultures, there was no relationship between age of the child and interpersonal distance from the men.

Women in Men-and-Women Groups. In 14 of 17 cultures, women were closer to younger children than to older children.

In three cultures there was no relationship between age of the child and interpersonal distance from the men.

In sum, for 50 of 67 comparisons (74.6%), the younger children were closer to the caretaking adults than were the older children. This bias occurred with men just as it did with women (Sign's test, n.s.)

Visual Orientation

Men in Men-Only Groups. In 10 of 16 cultures, younger children were kept within the visual field of the man more so than were older children.

In five cultures, there was no relationship between age and being in the adult's visual field.

In one culture, the older children were overrepresented in the adult's visual field.

Women in Women-Only Groups. In 13 of 17 cultures, younger children were overrepresented in the woman's visual field.

In three cultures, there was no relationship between age and visual field inclusion.

In one culture, the older children were overrepresented in the woman's visual field.

Men in Men-and-Women Groups. In 5 of 17 cultures, younger children were overrepresented in the man's visual field.

In 12 cultures, there was no relationship between the age of the child and visual field inclusion.

Women in Men-and-Women Groups. In 7 of 17 cultures, the younger children were overrepresented in the woman's visual field.

In nine of the cultures, there was not a relationship between age of the child and being in the woman's visual field.

In one culture, the older children were overrepresented in the woman's visual field.

In single-gender groups, 70.0% of the comparisons had the younger children overrepresented in the adult's visual field. The gender of the adult was not important (Sign's test, n.s.).

In two-gender groups, only 35.2% of the cases had the younger children overrepresented in the adult's visual field. The remaining cases, over half (61.7%) revealed no pattern in visual field inclusion by age of the child. Gender of the adult did not affect the pattern of the results (Signs test, n.s.).

SUMMARY

Once men were with their children, they interacted with their children (along the defined [coarse] dimensions) in much the same way that the women did. The one exception occurs when men and women are together, men—compared with women—decrease the level of activity, and women—compared with men—increase their level of interaction with the children. The gender of the child is not particularly important. For touch and physical proximity and to a lesser extent vision, younger children receive more interaction from adults—both men and women—than do the older children.

CONCLUSION

From the above data—both from the demographic and interaction indices—it appears that the "parenting template" is not gender dimorphic, but the threshold for activating or maintaining nurturing behavior is lower for women than for men. Once triggered, fathering seems very consonant (at this level of analysis) with mothering.

The question then arises: How does human fathering emerge? Why would men, across the globe, bother to spend so much time with and energy on their children? The next chapter addresses this basic question: Why?

CHAPTER 5

Those Two Filters Once Again

Tabula Rasa or Biocultural Paradigm?

The more people have studied different methods of bringing up children the more they have come to the conclusion that what good mothers and fathers instinctively feel like doing for their babies is usually best after all.

BENJAMIN SPOCK, M.D.

Possessive parents rarely live long enough to see the fruits of their selfishness

ALAN GARNER

Once the data are logged in and analyzed, the problem then becomes one of interpretation. A theoretical perspective becomes imperative.

THEORETICAL PERSPECTIVE

In what amounts to a totally arbitrary decision, the emergence or development of human social behavior is seen as a triune phenomenon—three major forces acting simultaneously on the actual emitted response. It is possible that a theoretician may be more comfortable with two forces; still others may find solace in four, five, or seven. For this project, however, three is a manageable, useful number and true to the notion of an epigenetic unfolding of the human condition. The three forces or tiers of analysis include

1. The symbolic tier.
2. The socialization tradition tier.
3. The biocultural tier.

What is being suggested here is that behavior development and variance can be conceptualized as emerging from two main effect variables (genotypic information and socialization information) plus the multitudes of interactions effects (from Jensen, 1972; Rowe, 1994). Because of the interdependency and short-term and long-term feedback loops that exist among these three tiers, any dissection of ongoing human social behavior will always have elements of the artificial and the arbitrary. With final interpretations tempered by this caveat, the three-fold analysis can be accepted as being diagnostically useful.

The Symbolic Tier

The universal proclivity by humans to symbolize and to form metaphor and simile has been richly documented by ethnographers for decades (e.g., Campbell, 1991; Douglas, 1978; Geertz, 1974; inter alios cf Jung, 1969). It is self-evident that analyses by symbolic anthropologists have constituted a broadly useful and informative discipline. However, a systematic relationship between symbols as a class of events and the referent behaviors is very difficult to ascertain (Harris, 1974a). Symbols can reinforce and parallel behavior tendencies, but they can also camouflage or obfuscate the accurate perception of empirical behavioral patterns. The symbol, in the form of an image or a rule or a spoken phrase that attempts to profile "the way things are" may be actualized more in the breach than in the observance. See Harris (1974a, 1974b, 1977) for examples. In addition, contrasting symbols or images can reflect the same trait; for example, "fools rush in where angels fear to tread," but "strike while the iron is hot." On the other hand, "haste makes waste" although "time and tide wait for no man"; on second thought, "make haste slowly." Then there is "well done is quickly done"; however, "the haste of a fool is the slowest thing in the world," which is countered by "and while I at length debate and beat the bush. There shall step other men and catch the bird." This same bird may be the "early bird that gets the worm," and last of all, "marry in haste, we may repent at leisure." The symbols of Western folklore give no real aid on how to manage one's time. Our symbolic view of children is no less diffuse:

> "It is dangerous to confuse children with angels."—David Patrick Maxwell Fyfe.
> "The smallest children are nearest to God, as the smallest planets are nearest the sun."—Jean Paul Richter.
> "A small child is a pig, a big child is a wolf."—Yiddish proverb.

"Every child comes with the message that God is not yet discouraged of man."—Sir Rabindranath Tagore.

"Small children disturb your sleep, big children your life."—Yiddish proverb.

"Children share with genius an open, inquiring uninhibited quality of mind."—Chauncey Guy Suits.

"Sometimes when I look at my children I say to myself, 'Lillian you should have stayed a virgin'."—Mrs. Lillian Carter.

"There is no finer investment for any community than putting milk into babies."—Sir Winston Churchill.

"Anybody who hates children and dogs can't be all bad."—W. C. Fields.

"Children are God's apostles, sent forth, day by day, to preach of love, and hope and peace."—James Russell Lowell.

"How sharper than a serpent's tooth it is to have a thankless child."—William Shakespeare.

"Feel the dignity of a child. Do not feel superior to him, for you are not."—Robert Henri.

"Parents are the bones on which children sharpen their teeth."—Peter Ustinov.

Folklore, being folklore, can give us an image to cover any version of childhood that is needed for any moment.

Because of the equivocal consonance between symbols, including verbal reports from informants and the referent behaviors, this study will concentrate on the socialization and biocultural tiers. This concentration can in no way be construed to suggest that work within the symbolic or verbal domain is not important. "Emic" analyses are, of course, necessary for a more complete understanding to the problem of what it means to be human. Nevertheless, the current lack of a paradigm, which allows the matching of empirically normative behaviors across cultures with parallel imagery or symbols across cultures, simultaneously severely limits and constrains the utility of a symbolic analysis toward the validation of causal agents generating the emergence of human social behavior.

Socialization Tier

In a rare display of consensus among social scientists, the notion has been accepted that socialization or enculturation of traditions that surround and immerse each citizen of a society influences the form and intensity of the individual's behavior. There is virtually no theorist who discounts the impact on a culture's citizenry of their assimilation of that culture. The importance of norms, expectations, and worldviews of each culture on its populace is agreed to be broad, deep, and pervasive.

To accede to the strength of socialization prerogatives on the ontogenetic development of human behavior, however, by no means disavows or argues against an additional causal influence on behavior by biological processes. Moreover, an acceptance of the power of social processes to affect behavior does not also necessitate a further acceptance of idiosyncrasy or total arbitrariness of each culture. Regardless of any proposed genotypic penetrance into any behavior, the notion that cultural elements often follow regular, predictable relationships with each other has been well documented (Easterlin & Crimmins, 1985; Fawcett, 1983; Handwerker, 1986; Mackey, 1995; White, Burton, & Brudner, 1977; White, Burton, & Dow, 1981; Whiting, 1964).

For this study, it is also accepted that culture and phylogeny track each other (i.e., coevolution) and that feedback loops align the biological substrate of *Homo* with the cultural manifestations that are found with that substrate (Barkow, 1980, 1989; Boyd & Richerson, 1988; Durham, 1979, 1990). The genotype shared in common by *Homo* is expected to generate thematic modes of behavior whereas the cultural circumstances generate variants of that theme.

Personality type and subsistence technique are good examples of a systematic linkage between theme and variation: (1) the acquisition of a personality is panhuman; (2) the various facets of the personality are differentially emphasized or deemphasized as a function of a culture's mode of procuring food from the environment (Barry, Bacon, & Child, 1957; Barry, Child, & Bacon, 1959; cf. Benedict, 1946; Mead 1935).

The ability to generate grammar (theme) and the myriad of language and dialects (variations) is an example of a linkage which, at present, points to no scaled relationship. The grand adventure between structural-functional anthropologists and the will-o'-the-wisp known as "kinship systems" is offered as a second example. All cultures seem to have kinship systems (theme). The reasons for the various forms and configurations (variations) are reluctant to reveal themselves.

The Biocultural Tier

This project accepts the proposition that the development of human behavior, in addition to human morphology and physiology, can be biased or canalized by genotypic information that is mediated by the neural and endocrine systems, that is, the motivation system. The central nervous system (brain and spinal column) in particular is viewed here as not only processing information originating from the external and internal environments, but also as autogenetically creating motivational states (Lorenz, 1958; Tinbergen, 1951). These motivational states are available for selection, both phylogenetically and ontogenetically, from a wide range of other potential motivations to be actualized into overt behaviors and finally to be directed and molded by the socially idiosyncratic milieu in which the individuals happen to reside.

This study also accepts the feasibility that the man-to-child bond is a partial function of genotypic information that in turn has eventuated from the phylogeny or evolutionary history of the human condition. The genotypic information, conceptualized within a "blueprint" or "recipe" metaphor, constructs the central nervous system and the endocrine system which, in concert, allow some behaviors to be learned more easily, more efficiently, and with more completeness than other behaviors (Garcia & Koelburg, 1966; Hinde & Stevenson-Hinde, 1973; Hamburg, 1963; Immelmann et al., 1981; Seligman & Hager, 1972). Operating within a normative environment consonant with the environment in which hominids developed the human biogram, the neurohormonal system would "forge" the putative man-to-child bond with particular characteristics. These characteristics should be recognizable as such and thereby become available to be recorded across societal boundaries.

Because all humans are included within the taxon *Homo sapiens,* a core commonality or constellation of genetic material is, by definition, shared among all humans. This shared genetic material can be hypothesized to generate thematic behavior patterns common to humans. The task then becomes ferreting out and delineating these thematic behavior patterns, that is, the validation of species-characteristic traits in humans. Given the likelihood that the central nervous system was positively selected for flexibility and plasticity in its adaptation to its varying environments, as well as selected for appropriateness in the sensory detection of stimuli and the accuracy of motor responses, the thematic patterns will be nested with the concept of a reactive range of behaviors (Freedman, 1974, 1979). The notion of a "reactive range" takes the blueprint metaphor one step further in that it is apparent that various readings of an architect's blueprint or that a lack of components required by the blueprint—for example, bricks, timbers, cement, or tiles—results in variations of the same type of house. Similarly, any genotype resides in a complex biological world with potentials of vitamin shortages, pH excesses, mechanical traumas, and viral invasions. It is expected, therefore, that variations of phenotypes occur from the same generalized genotypic instructions. The variations, however, are limited in range. Much higher or much lower variants would be lethal to the organism, either directly through gestation or indirectly in its inability to be socially competitive enough to have viable progeny. Plasticity is intrinsic to the genetic blueprint, but the plasticity is not infinite. Moreover, as stated earlier, some behavioral themes may be found only at very abstract levels. At those polar levels, for example, the knee reflex indicates that humans have reflexes or the breath cycle indicates that humans breathe, the genetic penetrance may be quite true but also remarkably uninteresting.

A few added points are useful here that involve two illustrative traits assumed to be shared by most humans: people have emotions and people dream.

One of the fundamental premises of this argument is that the affective segment or content of an emotion cannot be taught by one person to another. Although the label or the name of the emotion can be learned by one individual from the examples and teaching of other individuals, how that emotion actually *feels* is quite immune from pedagogy and is restricted to one individual at a time. Even *Sesame Street* and *Mister Rogers's Neighborhood* only instruct children on how to *deal* with emotions not on how to learn how they *feel.* The labels "hungry," "angry," "sad," "happy," and "lonely" can be transmitted from one generation to another. Nevertheless, how hunger, anger, sadness, happiness, and loneliness actually *feel* cannot be similarly transferred. In addition, although it is true that the behavioral, hence social, manifestation of emotions can be controlled or modulated by social rule and expectations, this manipulation is based on the prior existence of the emotions. The social manipulations can magnify, diminish, or orient; they cannot create.

For example, one society may deem weeping to be an acceptable release for pain or grief. Another society may view weeping as a totally unacceptable mode of response to pain or grief. What such social options cannot generate is the actual components of the subjective experience itself. On this matter, the epistemology of the solipsists seems well-found indeed: "one may know one's own emotional self, but one cannot know another person's subjective reality." At base, emotions are solidly individualistic and private domains, yet, yet, and yet again (sliding from solipsism to induction), the existence and ubiquity of human emotions are rarely challenged. They are tacitly accepted as being in existence. But, given that emotions do exist and their subjective content cannot be socially transmitted, the question arises: From whence do they come? Presuming that all events have causes and that human phenomena do not emerge out of nothingness, there must be a causal agent or set of agents causing human feelings to exist—at all.

Socialization traditions simply cannot be that agent. Socialization traditions can label or can direct emotions or can discourage and encourage the display of emotions, but socialization traditions cannot generate or create emotions. The only other available candidate that operates within the currently knowable time-space continua is the genetic material that act to blueprint the construction and functioning of the human motivational system. The ability to have feelings or emotions is the derivative of having a motivation system (a central nervous system plus a hormonal or endocrine system) which, in turn, is constructed from information blueprinted within the genetic material.

The inherent capacity to possess emotions can be actualized, and then, at this juncture, the emotion can be integrated into social structures and social expectations that amplify and modulate appropriate behaviors for the outward expression of those feelings. Conversely, some emotions and their behavioral derivatives known by the "natives" to exist can be inhibited or ameliorated by social censure and ostracism. For example, if someone were to anger a "native," what is the appropriateness for that native of an immediate violent escalating retaliation—a head for an eye, a carcass for a tooth?! The Yanomamo have one code on this philosophical dilemma. The Amish have another.

It should be made clear that this discussion emphasizes that it is the emotion's genetic template, or rephrased, as a template for a motivational state, that is inherited. The actual behaviors themselves, of course, cannot be inherited. However, the tendency—read emotions, read motivations—to behave in some way rather than in another and at some times or developmental stages rather than at others are inherited.

Some motivating states such as hunger, thirst, and cold can energize behavior quickly, and, according to one cultural circumstance, the procurement of manioc and water and an adjustment of fiber blankets will occur. Following another cultural circumstance, eggs Benedict, a sauterne, and a readjustment of the thermostat may defuse the motivations and return the individual to homeostasis. A third response may involve a hungry, thirsty, cold ascetic.

The overt, actual (voluntary) muscular patterns and sequences need not be closely aligned with the motivations, hence with the genetic material. The muscular patterns may be tightly aligned, such as in reflexes—for example, sneezing and swallowing—but the point here is that they need not be. On the other hand, the extreme plasticity of human behavior is not paralleled with an equally plastic motivation system. In more than an analogous manner, the motivation system may be conceived of as "fossilized behavior." The organization of our emotional apparatus has been honed by thousands and thousands of generations of survivors. Our current emotional apparatus is the latest version of humans who have met the environment head on and won and who have played social chess with each other and have also won that challenge.

A second human trait of interest is the ability to dream. Dreams, in addition to being able to have emotional overtones, are certainly cognitive events: scenes, strategies, scenarios, plots, jokes, and grammar are all available for dream content. Current documentation suggests that dreaming exists as a panhuman event (Hunter & Whitten, 1976, p. 134). Although the vocabulary in the dream, the grammar, and the format or story line or locale of the dream may reflect cultural variations, the sheer capacity, ability, and tendency to dream are a consequence of having a central nervous system biased to dream. The central nervous system, on its own, can generate this complex cognitive phenomenon.

As in the example of emotions, the logic involved in this argument is through the process of elimination: dreams exist. They must be caused. The capacity and dynamics of the dream phenomenon are well beyond the skills and techniques of socialization agents; yet dreaming still occurs. What other source could serve as a causal system? The choice here for that causal system is information coded in the genetic material. There is no third source to consider.

The argument is presented here that, at a minimum, the motivational system (central nervous system plus the endocrine system) can create emotions and intricate cognitive sequences (dreams). The construction of our motivation system is a consequence of the genetic blueprint or recipe. Although we can know the minimum of what our motivation system can do, a crucial question whose answer has a long procedural journey to make, becomes what is the maximum subtlety and intrusion that the genetic material can exercise into human social behavior? The minimum influence is impressive, the maximum may be even more admirable. See Rowe (1994) for a very readable introduction to the topic. See Plomin (1990) for a more technical discussion.

Part of the job description of behavioral scientists is the charge of separating which sets of information forging the various sectors of human social behavior are heavily biased by the genetic material and which sets of information are lightly touched by genetic material but are very sensitive to environmental histories and chance. Framed differently, the hoary nature-nurture versus nurture-only controversy is still alive and annoying. It will not do to announce that this problem is specious or unanswerable or to declare as an explanation that there is interaction between gene and environment. These are nonanswers to a real question. Both the variation (heritability) and the central tendency of human social behavior may be trivially or massively caused by genetic material operating through the motivational system. (See Volume

54 of *Child Development* for interesting exchanges.) See reviews for example, Fraser (1995) and Herrnstein and Murray's *Bell Curve* (1994) for an example of how difficult it is to have a serious dialogue on this controversy. Whether this influence will be found to be small or large will depend on the craft and enthusiasm of the behavioral scientists meeting their charge.

It is useful to point out that the validation of predictions concerning behavior must be achieved through behavior. Perfect knowledge of the structure and physiology of the neurohormonal system does not allow predictability of integrated social behavior of a human who has a past, a present, and a (planned) future, and who is behaving and living in a cathected social environment. Only behavior can validate hypotheses about behavior (Hinde, 1982; Immelmann, Barlow, Petrovich, & Main, 1981).

Note also that, although behavioral differences between populations can be argued to reflect genetic differences between populations, the demonstration of such an argument, though theoretically possible, is logistically and methodologically an awesome and most difficult task. A more feasible approach in a preliminary construction of a behavioral biogram of *Homo* is to seek behavioral consistencies across cultural boundaries.

1. Hold the genotype constant (*Homo sapiens* becomes the referent population) and
2. vary the societies, and, hence, vary socialization traditions. Then,
3. Test for the behavior in question.
4. If the behaviors are highly varied, then the *variable* in the project (different socialization traditions) becomes the candidate for explaining the variable behavior. The constant (*Homo sapiens'* genetic material) is a poor candidate to explain a variable.
5. If the behaviors are highly similar, then the *constant* in the project (*Homo's* genetic material) becomes the candidate for explaining the consistent behavior. The variable (socialization traditions) is a poor candidate in explaining a constant.

Ekman's work on facial expressions is, to date, the classic example of this method (Ekman, 1973, 1980). Scherer and Wallbott (1994), Buss (1994), and Fisher (1992) have followed in this tradition. Weissman et al. (1994) offer an analysis on mental illness with the use of this format. See Brown (1991) for a discussion of human universals. Freedman's (1974) work with infants, a quasi-deprivation study, is a good example of a useful type of controlled study wherein infants (who are too young to have incorporated much of their society's lessons) with different racial heritages behaved differently. Freedman argued that the different racial stocks are "built" to behave differently.

Assuming that the above model is reasonably accurate, then the researcher's task is to select likely behavioral candidates and then to survey the candidates' level and forms of actual occurrence in distinct cultures, that is, to seek the validation of their existence as a species-characteristic trait.

Four necessary, and it may be argued sufficient, conditions must be met to legitimize the claim that the behavioral candidates are in fact part of the human condition (Buss, 1984):

1. The thematic trait is catholic in scope. That is, the behavior is found in diverse cultures with distinct social structures and ecologies.
2. The behavior is potentially arbitrary in that the behavior is but one of many available response sets that could achieve the same results. To avoid an antinomous condition of competing hypotheses that cannot be logically disentangled, the behavior should not represent a technologically highly functional adaptation. The use of fire, weaving, the making of pottery, and the use of agriculture are examples of widespread traits; yet the universality of these highly utilitarian traits is undoubtedly a consequence of their technological efficiency rather than reflecting any relevant genotypic information. The widespread occurrence of these traits would thereby more represent cultural diffusion rather than genetic displacement. It should be noted that, among the six major dyads within a social structure, the man-child dyad operating within the diagnostic places and times of this study appears least mandated by the political, social, or economic imperatives of any society. The other five dyads (man-man, woman-woman, man-woman, woman-child, child-child) can be better argued to reflect a functional utility that emerged form social formulas operating over the eons (Fox, 1978, p. 126; Harris, 1979).

   High levels of man–child associations during the diagnostic observation intervals would *not* be predicted by current psychological or sociological theories.
3. To complement cross-cultural variability, a large number of observations with which the germane trait may occur is required to allow the emergence of the trait's prevalence in a culture.
4. The incidence of the trait or behavior must occur at a substantive level judged to be greater than "error variance": the behav-

ior of a demented lunatic fringe. The number of observed occurrences of the trait should not reflect either serendipity or examples of extreme deviance. With the occurrence of a sizable number of extant behaviors, the likelihood is increased for finding homologues rather than collecting coincidental analogues.

Once these four conditions are achieved, acceptance of a candidate as a species-characteristic behavior is enhanced by the demonstrated (inductive) predictability of the type and level of the trait in subsequent surveyed cultures.

So, at base, there are two explanations that are available to make more sense of the data that have been gathered: (1) a tabula rasa explanation and (2) a biocultural explanation.

Let's consider the highlights of the data in an encapsulated form.

- When social constraints were lifted, men systematically increased their levels of association with their children: both when women were present and when women were not present. The increase was systematic across cultural boundaries.
- If social expectations that separated the genders were imposed, then men decreased their presence with women but increased their associations with their children in the absence of women.
- Both men and women more associated with their younger children than with their older children.
- However, men had comparatively low levels of association with their youngest children, infants, in the absence of women. But, if women were present, the men (and women) were with infants in relatively high proportions.
- Men's association with his children, in the absence of women, was less social than the women (in the absence of men). Compared to women, men tended more to be with a single child and tended to be less with another adult (of the same sex).
- Of all the combinations of adult groups and gender of the child, the man—older boy dyad was uniquely elevated in proportions of occurrence.
- Men had a slight bias toward being with sons, and women had a similar bias toward being with daughters. When men and women were together, they associated with boys and girls in equal proportions.
- Once men were with children, they interacted with them, along the coarse, proxemic dimensions used in the study, in a manner highly consonant with that of the women.

- In terms of level of interaction, gender of the child was invariably irrelevant.
- If the man was with a child (in the absence of a woman), he would tend to interact with the child at a more active level than would a woman (in the absence of a man), but
- If men and women were together with a child, the woman would interact with the child at a higher level than would the man.

Now, let's go back to the basic experimental model:

1. Hold the genes constant (This was done. Everyone surveyed were *Homo sapiens.*)
2. Vary the cultures (This was done. Depending on the specific item being analyzed, the number of cultures varied from 16 to 23.)
3. Test for a behavior (This was done. The above 11 items were the tested behavioral indices.)
4. If variability, then look for different socialization traditions to explain the differences. (This was done. Division of labor by gender explains some of the variability.)
5. If consistencies, then look to a genetic bias in the species. (Consistencies were found.) We will now look at how this putative genetic bias may have arisen in our species.

A PHYLOGENY OF "DAD"

Men were found with their children in significant proportions (no women present) away from the domicile during the daytime. Clearly, they did not have to be there, but they were. It seems the most reasonable explanation that they were there, with their children, was because they wanted to be with their children. It was a priority that was exercised over other priorities.

As soon as the words "wanted to" are invoked, the large concept of motivation is similarly conjured. A man's motivational system is so configured that he would *want to* be with his child. This *want to* would have reasonable energizing power. This *want to* was found in diverse societies in five continents. I argue here that men are "built" to like their children. Liking his children and enjoying being with them is argued to be part of being a typical adult man.

If the above is more true than not, then the question becomes: how did man's motivational system become configured to like children? The following section addresses the question: How could our phylogeny have created a dad?

Paternity in the Animal Kingdom

Not an idle question: How or why?

Adult male nurturing of his young is not a feature of zoology. A good many of adult females from the fauna around the world are also not highly solicitous of their young. Fish seem cold, aloof parents. Amphibians and reptiles leave parenthood before their young hatch. After an ant or bee here and a wasp or so there, most bugs can be deleted from the rolls of devoted parents. It is when mammals and birds are introduced that parenting gets serious.

There are two routes to go when comparing the human species with nonhuman species: homologues (traits related by common ancestry) and analogues (traits related by convergent evolution that function to solve similar problems in similar ways).

Homologues to Human Parenting

Humans are often profiled by our taxonomic status as Primates. Primates, however, cover a wider swathe than is needed here. Primates cover the prosimians such as the loris, aye-aye, lemur, and pottos, and are thereby too removed to be useful here. We have very little in common with the ring-tailed lemur. The term Primate also covers the New World monkey (ceboidea). At the moment, they too are further removed from our bloodline to be useful in examining human fathers. We will return to them momentarily.

These deletions leave the Old World monkeys and the apes (the Catarrhinia) as cousins and as mirrors with which to better see ourselves.

Old World Monkeys. By all accounts, mothering behaviors are well developed indeed by baboons, langurs, macaques, and so on, in the Cercopithecoidea. Fathering, however, is much less reported (see Redican [1976], Taub [1984] and Smuts et al. [1986] for reviews). Caregiving or epimeletic behavior is virtually a female-only event. Two phenomena represent only apparent, rather than real, exceptions. One apparent exception is from the Barbary apes/macaques, and another is from the hamadryas baboon. Adult males of the Barbary apes often align themselves physically with infants. Because adult male Barbary apes will not aggress against an infant, the infant would thereby protect any less dominant adult male from aggression by a more dominant male: the infant buffers one adult male from agonistic behavior by another adult male. In other words, one adult male exploits the adult male-infant relationship in order to protect his position as well as life and limb rather than be with an infant in order to give nurturance to that infant (Deag & Crook, 1970; MacRoberts, 1970). The second apparent exception is the hamadryas baboon. A less dominant adult male hamadryas baboon may adopt a juvenile female (and only female). He will project and nurture that juvenile female. When the juvenile female reaches maturity, she becomes the mate of the adult male protector (Kummer, 1968). Here the nurturance seems better interpreted as a mating strategy than as a parenting strategy.

Accounts of an adult male leaving the perimeter of the band or troop in the company of one of its young are virtually nonexistent. Similarly, adult males do not leave the perimeter of their group, procure food, and then return to actively share that food with their young or even indirectly with their young through the mediation of the mother. Adult males do protect the young from danger by protecting the group from predators, and the survival chances of the young surely benefit from such protection. Nonetheless, the day-to-day care of the young is left to the females.

The Apes. The large-group living chimpanzees also have relegated nurturant parenting to the female as have the harem-living gorilla. The isolate orangutan male even stays away from the adult females except for episodes of reproductive behaviors.

However, when the arboreal lesser ape, the gibbon, is reviewed, the picture shifts. The gibbon, essentially arboreal and monogamous, has increased levels of adult male–young interaction. The adult male gibbon is much more solicitous than his more terrestrial cousins and arboreal peer: the solitary orangutan.

The gibbon brings us back to birds and back to some of the new world primates: the tamarins and the marmosets. All four groups are arboreal and are lightweight and tend to pair-bond.

Adult male birds—often very lightweight and, when not flying, arboreal—are charged with feeding their young, that is, leaving the nest, procuring food, and returning to actively share food with their young. If the adult males fail to help feed their young, the young will die. See Lyon, Montgomerie, and Hamilton (1987) for an example.

The monogamous, arboreal primates generally defend a territory as a pair and all of the members feed from the same source: they passively share food. However, unlike the birds, these adult male primates do not

(1) leave the group's space, (2) obtain food, (3) return to the group, and (4) give away the food to the young.

Analogues to Human Fathering

Whereas monogamous arboreal birds are a reasonable candidate for convergent evolution (similar solutions to similar problems) without the burden of a (recent) common family tree, a better candidate may be the canids. The adult males of the wolf (Allen, 1979; Mech, 1966; Mowat, 1963; Murie, 1944), the coyote (Dobie, 1949; McMahan, 1976; Ryden, 1974; Young & Jackson, 1951), fox and jackal (Alderton, 1994; Lawick & Lawick-Goodall, 1971; Moehlman, 1980), and hunting dog (Kuhme, 1965; Lawick & Lawick-Goodall, 1971) have all been reported to (1) leave the perimeter of the pack or den, (2) forage and obtain food, and (3) return to actively share food with their pups (Mech, 1970). See King (1980) and Thompson (1978) for discussions. In addition, and not incidentally, these adult males plays with their young. They frolic together. They tussle together. They play chase together. A parent, male or female, will take an older pup well away from the den and teach it the fine art of catching and scavenging for dinner (see Schaller & Lowther, 1969 for an overview of scavenging and hunting as ways to procure food). They then return to the den.

Compare this canid set of behavior with the isolate tiger or leopard or cheetah wherein only the mother nurtures her young. The adult male is totally irrelevant. Compare the canid set of behaviors with the social lion and the social hyena. Adult male lions and hyenas are considered a threat to the mother's young (Guggisberg, 1963; Kruuk, 1972; Lawick & Lawick-Goodall, 1971; Rasa, 1986; Rudnai, 1973; Schaller, 1972). In addition, the adult males do not return with food to relinquish the food for their young. Neither the adult male lion nor the adult male hyena play with their young.

As hunting and scavenging became a greater part of the early *Homo's* subsistence lifestyle, a la a canid characteristic, the pressures for division of labor intensified: men would hunt and women would not (cf. Brown, 1970; Murdock, 1937; Murdock & Provost, 1973). In temperate zones, where winter's cold and cessation of vegetable growth was a danger to life and limb, the reliance upon a successful male hunter would be further ratcheted. I argue here that shared feeding, a canid model, is an excellent candidate for the crucible to human fathering (see Mackey, 1976 for a discussion; cf. Lovejoy, 1981).

Well, how would this scenario have unfolded?

To wit: Because neither of our nearest phylogenetic cousins—the chimpanzees (bonobos or paniscus) or the gorilla—illustrates the canid model, it is presumed that *our* human fathering template arose after the Pongid-human split. This leaves "Lucy" (*Australopithecus afarensis*) or early *Homo* as the taxon that was the source of fathering. Which of the two is not germane. What is germane is eating. Birds (e.g., snow buntings; Lyon, Montogomerie, & Hamilton, 1987) highlight a truism: "two feeders are better than one (see Lovejoy, 1981 for a discussion on early hominid food sharing)."

The problem during that long ago era was to find men who would rather feed their children than spend their finite energy and time in finding additional fertile women to impregnate and thereby conceive additional siblings for his prior children. It is well beyond the scope and ken of this chapter to unravel those hurly-burly days of *afarensis* and early *Homo*. Hidden ovulation, continuous female sexual receptivity if not proceptively, foreskin alterations, brain size expansion, reactions to sexually transmitted diseases, language development, paternal certainty, and archaic kinship systems inter alia were all human traits that were developing in fits and starts. What caused what? versus What was a correlative of what? is simply an overload here. Others will have to unravel and untangle these interrelated dynamics.

But, what did result from this seedbed of humanity was a reasonably predictable pattern relating to paternalistic behavior for the *Homo sapiens* circa A.D. 2000.

1. Men court females.
2. Females and their kin evaluate suitors, in part, on the basis of their current ability to or promise of procuring resources: the more, the better (see Buss, 1989, 1994 for discussion).
3. Women select Mr. Goodgenes and Mr. Deeppockets.
4. Everyone involved assumes—as a given, with no discussion or debate—that the husband, turned father, will share his treasure, initially food, with *his* young. Across the world's community of cultures, fathers do precisely that: share (Human Relations Area Files, 1949). A father who provides for his children is an immutable fact of tribal life: "You are my children, and that which I have, I give to you." Men share.

Furthermore, not unlike the wolf, fox, coyote, jackal, and hunting dog, men play with their children. Any excursion to any playground on any Saturday (or the scholarly "Males Not Precluded Interval") will support the point. Two anecdotal examples will suffice to profile the rule: men play with their young. One example is from Charlottesville, Virginia and one form Reykjavik, Iceland.

Virginia. The man was probably 25 years old or thereabout. He weighed close to 250 pounds and, as measured later at the sliding board, was nearly 6 feet, 4 inches tall: a born tight end. The little girl was about 3-years old—small, bubbling, and evidently found squealing a terrific way to communicate. For about a quarter of an hour, our tight end would hoist the squealer to the top of the slide. Squealer then squeals as she zooms down the slide. Sometimes she lands on her feet, sometimes bottom, sometimes a combination. The tight end would hoot and lumber over to the squealer and pick her up and toss her into the air. More squeals. He would then place her on top of the slide and repeat the ritual.

Any interpretation of the tight end's behavior that did not include enjoying himself at an industrial-strength level is an interpretation from beyond the twilight zone.

Reykjavik. If the day is even remotely nice, the big park in the middle of Reykjavik attracts people by the hundreds. On one Sunday, one family that arrived at the park included a boy of 8 to 10 years, one girl 10 to 12 years, one mother, and one father. The father had brought reading glasses and a formidable tome. Scholarship was to be the order of this Sunday afternoon. The kids had other ideas.

A foot race was to be executed: Dad versus son versus daughter. The mother was the starter, timer, and judge. However "on your mark," "get set," "go" is said in Icelandic, those words were said. The race was on. Imagine Ichabod Crane with arthritis and poor fitting shoes being filmed in "slo-mo." Such was the dad. He came in third.

When he finally did cross the imaginary finish line, much guffawing and laughter was experienced by all. There was no time for ego or dignity, only a good howl. When all post mortems were exhausted, father returned to his book. The kids played and the mother attacked something in a large wicker basket.

Men play with their children. Why?

Another application of Occam's Razor intimates that men enjoy playing with their children because they *like* their children (and they like to play).

Coming at the same phenomenon of the man-to-child affiliative bond in a more structured way:

- In the Plio-Pleistocene era, men who had a neurohormonal system that facilitated the development of an affiliative bond with their children would also be more likely to share food with and protect those children, his children.
- Children who were better fed and better protected had a better

chance of surviving to fertility and on to adulthood than children who experienced malnutrition and vulnerability to predators: human or otherwise. Live fertile adults have a much better chance of giving their parents grandchildren than do dead pre-pubescents.

- Women who selected as mates those men who would feed and protect her and *his* children were better fed and protected than women who mated with men less nurturing toward her and her children.
- Women who are better fed and better protected and who have surviving children have a better chance of having grandchildren than women who are malnourished, physically vulnerable, and whose children die prior to puberty.
- Having an added ply of survivability, children of nurturant men are more likely to pass along those alleles (which constructed a motivational system that, in turn, created a nurturing father who liked his children) than those children of less nurturant men (who would be less likely to pass along these alleles that con-structed a motivation system which, in turn, created a less nur-turing man who was indifferent to any consequence of his copu-lations).
- Over geological time, alleles that created men who liked their children would displace alleles that created men who found his children irrelevant.
- Ergo, therefore, and consequently, most adult male *Homo sapi-ens,* given any opportunity, are sublimely willing to *like* to provi-sion and protect their children. They are built that way. Men have about as much option of being fond of their own children or not as they have in digesting a protein. The twin juggernauts of time and Mother Nature have already decided the issue about their issue.
- However, it should be clear that the father was not selected to be a mother. He is different. Whereas the mother is an infant special-ist, he is not. He is a toddler-and-beyond specialist in the domain of rough-and-tumble play and exploring the environment. When he is with the mother, he yields to her and her caretaking skills. When the mother is not there, he will perform admirably as a caretaker of the "toddler-and-beyond."

Any questions?

If the above is more right, than wrong, then the proposed indepen-dent man-to-child affiliative bond ought to be found in the United States among the U.S. men. Furthermore, such a proposed bond ought to be findable. The next section attempts to find the bond in the United States.

A TEST FOR THE FATHER-TO-CHILD BOND:
A U.S. EXAMPLE

The fundamental conclusion to the preceding section's results was that there is an independent father-to-child bond, that is, men are built to like their own children. There is no reason to expect that U.S. men and fathers are exceptions. If the fundamental conclusion is more correct than not, then it should be testable, and testable within the United States (see Popper [1959, 1962] for a discussion on testability, also known as falsifiability).

The argument is that U.S. fathers bond to their children and enjoy being with them. Accordingly, it is unlikely that fathers take actions that would separate them permanently from their children. Divorce is a proceeding that legally separates parents from children. If it can be shown that the addition of children with all of their attendant costs, including financial costs, emotional costs, stress, dysphoria, social costs, and freedom of movement costs, *increases* men's propensity to divorce, then the notion of an independent father-to-child bond is considerably weakened. Let's look at divorce: U.S. style.

Divorce in the United States

Just as marriage in various forms exists in all the world's cultures, the formal dissolution of a marriage is also ubiquitous (Levinson & Malone, 1980; Schlegel, 1972; Seccombe & Lee, 1986; Stephens, 1963). The U.S. divorce rates (number of divorces per 1,000 population) are quite high when compared with other countries that keep records (U.S. divorce rates = 4.9 in 1986 [U.S. Bureau of the Census, 1990] versus the mean of alternate countries of 1.1 sd = 1.2; N = 127 [United Nations, 1982]. It is important to note that most children in the United States stay with their mothers after their parents divorce, up to 90% in some states (Cherlin, 1988; Chesler, 1986; Luepnitz, 1982; Sack, 1987; Sitarz, 1990).

In the United States, the divorce rate (number of divorces per 1,000 population) from 1900 to 1986 increased 700%, from 0.7 to 4.9 (National Center for Health Statistics, 1950–1990). Such a rapid increase argues forcefully against any putative father-to-child bond. Fathers are separating themselves from their children.

Table 5.1. Percentage of People Who Did and Did Not
Remarry after First Divorce

	Remarried		Not remarried	
Age in years	Male	Female	Male	Female
31–35	75.1	64.4	24.9	35.6
41–45	78.1	69.7	21.9	30.3
51–55	83.0	73.5	17.0	26.5
61–65	85.6	78.0	10.7	22.0

Source: U.S. Bureau of the Census (1976).

As current marriage and divorce statistics illustrate, remarriage after divorce has been and still is the norm for both men and women. For men who completed their marital histories, nearly 90% who divorced eventually remarried (U.S. Bureau of the Census, 1976). See Table 5.1. Increasing numbers of men thus are placing themselves in the position of losing their children, while they also are given (and accept) responsibility for nurturing the children of other men when they remarry a divorced mother. Such a marital strategy is strongly antithetical to a father-to-child bond.

Furthermore, social glues that normally adhere a man to his children have all but evaporated. The government (state, local, and federal) has clearly inserted itself as a competitor for the role of provider. Governmental support for the isolated mother-child dyad has increased in scope to include cash, housing, medical care, food, and fuel. Hence, if a man were to desert the father role, his children may (or may not) experience a decrease in lifestyle, but if there is a decrease it is not to the point of lethal privation. His departure may result in a suboptimum existence for his children, but they certainly would not die from his departure. In fact, infant mortality has continued its decades long decline from 85.3 infant deaths per 1,000 live births in 1900 to 26.0 in 1960 to 8.9 in 1992 (U.S. Bureau of the Census, 1994). As divorce rates systematically increased, infant mortality has systematically decreased.

Simultaneously, the social sanctions that traditionally adhere a father to the mother–child dyad are dissolving. In other words, when fathers desert their children, there are no social opprobium directed against the father. Even if child payments are effectively and legally coerced, the payments are quite low. For example, there was a mean monthly payment of $81.00 in 1988 (Seltzer, 1991; cf Weitzman, 1985). Blankenhorn (1995) reported a mean of $188 per month in 1989 re-

Table 5.2. Mean Percentages of Divorces by Number of Children and Year of Cohort

| Cohort | Number of children | | | | N |
	None	One	Two	Three or more	
1982–1986					
Mean	46.3	25.6	19.8	8.2	1,173,000
sd	0.70	0.16	0.16	0.39	
1971–1975					
Mean	41.1	25.4	18.9	14.6	909,200
sd	1.30	0.28	0.11	1.49	
1960–1964					
Mean	39.7	23.9	18.4	18.0	419,600
sd	2.33	0.81	0.59	0.59	

ceived by all women who were due child support payments. Any social stigma associated with divorce or unmarried motherhood either had dissipated or had been minimized by most groups.

In terms of incentives, there are virtually no economic gains for men who embrace the father role or who remain in the father role (Huber, 1980; Murray, 1984). As mentioned earlier, such economic factors are important in affecting birthrates, that is, in accepting the parenting role (Aghajanian, 1979, 1988; Arnold et al., 1975; Bradley, 1984; Caldwell, 1982; Cochrane, 1983; Day & Mackey, 1986; Easterlin & Crimmins, 1985; Handwerker, 1986; Ross & Harris, 1987, cf Zelizer, 1985). It is easier to make economic gains in the United States by avoiding entry into the father role or by leaving it once fatherhood has been achieved. In addition, the social and psychological benefits (versus similar types of costs) received by the father for fatherhood were and are equivocal at best (Adams, Miner, & Schrepf, 1984; Bumpass, 1990; Heaton, 1990; Hoffman & Manis, 1979; Lamb, Pleck, & Levine, 1987; Landers, 1976; Mackey & White, 1993; Neal, Groat, & Wicks, 1989; Patterson, 1980; White & Kim, 1987).

U.S. Divorce Data. Divorce rates by number of children for the three intervals—1960 to 1964, 1971 to 1975, and 1982 to 1986—are presented in Table 5.2. The data were analyzed by averages per interval. For all three intervals, the modal number of children (under the age of 18 years) per divorce was zero. The median number of children per divorce was *less* than one for all three intervals (.43, .35, .14, respectively).

A majority of divorces involved less than the replacement value of two children (63.6%, 66.5%, 71.9%, respectively). Note that the percent of childless divorces has increased rather than decreased from the 60s to the 80s. Framed differently, the percentages of divorces involving children decreased from 60.3% in 1960–1964 to 53.7% in 1982–1986 ($z = 73.8$; $p < .001$; 2-tailed). The 1971 to 1975 interval was intermediate at 58.9%. Note that in the 1982 to 1986 interval, the percentage of divorces decreases as more children are involved (one child = 25.6%, two children = 19.8%, three or more children = 8.2%). Part of this reduction is, of course, due to the smaller proportion of families with three or more children, but note that, although the mean number of children born per woman between 1982 and 1986 was 1.8 ($sd = 0.0$), the mean number of children under 18 years of age per divorce was approximately half that figure (0.92, $sd = .02$). The average median number of children under the age of 18 years per divorce was lower still (0.14).

Therefore, there is no evidence that, as more children and hence more expenses are being incurred by the men, they are making the economically wise strategic choice of deserting those children. Score one for an affiliative bond from father-to-child over the dismal science of economics.

Yet divorces are occurring. Men are being separated from their children. Two points need to be examined: first, how many men are involved with this separation of father from child, and second, what or who is driving this separation?

Let's follow a cohort of 100 married men to see how their marital, also known as reproductive, histories unwind (from Mackey, 1980): (a) 60 to 80 men will marry but not divorce; (b) 20 to 40 men will divorce: two-thirds of the divorces involve 0 to 1 child (13 to 27 men); and one-third of the divorces involve two or more children (7 to 13 men).

Thus, most men who become biological *and* social fathers have entered fatherhood for the long haul. They marry, become a parent, and stay put.

Those fathers that do separate (or are separated) from their children represent a small minority of fathers as a class. Parenthetically, although impolite to introduce, the idea of cuckoldry is relevant. Men do initiate divorce proceedings. If a husband becomes aware that the child whom his wife had just delivered was not his but another man's biological child, he has a choice to make. He can decide to be a social father to another man's lineage. On the other hand, he may have no intention of raising another man's descendant (genes). At that moment, were he to petition for a divorce, from his perspective, he has jettisoned a childless marriage. And, again from his vantage point, his divorce involved zero children. Husbands generally have a dim view of being cuckolded (Shapiro, 1987). Jealously cum cuckoldry have resulted in many a violent denouement (see Daly & Wilson, 1987, 1988, and Blankenhorn, 1995 for discussions on family violence).

In the context of the wife and mother, the tendency of the husband and father to be the petitioner, rather than the respondent, in a divorce proceedings will now be examined. But first a methodological note.

The divorce statistics presented here were derived from the *Vital Statistics* 1960 to 1988 (National Center for Health Statistics, 1960–1991). (See Barkow, 1989 and Van den Berghe, 1979 for discussions on data gathering techniques to test bioculturally oriented hypotheses). I emphasize that the micro politics of divorce are convoluted and divorces are not always predicated on simple, straightforward truths. Legal systems, deeply felt emotions, and ambivalence of divided loyalties create a multidimensional human map and complex stratagems and motivations (see Chesler, 1986; Luepitz, 1982; Maccoby & Mnookin, 1992; Wallerstein & Blakeslee, 1989; Wallerstein & Kelly, 1980). For example, a petition may occur more as a preemptive strike than as a marker for the more dissatisfied partner. On the other hand, a petition may come as a bolt from the blue. The unsatisfied partner (petitioner) initiates the divorce and the other partner (respondent), whether happy with the marriage or not, must respond to the legal mechanisms involved. In gist, although there is probably not a perfect consonance between marital reality and who petitions versus who responds, there is probably a substantial overlap between the stated, overt dissatisfaction and the actual, covert dissatisfaction of a marriage entering into the legal swamp of dissolution. Onward to the data.

Petitioning for Divorce by Gender of Spouse.   In the interval for which data are available, 1982 to 1986, the mean percentage of divorces petitioned by men was less than the percentage petitioned by women at all numbers of children surveyed (zero children to three or more). See Table 5.2. The low percentage for the wife was 55.88% at zero children and the high was 65.66% at three or more children. The low percentage for the husband occurred at three-or-more children (27.44%) and the high was at 35.52% when zero children were involved.

Of special interest to this argument is what happens when at least one child is involved in the dissolution. Compared with childless divorces and for marriages with at least one child, the percentage of women petitioners increased and the percentage of men petitioners decreased. The following detailed findings are of special interest. The percentages of husbands' petitions in marriages with no children were higher (35.52%) than in marriages with one child (27.82%), two chil-

**Table 5.3. Percentage of Divorces by Number of Children
and by Status of Petitioner, 1982–1986**[a]

Number of children	Status of petitioner				
	Husband	Wife	Husband and wife	Other	Total
None	35.52	55.88	5.40	3.20	100.0
sd	0.33	0.88	1.40	0.99	
One	27.82	64.80	5.66	1.72	100.0
sd	0.45	0.99	0.22	0.86	
Two	27.64	64.74	6.04	1.58	100.0
sd	0.67	0.69	0.39	0.79	
Three or more	27.44	65.66	5.16	1.74	100.0
sd	0.65	0.77	0.40	0.69	
All children	31.26	60.20	5.84	2.70	100.0
sd	0.42	0.78	0.22	0.83	

[a]Mean number of divorces = 573,931.

dren (27.64%), and three or more children (27.44%; Z-scores of 49.8, 46.7, and 33.7, respectively; $p < .001$; 2-tailed). This pattern contrasts sharply with that of the wives' pattern, whose percentages of petitions in marriages with *no children* (55.88%) were *lower* than the percentages of petitions in marriages with one child (64.80%), two children (64.74%), and three or more children (65.66%; Z-scores of 55.1, 50.1, and 39.1, respectively; $p < .001$; 2-tailed). Also note that as additional children are involved in a divorce, the father's tendency to divorce does not increase, the figures being virtually identical (one child, 27.82%; two children, 27.64%; three or more children, 27.44%). See Table 5.3. An affiliative father-to-child bond explanation, not a socioeconomic position, more accurately predicts the correct direction.

When considering all of the divorces petitioned by the men, 51.3% of all petitions were from childless marriages. For women only 41.8% of all petitions were from childless marriages. The percentage of husband's petitions (51.3%) in childless marriages was significantly *higher* than that of the wives' (Z score = 64.7; $p < .001$; 2-tailed). However, for divorces with one, two, and three or more children, the percentage of women who petitioned for divorces was *higher* than similar figures for men (Z scores of 35.8, 30.8, and 21.0, respectively; $p < .001$; 2-tailed). (See Table 5.4.)

Let's return to those fathers who were separated from their children via divorce. Almost two-thirds (65.1%) of the divorces involving children were petitioned by the mother, not the father. Again, the cave-

Table 5.4. Percentage of Divorces by Number of Children, by Husband as Petitioner, and by Wife as Petitioner Separately, 1982–1986

Number of children	Status of petitioner %		Z score	$p <$ (2-tailed)[a]
	Husband	Wife		
None	51.3	41.8	64.7	.001
sd	0.87	0.07		
One	22.2	26.8	35.8	.001
sd	0.15	0.12		
Two	17.1	20.7	30.8	.001
sd	0.35	0.84		
Three or more	7.0	8.7	21.0	.001
sd	0.30	0.34		
Number not specified	2.4	2.0	9.4	.001
sd	0.67	0.39		
Total	100.0	100.0		
Mean number	170,003	353,191		

[a]Because of the large n's, even small differences in percentages will generate statistical significance. Hence, the direction of the patterns is emphasized more than the probability levels.

at of the intricacies and machinations of divorce strategies and counter-strategies should be remembered. Nevertheless, it is the mother who is mainly responsible for the legal separation of the father from his children. Returning to the marital, also known as reproductive, histories of the 100-man cohort: for the 7 to 13 men who marry and divorced with 2 or more children, only 2 $(7 \times 27.5\% = 1.925)$ to 4 $(13 \times 27.5\% = 3.575)$ initiated the divorce proceedings. These figures are approaching error variance.

Still and yet, the figures are not nil. Men with two or more children have taken the steps to separate themselves from their children. These men need to be explained. First, some of the men gain custody so that no separation occurs. Most, however, do not. It is these "most men" that are to be addressed.

What is being indicated by these data is that there is an independent father-to-child bond. The bond is conceived to be mediated by the motivational systems (nervous system, hormonal system) which, in turn, were results of the genetic blueprint or recipe inherent in our species. Such a putative bond is just one motivational impetus competing against and with a number of alternative pushes and strains operating within a single person across time (i.e., the man's developmental ontogeny). The age, health, number, and developmental status of the child(ren) also affect the father's cathexes. The age, health, fidelity, and fertility of the wife also influences the husband's motivations. Availability of alternative women refract his paternalistic motivations from nurturer–protector to procreator. And, of course, from any cohort of 100 men, there may be found a scoundrel or so.

Thus, it seems reasonable to view fathering as a very normal flow of the human condition. However, of very recent vintage, alternative demands from distantly related quarters have created forces antithetical to what would otherwise be normal flow of humanity. These forces and how they came to be will be examined in the subsequent chapters.

CHAPTER 6

Father

Perceptions until the 1970s

There was a time when father amounted to something in the United States. He was held with some esteem in the community; he had some authority in his own household; his views were sometimes taken seriously by his children; and even his wife paid heed to him from time to time.
ADLAI EWING STEVENSON

My daddy doesn't work, he just goes to the office; but sometimes he does errands on the way home.
LADIES' HOME JOURNAL (1946)

Leaving the cross-cultural behaviors for a moment, this chapter will focus on the United States and its relationship to the American father. As in any other society, the contemporary American society can be analyzed via the triangulation of three sets of phenomena that circumscribe any observable behavior pattern: (1) a symbolic or myth system referenced by the behavior, (2) a scientific paradigm, with variable levels of consensus, and (3) the actual behaviors themselves. These three sets clearly overlap, but the three can also be separated out.

While image, as the sports icon suggests, may or may not be everything, it is certainly important. Again, if actual behavior is the focus of examination, only surveyed behavior will validate or refute any hypothesis about behavior. The difficulty is in being able to witness and record the behavior. Humans can sometimes be very private, if not shy, subjects.

HISTORICAL PERSPECTIVE

Data about fathering behavior, especially before data gathering and data analysis disciplines were created, are sparse. Church records may indicate demographic trends, but the day-to-day habits of the recorded worshipers are immune from analysis. The images, however, can be anecdotally sampled, and sampled they were. Surviving letters and sermons and diaries have been found and perused to lend insight into what and how fathering was viewed by the literate natives. See LaRossa & Reitzes (1993) for a fascinating review of letters from fathers during the great depression.

How social class, the famous SES (socioeconomic status), age of child, gender of child, number of children, and religion all perturbed the basic worldviews is not going to be findable. *How* well normative behaviors—central tendencies—mirrored these images is also unavailable. Nonetheless, some fundamental common threads have emerged.

The man was assumed to be the titular head of the household and responsible for the moral development of his children (Demos, 1986; Griswold, 1993; LaRossa, 1988; Nash, 1965, 1976).

Although rarely mentioned, there was an assumption (at least here) that men presumed that it was their responsibility to provide bed and board for their children and to protect them from harmful forces. The French proverb: "A father is a banker provided by nature" supports such an assumption, as does the aphorism "Children suck the mother when they are young, and the father when they are old". Day-in and day-out care of children was not included in these early written documents as part of fathering. Therefore, how little or how much men actually participated in the rituals of nurturing children from birth to independence can only be conjectured. The current imagery of the dreaded patriarchy infers that our paternal ancestors were distant and aloof. Although this inference, too, must remain conjectural.

A point about ancestor evaluation may be useful at this juncture, and that point involves the concept of temporocentrism. Temporocentrism is a parallel cousin to ethnocentrism and concerns the evaluation of one time frame by using the worldview, zeitgeist, mores, folkways, and benchmarks of the current social structure. Whereas the more celebrated ethnocentrism (a la Benedict and Mead) cautions against interpreting one group using the cultural barometers of an alternate group, temporocentrism intimates similar caveats when two temporal intervals are involved.

To wit: Let's go back to the epitome of infamous patriarchy: the Victorian era (circa 1837 to 1901) as celebrated in the United States around the turn of the century. The (crude) death rate was 17.2 deaths per 1,000 population (U.S. Bureau of the Census, 1975), which is about double the current (crude) death rate of 8.6 (U.S. Bureau of the Census, 1994). Life expectancy was approximately 34 years (U.S. Bureau of the Census, 1975), which is less than half of the current life expectancy of

75.4 years (U.S. Bureau of the Census, 1994). The (crude) birthrate was 32.3 births per 1,000 population (U.S. Bureau of the Census, 1975), which is nearly twice the current (crude) birthrate of 16.3 (U.S. Bureau of the Census, 1994). For Massachusetts, the infant mortality rate (deaths under one year per 1,000 live births) was 141.4 (U.S. Bureau of the Census, 1975), which is nearly 16 times the current nationwide infant mortality rate of 8.9 (U.S. Bureau of the Census, 1994). Maternal mortality rate (deaths of the mother per 1,000 live births) in 1915 was 6.1 (U.S. Bureau of the Census, 1975) compared with a current rate of less than 0.1 (U.S. Bureau of the Census, 1994): 89 times as high. Nearly 40% of the labor force was engaged in (mostly small farm) agriculture (U.S. Bureau of the Census, 1975), which is almost 15 times the current percentage of 2.7% (U.S. Bureau of the Census, 1994). Medicine was pre-sulfa drugs and pre-polio vaccines. In other words, life was different (see Richards, 1977 for a discussion). Parenting in general and fathering in particular might well be affected by the expectations of 4 to 6 children rather than 1 to 3 children and by the lurking expectation that all of our children will probably not reach adulthood. The actual death of a small child might well affect the parent–infant relationship in subsequent births. Any visit to any children's hospital will reveal the anguish of parents, who, through no fault of their own, have to experience and witness an inevitable and often slow death of one of their children. It may be bold indeed to assume our ancestors were any less affected. Division of labor in child care, infants versus toddlers versus prepubescents, might well affect paternal versus maternal roles. See Stewart (1990) who examines how current fathers become better integrated into caretaking when (even) a second child is brought home.

Let one example serve to highly the triangulation among (a) cultural symbols that are more ethereal and abstract, (b) physical realities that are often raw and gritty, and (c) historical continuity: the example is under the rubric of the "sexual double standard."

THE COLLECTIVE WISDOM OF OUR FOREBEARS: THE "DOUBLE STANDARD" RECONSIDERED

A number of current political and social groups have decried the existence of the sexual double standard as an example of suppression or oppression of women by a male patriarchy (Bird, 1976; Greer, 1971; Millett, 1978; Polatnik, 1973; Smuts, 1995). The sheer existence of the double standard does not seem to be questioned. The reason that it does exist, however, is subject to a good deal of questioning. I suggest here that the origin and maintenance of the double standard may have less to do with preserving male power and dominance than with preventing female infertility and infant mortality.

The Ubiquitous Double Standard

A cross-cultural analysis of extramarital sexual norms illustrates that men's behaviors are more likely to be *less* restricted and that women's behaviors are more likely to be *more* restricted. See Table 6.1.

One explanation that is often invoked to explain the basis of the asymmetry is that of "paternal certainty" (Kulrand, 1979; Smuts, 1995). That is, for a man to maximize his certainty that he is, indeed, the father of his wife's child, his best strategy is to cloister his wife. The more complete is the cloistering, the more confidence the man has in his paternity. Enforced, coerced cloistering seems like a good definition of oppression. This explanation of the double standard is testable.

Some societies (roughly 12%) are matrilineal such that inheritance passes from mother to daughter. Note that matriliny—a system of inheritance—is not the same as matriarchy—a system of power. Whereas some societies are matrilineal, none is matriarchal. In a matriliny, a child, whether a son or a daughter, belongs to the woman's clan or lineage. The father's lineage includes his maternal aunts, his mother, his sisters and their children and his brothers. Accordingly, the father has no claim on or no kinship with his wife's children. They belong to a separate kin group than his own. Thus paternal certainty has no social importance to the father. Because of the social meaning of the child belonging to the mother's kinship circles, it would thereby be expected that the double standard—if it is generated by a need to certify paternity—would not be needed nor be found in these matrilineal societies.

Table 6.1. Extramarital Sex Norms for Husbands and Wives: 216 Cultures[a]

Norms	Spouse		Total
	Husband	Wife	
Permissive	60	13	73
Restrictive	48	95	143
Total	108	108	216

[a]$X^2 = 45.7$; $df = 1$; $p < .001$; $C = .42$
Source: Adapted from Broude (1980).

Table 6.2. Frequencies of Adultery Norms
for Women by Inheritance Type: 105 Cultures[a]

| | Adult norms for women | | |
	Permissive	Restrictive	Total
Lineage type			
Matrilineal	2	10	12
Patrilineal	6	41	47
Other	5	41	46
Total	13	92	105

[a]$X^2 = 0.31$; $df = 2$; $p > .05$. Note that not all of the cells have a
minimum expected value of five: a number generally viewed as the
minimum for a valid test. However, the small expected frequency
would tend to inflate the X^2 value. Given the exceedingly small
overall X^2 value of 0.31, the test is presented with the *caveat* that
there are cells with expected frequencies less than five.
Source: Adapted from Broude (1980).

But such is not the case. As Table 6.2 clearly illustrates, the adultery
norms are virtually identical in matrilineal societies as in patrilineal
societies as in alternative forms (such as ours: bilinear). Clearly, an
additional social force is in operation.

The Threat of Sexually Transmitted Diseases

A part of the human condition is our ability to become ill. A number of parasites specialize in exploiting humans as quite congenial, if unwilling, hosts. Several of these parasites are transmitted through human sexual behavior: hence sexually transmitted diseases (STDs). There are more than 50 sexually transmitted organisms and subsequent maladies recognized by the Division of STD/HIV Prevention (1990). Over and beyond the distress these organisms create for the affected individuals—one at a time—the threat to the community is at least as important.

Because, over long periods of time, host and parasite adjust and readjust to each other, it is impossible to document the level of lethality or impairment current organisms caused in prior centuries. However, it is probably not unreasonable to suspect that, in preantibiotic eras, STDs, in variant forms, were at least as debilitating as are their current counterparts. For example, earlier forms of syphilis were far more fatal than are the present cases (McNeil, 1976).

What then, over and beyond the infected patient, would be the threat to the commonweal? There are four unique facets of STDs that expand their influence over human hosts and are relevant to this argument.

1. The best preventative for an STD epidemic in a community is complete abstinence. However, this cure would last only one generation. Complete abstinence means that there would be no further generations. The next best tack is a compromise and allows sexual contact, but reduces the number of sexual partners, that is, institute monogamy. While STDs occur in both males and females, there is an asymmetry between the genders in two important respects.
2. Man-to-woman transmission of STDs is easier, that is, more efficient, than is woman-to-man transmission (Hook & Handsfield, 1990; Moore & Cates, 1990). Said a little differently, an infected man can infect a symptom-free woman more easily than an infected woman can infect a symptom-free man.
3. An infected woman is far more likely to be rendered infertile than is an infected man (Westrom & Mardh, 1990). Currently, PIDs (pelvic inflammatory diseases), for example, salpingitis, are the primary sources of female infertility (Mosher & Aral, 1985). See Table 6.3 for an example from Sweden. It is rare for a male to be rendered infertile by an STD.
4. A pregnant woman infected by an STD increases the chances of maternal deaths via ectopic pregnancies (Lurie, 1992; JAMA, 1995), infant mortality and infant morbidity, for example, prematurity, low birth weight, and spontaneous abortion (Brunham, Holmes, & Embree, 1990; Westrom, 1991), ophthalmia, conjunctivitis, pneumonia, and arthritis (Gutman & Wilfert, 1990; Schultz, Murphy, Patamasucon, & Meheus, 1990).

Societal Responses to STDs

At whatever level of consciousness the connection was made between multiple sexual partners and sterile mothers and sickly infants, it is suggested that this connection was made across the world's community of societies. There was a systematic restriction of sexual partners. If a family or tribe wished to minimize STDs and still have children for the next generation, then the best course was to institute and maintain strict monogamy. The next best route was to institute polygyny: plural wives allowed for men and one husband (monogamy) for

Table 6.3. Reproductive History of Women, Who, after Index Laparoscopy,
Were Diagnosed as Having Abnormal (e.g., Occluded) Fallopian Tubes
(Patients) or as Having Normal (i.e., Symptom-Free) Fallopian Tubes (Controls)[a]

	Patients (n = 1732)		Controls (n = 601)		
Reproductive events	n	%	n	%	Z
Avoided pregnancy	370	21.4	144	24.0	1.33 ns
Attempted pregnancy	1309	75.6	451	75.0	0.29 ns
Became pregnant	1100	84.0	439	97.3	7.34[b]
(first pregnancy ectopic)	(100)	(9.1)	(6)	(1.4)	5.38[b]
No pregnancy occurred	209	16.0	12	2.7	
(examination found tubal infertility)	(188)	(14.4)	(9)	(2.0)	
(examination indicated nontubal infertility)	(21)	(1.6)	(3)	(0.7)	
Not pregnant for unknown reasons	53	3.0	6	1.0	
Totals	1732	100.0	601	100.0	

[a] n = number of women; Z = z-score, a statistical instrument
[b] p < .001 (two-tailed)
Source: Adapted from Westrom et al. (1992).

women. Nearly 99% of the known cultures of the world either mandate
monogamy (15%) or allow polygyny (84%). Less than 1% of the cultures entertain polyandry (one wife and plural husbands; Divale Harris,
1976). The more vulnerable, more susceptible gender (in this instance
the female) was more cloistered than the less vulnerable, less susceptible gender (the male). As with any other strong emotion, the social
benefits are maximized if the behaviors in question are placed under a
moral rubric. Across the world, sexual promiscuity is generally considered improper behavior: more so for the woman, and less so for the
man. This two-pronged strategy—avoid polyandry and cloister the
women more than the men—is consonant with the solution of procreating the next generation with minimal dangers from STDs. However, the
linkage between images and the consequences of acting in concert with
those images is neither immediately apparent nor formally instructed.

Consequences of Loosening the Double Standards

For the sake of discussion, let's assume that in the contemporary
United States, the double standard has been challenged and, accordingly, has been loosened. If the above argument on societal strategy is
valid, then the ancestral prediction is that in those places where the

double standard is less challenged fewer STDs would occur. This notion, too, is a testable prediction.

Across the 50 states, the percentage of children born to single
mothers varies. By definition, a child born out of wedlock is born to an
extramarital relationship. Across the 50 states, the incidence of reported gonorrhea, an STD, also varies. If the ancestors were adequately
insightful, then the level of STDs ought to vary with the level of single-
parent births. The higher level of out-of-wedlock births would be expected to be aligned with a higher rate of STDs.

METHOD

For 1990, the percentage of all births in the United States born to
single-parent mothers was gathered across the states (U.S. Bureau of the
Census, 1994). For 1990, the rate per 100,000 population of reported
gonorrhea was gathered across the states (Division of STD and HIV
Prevention, 1990). See Table 6.4.

RESULTS

Our forebearers were sustained. There was a robust relationship
between rate of STDs and the percentage of out-of-wedlock births (r_p =
.661; $p < .01$; 2-tailed). As the percentage of single-parent births increased, so did the rate of STDs. Over 40% ($.661^2$) of the differences in
STD rate can be attributed to the varying level of single-parent births.

CONCLUSION

There are two points to be gleaned from the above exercise: one
specific, one general. The specific point is that, if multiple partners or
extramarital sexual relationships are to be extant in a community, then
elevated risks for STDs ought to be expected. If the STDs are left un-
treated, or treated late, then elevated rates of infertility, dead women,
and infant morbidity, including infant mortality, ought to be similarly
expected. For the great bulk of our ancestry, there was little medical
intervention available to treat STDs. Here an ounce of prevention
would be worth a pound of cure—a cure which was not available.

The general point is that traditions and folklore exist the way they
do for reasons. Cultural traditions are not random events that are established willy-nilly or maintained by whimsy. As Fox (1978) suggested:

Table 6.4. The Relationship, across States, between the
Percentage of Out-of-Wedlock Births and the Rates of
Gonorrhea, 1990 ($n = 50$) (Division of STD/HIV
Prevention, 1990)

State	Percentage of births born out of wedlock	Rates of gonorrhea (per 100,000 population)
Alabama	30.1	576
Alaska	26.2	221
Arizona	32.7	96
Arkansas	29.4	346
California	31.6	271
Colorado	21.2	97
Connecticut	26.6	269
Delaware	29.0	515
Florida	31.7	390
Georgia	32.8	790
Hawaii	24.8	51
Idaho	16.7	14
Illinois	31.7	340
Indiana	26.2	142
Iowa	21.0	95
Kansas	21.5	206
Kentucky	23.6	164
Louisiana	36.8	300
Maine	22.6	16
Maryland	29.6	499
Massachusetts	24.7	136
Michigan	26.2	350
Minnesota	20.9	125
Mississippi	40.5	545
Missouri	28.6	424
Montana	23.7	31
Nebraska	20.7	113
Nevada	25.4	249
New Hampshire	16.9	25
New Jersey	24.3	214
New Mexico	35.4	77
New York	33.0	277
North Carolina	29.4	451
North Dakota	18.4	19
Ohio	28.9	393
Oklahoma	25.2	196
Oregon	25.7	88
Pennsylvania	28.6	215
Rhode Island	26.3	109
South Carolina	32.7	424
South Dakota	22.9	37

(*continued*)

Table 6.4. (*Continued*)

State	Percentage of births born out of wedlock	Rates of gonorrhea (per 100,000 population)
Tennessee	30.2	398
Texas	17.5	255
Utah	13.5	22
Vermont	20.1	11
Virginia	26.0	287
Washington	23.7	121
West Virginia	25.4	81
Wisconsin	24.2	183
Wyoming	19.8	38
Mean =	26.1	226
sd =	5.5	178

Source: Division of STD/HIV Prevention (1990).

centuries know more than behavioral scientists. For those individuals who wish well for their own commonweal, there may be some advantage in examining the costs in addition to the putative benefits in jettisoning any worldview that has survived the filters of time and has served the adherents well in those times and places that were not always benign.

The above example is not to deny that there are tacky, tawdry men. The above example urges that "tacky, tawdry" be applied with circumspection.

THE U.S. DAD IN ACADEMIA

Until the late 1970s and early 1980s, three images dominated the behavioral sciences. The three images came from one psychological primatologist, Harry Harlow, from one psychoanalyst, John Bowlby, and one social anthropologist, Margaret Mead. Harlow's "white rat" was the rhesus macaque. His classic studies of the impact of isolation and mother-surrogates on the rhesus macaques have become a staple especially in introductory psychology courses. When viewing the paternalistic qualities of the adult male rhesus macaques, Harlow viewed adult male-young interaction as a derivative effect: (1) adult male macaques enjoyed being around (2) adult female macaques who in turn (3) enjoyed being around infant macaques. Thus (4) adult male macaques associated around infant macaques because they, the infants, were with adult female macaques. As was visited earlier in Chapter 2, Harlow's observation about adult male macaques not exhibiting high levels of epimeletic or caregiving behaviors toward their infants or their young is quite correct.

Harlow then generalized that, based on the rhesus macaque model, there was no independent human male-to-child bond. Men's association with children was a derivative effect: Men like women and like to be around them. Women like children and like to be around them. Therefore, men are around children because women are around children (Harlow, 1971). See Adams (1960) for a similar discussion, and see Smuts (1992) for a resurrection of this theme. Smuts views an enhancement of men's child care quotient as being a reproductive strategy by the men to impress the women of the men's potential of being a nurturing man. Hence, an icon in developmental psychology, Harry Harlow, had placed his imprimatur on a ratchet turn of distance between men and their children.

Harlow's work on early imprinting also known as "bonding"—the flip side of deprivation—influenced Bowlby, who reinforced the notion of an exclusivity of the mother-to-child bond at the expense of any possible father-to-child bond. His concept of monotropy, the primacy of the mother-child bond, gained considerable currency within the realm of developmental psychology (the work of Schaffer & Emerson, 1964, which indicated a plasticity of *which* an adult to whom a child may bond was noted, but often relegated to a footnote).

The final trendsetter and eminent "tabula rasa-ist," Margaret Mead, coined the highly quotable "Human fatherhood is a social invention" (Mead, Chapter 9, 1949). Sometimes her sentiment is translated as social accident (Parke & Sawin, 1977). For example, she wrote:

> But the evidence suggests that we should phrase the matter differently for men and women—that men have to learn to want to provide for others, and this behaviour, being learned, is fragile and can disappear rather easily under social conditions that no longer teach it effectively. Women may be said to be mothers unless they are taught to deny their child-bearing qualities (p. 192).

She continues:

> So that when it is said that men have no *natural urge* to paternity and so do not necessarily suffer from refusing paternity, we still must recognize that refusing the responsibilities of parenthood in most societies is a very expensive matter for the individual. (p. 226; italics added).[1]

[1] It may be useful to address Margaret Mead's often cited discussion of the Tchambuli (*Sex and Temperament in Three Primitive Societies,* 1963). Mead suggests that the Tchambuli have developed a culture in which the roles of men and women are reversed when

Thus, this trio—each one complementing the other two—created an academic base in the post-World War II United States, which gave an intellectual and scholarly basis to the supremacy of the inherent mother-child bond with fathering a supernumerary learned bundle of behaviors, a thin veneer of paternalistic solicitude.

It is important to note that *actual* indices of normative, typical—central tendencies—of fathering were not gathered and, hence, not presented, to support the trio's positions on U.S. fatherhood. Any correspondence between what fathers were actually doing and what scholars said they were doing was simply unknown.

THE PROFESSIONAL PRESS

The father's impact on the psychological development of his children was given little attention by professionals researching how children develop. For example, in the Foss series *Determinants of Infant Behavior,* there are over 600 references (Foss, 1961 to 1969). Of those 600, 91 (15.2%) refer directly to mother or maternal, while only one reference (0.2%) refers directly to father or paternal, and this one representative is Itani's (1963) work with the macaque monkey.

Spitz's (1968) *The First Year of Life* has little more than two sentences devoted to father: ". . . the reader must surely have wondered why I did not mention that the baby also has a father; and the mother a husband! After all, the father of the baby is the ultimate culmination of the mother's first object relation. He is the ultimate product of the vicissitudes which the mother's object relations have undergone" (p. 203). Perhaps after one's "vicissitudes" have been "culminated," there is little more to say. Dodson's (1974) most interesting and illuminating subtitle to his offering *How to Father* was "The first truly comprehensive guide for fathers that every *mother* should read (emphasis added).

The relatively rare professionals who were interested in fathering tended to focus on the differences in psychological indices in children as a function of differences on fathering behaviors": I.Q., self-esteem, gender identity. At base, the question asked was: if one changes fathering behaviors in degree or kind, does this change affect the child's

compared to the gender roles in traditional American society. Mead's interpretation of her own research leaves a good deal of room for debate. But, that point aside, there is no evidence presented by Mead or mention by her of the Tchambuli men assuming the role of either equal or primary child caretaker. Accordingly, the Tchambuli are not available as either an exception that profiles the rule or as an exception that disproves the rule. There is no evidence that the Tchambuli men are an exception.

psychology?: more or less smart; more or less secure, more or less masculine or feminine (Biller, 1971; Fagot, 1973; Hamilton, 1977; Lamb, 1976; Lynn, 1974; Mead & Rekers, 1979). Father absence had a moderate-sized coterie of experts. The generic formula for analysis was (1) find out what children cum fathers were like. Then (2) find out what children sans fathers were like. Subtract (2) from (1) and some insight was gained on the contributions a father made to his child's psycho-social-emotional-cognitive development (Biller, 1968, 1971, 1974; Block, 1973; Hetherington, 1970; Lynn, 1974; Lynn & Sawrey, 1959; Maccoby & Jacklin, 1974).

In the gap from the 1940s to 1970s, the general consensus was that yes, the caring, concerned, supportive, and loving father increased I.Q., confidence, and gender identity compared to either a nonexistent social father or a cold, primitive, indifferent father. See Sexton (1973) for a discussion on the problems of divining the specific nature of how the dynamics actually functioned and of how to ascertain a threshold.

Of interest, virtually no theorist noticed or highlighted the bread-winner or provisioning role *as an example of fathering.* That is, even though U.S. men inter alia are thoroughly convinced "bread winning" and "bread sharing" is a profound part of fathering, the differential impact of differential "bread" (both food and money) was rarely tucked under the aegis of fathering. As an exception to the trend, Adams, Milner, and Schrepf's (1984) stated purpose of their study was to look at behavioral or social dysfunctions in relation to absence of father versus absence of income. The two variables—availability of father vis-à-vis availability of income—were intractably intertwined, and it took a valiant swashbuckler to make the attempt. While not coterminus, the two indexes (father absence and income absence) were highly interrelated.

Because (1) SES and income are strongly correlated and (2) anyone's life-chances are profoundly affected by SES, the addition of the bread-winning capability of a father (and remember that around the globe men willingly share their treasure with their children) can profoundly affect the life-chances of a child. Hence, men see the role of provider as an important facet of their fatherhood. The sociologists view SES, also known as income, as a potent variable in life-trajectory of a growing child. The connection was glaring. The group that missed the connection were childhood specialists.

THE POPULAR PRESS

In the 1950s and 1960s, an era of economic prosperity for the United States, a number of publications presented the premise that the

U.S. father had become irrelevant and an object of chidable whimsy (Bednarik, 1970; Brenton, 1966; Greene, 1967; LeMasters, 1974; Rebelsky and Hanks, 1972). See Margolis (1984) for a complementary discussion of the maternal image.

In their review article of this era, Rapoport, Rapoport, Strelitz, and Kew (1977, p. 73) reported the then current expectations of parenting were that mothers were the main figures involved in parenting and that fathers were peripheral. Gorer (in Nash, 1965) suggested that because the child's early life was inundated by females, the father had become vestigial. Biller (1971) encapsulated the father's role in the first half of the twentieth century as being often ineffectual. Child rearing was viewed as the mother's responsibility and the father was not important in the socialization process. Parsons and Bales (1955) described women as the individuals who bear, nurse, and nurture children, whereas the alternative left to men was within the domains of achievement in power and mastery of the environment. LeMasters (1974) wrote that U.S. men were something less than good parents. In more than metaphorical manner, he wrote that the human primate father is incompetent enough to give primate fathers in general a bad name. Arguably, LeMasters knew even less about primates than about fathers.

Reports on father figures were often indirect, that is, mothers' reports (e.g., Pedersen & Robson, 1969, note that this trend continues as a major source of information on fathers [Koestner, Franz, & Weinberger, 1990; Harris & Morgan, 1991; Smith & Morgan, 1994]), or children's reports (e.g., Biller, 1968), and father-absent studies (see Pedersen, 1976). The few reports (e.g., Tasch, 1952) on fathers were usually from questionnaires or interview formats. As an exception, Rebelsky and Hanks (1972) collected data on actual man–child interaction. This study received a good deal of coverage. The study placed a voice-

Table 6.5. Incidence of Incompetent Parenting Behavior in Cartoons When at Least One Parent and at Least One Child Are Depicted, 1922–1968

| Parental behavior | Cartoons with | | | | | |
| | Mother shown | | Father shown | | Total | |
	n	%	n	%	n	%
Incompetent	37	26.8	108	73.0	145	50.7
Competent	101	73.2	40	27.0	141	49.3
Total	138	100.0	148	100.0	286	100.0

[a]$X^2 = 60.87$, $df = 1$; $p < .01$
Source: Adapted from Day and Mackey, 1986.

activated microphone on men and recorded the length of verbalizations from fathers to their infants. The average amount of recording verbalization was 37.5 seconds per day.

In an analysis of cartoons in the stolidly middle-class magazine *The Saturday Evening Post*, Day and Mackey (1986) found that fathers were significantly more likely to be caricatured as bumbling or incompetent than were mothers. (See Table 6.5.)

See LaRossa, Gordon, Wilson, Bairan, and Jaret (1991) for a complementary, more finely grained analysis of similar data. Parenting, already a womanly specialty, was viewed as becoming increasingly irrelevant for the man. Fathers' breadwinning efforts were not calculated into a father-quotient, and theorists profiled them as ad hoc assistants to mothers.

Then from the middle 1970s to the latter 1980s, father the irrelevant became father the underachiever.

CHAPTER 7

Father the Irrelevant Becomes Father the Underachieving

I perceive affection makes a fool of any man too much the father.

BEN JONSON

There is no good father, that's the rule. Don't lay the blame on men but on the bond of paternity, which is rotten.

JEAN-PAUL SARTRE

By the time the 1970s arrived, America was undergoing some very basic shifts in its demographics. First and foremost, the birthrate—after the profusion of postwar baby boomers—continued its long-term downward trajectory and, in 1972, dipped below the replacement value of 2,100 children per 1,000 women. Given that the United States has stayed below the 2.1 (children per woman) figure ever since, this dip appears to be permanent.

Second, mothers, released from a succession of births, began entering the labor force in unprecedented numbers. For example, in 1955, 18.6% of married women with children under the age of six years were participating in the labor force. By 1970, this percent had increased to 30.3. By 1980, the increase had reached 45.1% and by 1993 over half (59.6%) of the married women with children under the age of six were in the labor force (U.S. Bureau of the Census, 1994). The women's movement, however defined, which had been somewhat quiescent during the great depression, World War II, and the aftermath of the 1950s, reemerged and pushed for gender equality in the work place (wages, hiring, and promotions) and then pushed for equality in the nursery (diapers, feeding, and caretaking).

The image of "father-the-irrelevant" was awkward if quality parenting were to be a coed activity. The feedback loops of science and society are rarely the null set (Kuhn, 1970). The behavioral sciences have a tendency to discover that which important segments of society would like to have discovered. A discovery of a new and improved image of fathering would not prove to be an exception.

THE PROFESSIONAL PRESS

Studies in the professional press began to appear that readjusted the premises that profiled and defined U.S. fathering. The focus on fathering began to shift from the premise that fathers were not fundamentally important in the healthy development of their children to the premise that fathers theoretically are quite significant in the healthy psycho-socio-emotional development of their children, but that U.S. fathers were not actualizing their potential, and, thereby, were not meeting appropriate standards of paternalistic behavior. In other words, fathers can be influential but U.S. fathers were not fulfilling that promise. Clark-Stewart (1978) wrote of how American fathers were "underutilized." Price-Bonham and Skeen (1979) and Parke (1979a, p. 15, 1979b, p. 577) suggested that fathers need more education and practice in their roles of father. Biller (1974, p. 4), in his book with the chilling title *Paternal Deprivation,* found a picture in America of general paternal dereliction in which large numbers of fathers had little or minimal interaction with their children. (A decade later Biller, with Solomon [Biller & Solomon, 1986], offered palliatives with *Child Maltreatment and Paternal Deprivation: A Manifesto for Research Prevention and Treatment.* Biller then coauthored a book with Meredith (Biller & Meredith, 1975) in which they wrote: "Father neglect is such a profound problem in this country that a significant number of children have become 'walking wounded'—victims of subtle psychological violence, a result of the void of chronic father neglect." (p. 9). With rare exceptions, for example, Hetherington (1970) and Peters and Stewart (1981), no one seemed willing to consider the notion that U.S. men, as a class, were doing just fine in the fathering department. The conventional wisdom was being solidly planted in the premise that a deficiency existed. The problem at hand was to identify the characteristics of the deficiency with some specificity and then remediate that deficiency and thereby fix the problem: that is, fix the men so that they would become the acceptable parents that they were capable of being. In 1976, two publications—one professional and one popular—appeared that proffered the very concept that a large proportion of Americans were delighted to hear. Their best hopes were crystallized and confirmed: American fathers were not irrelevant, they were merely underachieving. The professional book was Michael E. Lamb's *Father's Role in Child Development* (1976). In his overview, Lamb writes: "Many social scientists believe, moreover, that, even in families in which the father is nominally present, his participation is often minimal. Although I have been concerned in this essay with detailing the contributions that fathers make to their offsprings' development, it is regrettably true that many fathers have little to do with their children, interact minimally with them and hence, make little positive contribution to their psychological development. . . . Fathers can hardly be expected to maintain a belief in their importance when they are continually being told of their irrelevance, other than as economic supports of the family unit" (p. 29).

A few technical points should be made at this juncture. (1) No one has developed a threshold of parental caretaking indices wherein the child has demonstrable deficiencies if that child's receipt of caretaking falls below that threshold; yet the child is demonstrably improved if the child's receipt of caretaking falls above that threshold. We just do not know how much of what is enough. (2) Hard data, especially in the 1970s, were quite sparse. And Lamb's comment of "have little to do with their children" becomes an excellent candidate for the "woozle" effect (based on Milne's *Winne the Pooh*) wherein various commentators comment on each other's comments frequently enough so that the initial comment becomes increasingly solidified as an obvious verity. That is, familiarity breeds acceptance. The vast bulk of the fathering literature available from the 1970s was from (1) the symbolic domain, often in elegant prose; (2) questionnaires that may or not have reflected behavioral central tendencies (Tasch, 1952); (3) reports from the wife or mother that may or may not have reflected behavioral central tendencies of the husband and father (Pedersen & Robson, 1969); and (4) children's recollections (Healy, Malley, & Stewart, 1990). (3) Food, clothing, and shelter are necessary, if not sufficient, conditions for more glamorous human psycho-socio-cognitive characteristics to flourish.

James Levine (1976) published his *Who Will Raise the Children? New Options for Fathers (and Mothers)*. The answer was fathers and mothers on an equal footing. (Oddly enough, grandparents—logical candidates to answer his question—were not included as potential recruits).

The news of the metamorphosis from irrelevant to underachieving was well received by academia and the literati. Examining the new and improved (especially U.S.) fathers became a growth industry. Various disciplines each configured their own model to analyze the U.S. dads who were not primed to be remedial.

Developmental psychologists asked for volunteers (white middle-class graduate students with infants in prestigious universities seem to be the most amenable to recruiting efforts). In a review of the field, Berman and Pedersen (1987) surveyed eight studies on men's transition to parenthood: six of the eight were white only, the other two were majority white; seven of the eight were middle class to professional class and the eighth was a cryptic "wide range"; six of the eight had either exclusively one child per family or a majority of one-child-only families and two studies had first-and-later children. If our ancestral families averaged more than two children per female (and they had to have done that or their descendants "us" would not be here), and if, as this book suggests, that fathers more specialized in toddlers and above, then a focus on the father–infant dyad as representing fathering may hit the nail squarely on the thumb in terms of profiling normative fathering in normative families (cf. Pedersen, 1980; Yogman, 1982).

Once the volunteers had been gleaned, data on mother–child dyads, father–child dyads, and mother–father–child triads were analyzed. The mother's profile was then compared to the father's profile: for example, Barnett & Baruch, 1988; Baruch & Barnett, 1986; Berman & Pedersen, 1987; Blakemore, 1981; Golinkoff & Ames, 1979; cf. Heath, 1978; Hoffman & Teyber, 1985; Main & Weston, 1981; McLaughlin, White, McDevitt, & Raskin, 1983; Neal, Groat, & Wicks, 1989; Osofsky & O'Connell, 1972; Pakizegi, 1978; Spelke, Zelazo, Kagan, & Katelchuck, 1973; Stoneman & Brody, 1981. See Hames (1988), Roopnarine, Talukder, Jain, Joshi, and Srivasstav (1992), Ninio and Rinott (1988), and Levy-Shiff and Israelashvili (1988) for non-U.S. examples: Ye'kwana, India, and Israel. Risman (1986) encapsulated this notion of evaluating fathers with the mother-template with the title: "Can Men 'Mother'? Life as a Single Father." (cf. Suiter, 1991; Thompson, 1983; Radin & Harold-Goldsmith, 1989). From the world of psychiatry, Earls (1976, p. 224) made the sociological observation that:

> "It could be speculated that the neglect and omission of fathers in the work of psychiatry and the social sciences is bound to the nature of patriarchy, which renders to it a relative degree of immunity. But the social order, at least of contemporary American society, is changing rapidly in critical ways that indicated increasing deviation from traditional patriarchy".

Bridges, Connell, and Belsky (1988) compared fathers with mothers, but emphasized qualitative differences in parenting style. Unsurprisingly enough, men were found to be *equally* capable of dealing with children. However, the typical result was that, although men were quite capable of nurturing their children, their nurturing quotient was lower than the mothers'. No 50:50 split was unearthed. Note that the template of parenting was generally developed along the lines of traditional tasks performed by the traditional mother. That is, parenting was being redefined as mothering. Fathering was on the way to being transduced into mothering. The value of a steady, proficient breadwinner was, by this time, irrelevant.

Festinger's (1964) idea of cognitive dissonance is germane here. Part of the greater crusade was that men were making too much money compared to women (normally phrased: women were being discriminated against economically). If enriched breadwinning on the part of the father was to be seen to aid in the optimum development of the child, then such enrichment for the child would be a fine happenstance. However, if the mother template is the appropriate route to evaluate fathers, then the larger paychecks by fathers—more likely to be referred to as men rather than as fathers—were an awkward inconvenience. Consequently, an enrichment from the breadwinning role was not to be included in the calculus.

As the above quote by Lamb had foreshadowed, the breadwinner-provider role was thereby shunted into near oblivion by those who were writing about the father. Lamb's revised edition (1981) continued the shunt. While a majority of men continued to assume their task was to provide for their family, the pundits had voided that assumption. For example, McCall (1985) wrote in his column *About Fathers*: "They're much more than breadwinners—their influence is unique" (p. 120). The negative consequences upon children of their father being laid off from his job were virtually ignored. But when analyzed, the consequences were generally quite negative (McLoyd, 1989). Father's increased earning power versus the mother's earning power was almost never viewed as a boon for his children—that their lives were being enriched or enhanced through his work ethic and sharing. The income differential was invariably viewed as proof positive of gender discrimination as well as of the victimization of women. See Blankenhorn (1995) for a complementary discussion.

Sociologists did "who-does-what" studies and found that, unsurprisingly enough, women did the predominant amount of the day-to-day maintenance and scheduling of the children (Coltrane & Ishii-Kuntz, 1992; Coverman & Sheley, 1986; Hochschild, 1989; Lewis, 1986; Nakhaie, 1995; Palkovitz, 1987; Shelton, 1992). Hanson and Bozett (1985) summed up the hopes and wishes of the academics and the literati with their creed: "In general, we believe that men need to assume more responsibility for child rearing and homemaking . . . many (men) are relatively ineffective in child care, seem reluctant to increase

their participation or are unable to participate because of external circumstances." (p. 14). On the other hand, men's intransigence was neatly encapsulated by Bartz (1978): "However, fathers' unwillingness to
seek educational help with the parental role is a problem more resistant
to change. There are emotional and attitudinal factors involved here
which have not yet been thoroughly explored." (p. 213).

Ergo, (1) if men were capable of quality parenting, and (2) if men
were underrepresented in the actuality of parenting, then (3) men must
be underachieving. The rest of the argument went unstated: Equality is
just, good, and ennobling. Men should be just, good, and ennobled.
Men should perform 50.5% of the child care. They are *his* children,
too! Enough said, case is closed.

To buttress the conventional wisdom of parenting equality, a serious effort was initiated in Sweden to *officially* make parenting a gen-
der-neutral status. In Sweden, there was a maternal leave policy. The
woman who gave birth was ensured time off from her job with full pay
for a year (and an additional three months with a slightly less income
compensation) to be with her infant. Job security was assured. To
match the maternal leave policy, a paternal leave policy was enacting
for the Swedish men, and the new Swedish fathers were urged (with
the aid of an aggressive advertising campaign) to avail themselves of
the opportunity. In 1974, the Swedish government's official rationale
for extending parental leave to cover men read:

> The change from maternity leave to parental leave is an important sign that
> the father and mother share the responsibility for the care of the child. . . . It
> is an important step in a policy which aims through different measures in
> different areas to further greater equality, not only formally, but in reality,
> between men and women in the home, work life, and society (translated by
> Haas, 1990).

The results of the Swedish experiment will be revisited in Chapter 14. With hindsight, when looking back at the U.S. version of im-
proving the father, the naïvete of the well-intentioned innocents becomes impressive. Academics and the literati had the social calculus
well in hand.[1] The only fly in the fondue was that the American men
were not consulted. Voting with their feet, they said, Thank you, no.

A little prior reflection might have anticipated this disinclination.
Whatever the forces that had pulled women from the nursery (again,
the birthrate was below replacement value), those same forces would
be unlikely candidates to pull men into the same nursery. Harkening
back to Patterson's (1980) study—(*Mothers: The Unacknowledged Vic-*

---

[1]One fears that these academics and literati are the same fine folks who envisioned that
forced school bussing would singularly solve racial and education differentials.

tims)—raising children is very hard on those people who are raising the children.

The cross-cultural data on the associations between men and children surveyed earlier in Chapter 4, as well as the surveys by Hewlett (1992) and Barry and Paxson (1971), indicate that men are better built for children who were toddler and above with brief, high-intensity bouts of interaction (read: "play") and dealing with the environment as their forte. To repeat the fundamental conclusion of Chapter 4: "Parenting behaviors are not gender dimorphic; however, the threshold for activating or maintaining parenting behaviors is lower for women than for men; more lower for infants, less lower for older boys."

That men *could* change a diaper, *could* bathe their child, *could* fix formula was not the issue. Many men did and do. At this point, the second *a reminder can trump inspiration* maxim will be presented. If given a chance, people tend to do things, that is, behave the way they want to. If given a chance, people tend to avoid behaving in ways that cause themselves grief. People tend to maximize pleasure and comfort and satisfaction if they can and tend to minimize pain, discomfort, and unhappiness if they can.

I suggest here that, while men can change diapers, the threshold that impels them to do so is higher than for women, especially when the wife or mother is also available. As an analogy, many women can and do change tires on their cars. Nonetheless, they may not be as enthusiastic in doing so as their husbands, especially if the husband were present. It is rare when a woman stops on the highway to change the flat tire for a distressed man.

Across the world's community of cultures, primary infant care is exclusively a female prerogative (Weisner & Gallimore, 1977; Barry & Paxons, 1971; Josephson, Barry, Lauer, & Marshall, 1977). Cultural traditions react to infant care seriously. If a task in a culture interferes with proper child care, that task is systematically given to men (Brown, 1970; Murdock & Provost, 1973). Hunting for large animals and metal working are two examples which are incompatible with taking care of infants, and, across the world's community of cultures, these two activities are for men only (Murdock, 1937).

As the 1980s ended and the 1990s began its decade-long tenure, three trends began to crystallize: (1) a few good, conscientous men—generally middle-class professionals with one infant child—strove to emulate the imagery of the new, improved androgynous father, which was based on the traditional mother template. This trend also included two additional facets: marriages with highly nurturant androgynous fathers (i) were more prone to dissolution than a more traditional marriage, and (ii) the addition of more children eventuated in a restructuring of their families in the direction of the traditional family division of labor by gender (Booth & Amato, 1994; MacDermid, Huston, & McHale, 1990; Radin, 1988; Radin & Goldsmith, 1985, 1989; Russell, 1983; Williams & Radin, 1993). (2) Many, if not most, fathers blithely ignored the supplications of the literati and academics and fathered in a way that was comfortable for them and their children. (3) As was mentioned in Chapter 1, the severe abrading of men from the father role via no-fault divorce and out-of-wedlock births separated men from children in large numbers and high percentages. Both phenomena are immune to what men may want or prioritize. That is, both no-fault divorce and out-of-wedlock births may occur whether the man is agreeable to them or not. Legally, the man's wishes are totally irrelevant. Furstenberg (1988) succinctly pinpointed the gap between the few good men and the fatherless children with his essay: "Good dads—bad dads: two faces of fatherhood."

When it became clear that men were not going to be second mothers, a subtle shift occurred in the presentations of those who believed that U.S. fathers, as then currently configured, should be upgraded. The shift changed focus from increasing father–infant nurturing along the lines of the mother template to increasing the aid that a husband can lend to his wife. Father Theodore M. Hesburgh caught the spirit of the times with his sentiment: "The most important thing a father can do for his children is to love their mother." That is, the neo-newer, even more improved man of the 1990s was to increase his quotient of housework—again, based on traditional chores nominally performed by traditional mothers. The men were to help their wives by lightening their domestic duties. Studies were published that indicated women were still executing most of the housework. Hochschild's (1989) seminal work *The Second Shift: Working Parents and the Revolution at Home* received nationwide attention (*Newsweek,* 1989). (It may be of interest to note that Hochschild surveyed 50 families, ten of which were profiled. The average number of children per the 50 families was 1.6 children. None of the families had three or more children. In terms of replacement value, this sample was dysfunctional. No group can maintain itself with an average of 1.6 children per woman.) The thesis of Hochschild was that women were overworked in the home and men were underworked. Other researchers followed suit, e.g., Shelton's *Women, Men, and Time: Gender Differences in Paid Work, Housework, and Leisure* (1992, p. 43). Coltrane and Ishii-Kuntz's (1992) introduction to their research project began: "In response to the recent dramatic entry of women into the paid labor force, social analysts have asked why men have not assumed more responsibility for household tasks traditionally performed by women." In their results section, they note:

"Like previous researchers, we found that husbands' average contributions to housework were relatively small. The mean number of hours husbands devoted each week to the five tasks of cooking, dishes, cleaning, shopping, and laundry was 8.6, with a mean proportionate contribution to the total number of hours spent on these tasks of 19.3%." As a contrast, they offer that 80% of the surveyed wives performed 20 or more hours of housework per week. Deutsch, Lussier, and Servis (1993) covered both "husband-as-wife" and "husband-as-mother" in their article "Husbands at home: predictors of paternal participation in child care and housework." After reviewing their results on the level of paternal child care, they wrote: "Fathers of infants do very little to care for them. According to mothers, fathers' involvement in the basic caretaking tasks like feeding, soothing, and getting up at night is quite low. As in previous research . . . these mothers are not getting what they expected. Fathers' own reports of their performance are only slightly better. These men do less than they had anticipated." Moving on to results from the survey of housework, Deutsch, Lussier, and Servis (1993) found that "levels of husbands' contributions to housework were also low." Lindsey (1994) neatly encapsulates the shift: ". . . parents in the nearly four decades that these changes have been taking place have largely failed to establish a new and equitable equilibrium in their family responsibilities. . . . (Calasanti and Bailey (1991), examining the division of household tasks among working couples, found that in the United States, women performed between 73% and 84% of all domestic labor. The issue of who is responsible for what household chores remains an area of conflict in many families (p. 72)." U.S. men's reluctance to do traditionally female chores has some longevity. Coverman and Sheley (1986) reviewed men's housework and child care time from 1965 to 1975 and found low levels of male participation throughout the target interval.

THE POPULAR PRESS

Literature on the father, which aimed at a wider, nonspecialist audience, was also making the transition from *father the irrelevant* to *father the underachiever*. When discussed at all, U.S. fathers tended to be depicted as either remaining aloof from their children, and thereby abdicating paternalistic responsibility, or as being good naturedly amiable toward the father role, yet uncomfortable or incompetent in exercising that role; for example, Brenton (1966), Coon (1971), Sexton (1969, 1970), Greene (1967), Bednarik (1970), and McLaughlin (1978). A syndicated cartoon exemplified this theme with the caption: "You can always tell the father on TV shows. They're the mindless, ineffectual buffoons." Fasteau (1976) wrote:

> Being a father in the sense of having sired and having children is part of the
> masculine image; but fathering, the actual care of children, is not. Men who
> spend a lot of time taking care of their children—washing, dressing, feeding, teaching, comforting, and playing with them—aren't doing quite what
> they should be.

In the mid-1970s, the premise began to emerge that fathers, too, could and should be positive influences upon the growing child (Fein, 1978; Levine, 1976; Rossi, 1977). In an article in the *Ladies Home Journal,* Maynard (1979, p. 152, quoted a wife as lamenting: "The truth is . . . my husband really doesn't know how to be a father." Maynard continued that "an enormously large percentage of fathers in this country are simply not involved enough in caring for their own kids." Biller and Meredith (1975) speculated that paternal deprivation is widespread enough to generate large numbers of "psychologically wounded children."

Yarrow (1982) noted:

> Although many mothers want and may expect their husbands to be involved parents, sharing the tasks and the fun involved in rearing a child,
> men's attitudes toward their roles as fathers have been changing more gradually than their wives' expectations.

Giveans and Robinson (1985) seemed hopeful with their impressions that "In short, fathers are becoming 'hooked' on their children, thereby modeling a more human parenting style for subsequent generations to emulate."

Although a little later than her colleagues, a standard-bearer for the women's movement, Germaine Greer (1990), joined the fray with her book *Daddy We Hardly Knew You.* In her discourse, Greer seemed somewhat annoyed that her father would have been adversely affected by military duty in World War II. In a remarkable use of logic, she viewed her father's reaction to being bombed by the German Luftwaffe as the basis upon which he would construct his paternalistic philosophy vis-à-vis a highly literate and independent-minded daughter.

Once the academics and literati explained to men that they were important to their children, a number of feel-good offerings began gracing the newsstands. Martin Greenberg's *The Birth of a Father* (1985) extolled the intrapsychic joy and satisfaction of bonding with his son (his only child to that point). The best seller by Bob Greene (1984), *Good Morning, Merry Sunshine: A Father's Journal of His Child's First Year*, chronicled his happiness with his one daughter for one year (his only child to that point). Greene's book had followed Mike Clary's (1982) diary entitled *Daddy's Home: The Personal Story of a Modern*

Father Who Opted to Raise the Baby and Mastered the Craft of Mother-hood (his only child to that point). Clary had evidently accepted a notion that the modern father was a good mother.

Crittenden (1985, p. 145) summed up this new age of Aquarius of modern fatherhood with her admission: "I also have to admit that another part of me reads books like Greene's and gets teary eyed at the thought of all those men finally discovering what amazing little creatures their children are—and, not incidentally, giving their wives a little time to relax and enjoy them, too." Blakely (1984) lent a unique perspective on the new phenomenon. She wrote: "Many men are hard put to find a woman with whom they can empathize. The lucky, and loving, find her in their own homes. Their daughters often help set them free. . . . For the love of the women they live and work with, I hope they (the men) grow up before their daughters do."

It is useful to reiterate that this time frame is the very same time frame in which (1) no-fault divorce rates are occurring at comparatively high levels (and again, women dominate as petitioners in divorce cases, and increase that dominance when children are involved), and (2) the proportion of out-of-wedlock births is increasing rapidly. The modern father was being lauded and erased at the same time.

CHAPTER 8

Fathers in the 1990s
Dr. Jekyll and Mr. Hyde

*To make the child in your own image is a capital crime, for
your image is not worth repeating. The child knows this and
you know it. Consequently you hate each other.*
                                                    KARL SHAPIRO

*I have found the best way to give advice to your children is to
find out what they want and then advise them to do it.*
                                                    HARRY S. TRUMAN

As the 1990s indefatigably continued toward the 21st century, a crisp
dilemma has occurred on the American scene: What to do with U.S.
fathers? Two very separate images were being generated (see Furstenberg's 1988, pp. 193–218) *Good Dads-Bad Dads: Two Faces of Fatherhood* and Coolsen's (1993) *Half Full or Half Empty?* for complementary
discussions). One image was pleasant and congenial: the modern, caring, in touch-with-their-feelings men, many of whom, along the way,
had somehow managed to view themselves as morally superior to their
own fathers. The second image was anything but congenial: the *Deadbeat dad.* These were tacky, tawdry men who absconded from their
wives and children with the family's treasure. The good news will be
examined first.

THE IMAGE OF THE GOOD DAD

A plethora of literature appeared noting the newer, and even more
improved, father had arrived. These newest new fathers were seen as
quite distinct from their male ancestors: ancestors who were clearly
deficient as fathers. Kimball's (1988) *50–50 Parenting* advocated the
equality of parenting: mostly based on the mother template. Kort and
Friedland's (1986) edited volume *Father's Book: Shared Experiences*

painted a human face on fathers. Osherson's (1986) *Finding Our Fathers: The Unfinished Business of Manhood* shared with the reader biographies of nurturing and caring between grown sons and their fathers. Pruett's *The Nurturing Father* (1987) (with an *n* of 17) reassured the reader that fathers, too, can be nurturing.

Ritner (1992) had one of the more descriptive titles: *Fathers' Liberation Ethics: A Holistic Ethical Advocacy for Active Nurturant Fathering.* The definitive, antithetical volume that advocates oppressive, fragmented, immoral, passive, exploitive fathering is still waiting to be published. Garbarino (1993), who is undoubtedly dissatisfied with current fathers, wrote *Reinventing Fatherhood* in which he asks and then answers his own question: "What must we do? To develop a new kind of father, we must encourage a new kind of man." In *My Fair Lady,* Professor Higgins asks, Why can't a woman be more like a man?" It's time to ask the opposite question. If we are to rewrite the parenting scripts to emphasize nurturing and the investment of self in children's lives, we need to ask, Why can't a man be more like a woman?.

Louv (1994) is also in favor of a reconstruction of father. In *Remaking Fatherhood,* Louv writes (p. 182): "As men work toward redefining what fatherhood means, they need to call upon all their talents and capacities and hopes . . . Although these instincts are common to virtually all fathers, men are only beginning to find the words to describe what fatherhood makes them feel."

Coolsen (1993) asks a question, but does not provide an answer: "Can we create a society . . . in which fathers themselves are willing to give up their old authoritarian role and act as partners with their spouse in child rearing and everyday family life? On the dust jacket of Sears' (1991) book *Keys to Becoming a Father,* a blurb reads: "Fathers today are playing a larger parenting role than ever before. Here is a doctor's advice to men on all aspects of fatherhood, from assisting at childbirth through sharing child care functions with Mom. Most of all, this book offers insights into getting joy from being a father."

Colman and Colman (1988) synthesize a problem and then solve it, to wit: ". . . we summarize the dilemma: The behavior of fathers is under attack, but the concept of *father* has remained relatively stable. Men who become nurturant in the family often feel that they are mothering rather than fathering. It is difficult for a man to feel like a gentle, caring parent and like a man at the same time."

Bronstein and Cowan's (1988) edited book is entitled *Fatherhood Today: Men's Changing Role in the Family.* The editors seemed convinced any changes would be for the better.

In a book that was hard to confuse with *Rebecca of Sunnybrook Farm,* Rothman's (1989) publication was entitled *Recreating Mother-*

hood: Ideology and Technology in a Patriarchal Society. Just for the purposes of closure, the society to which Rothman is referring is the United States. On page 213, Rothman writes: "Freud was right; mother-rearing has consequences that are not good. Freud was wrong: it is not women who are so horribly damaged, but men. . . . The loss, the ominous subhumanity, is men's. The solution is to involve men fully in child care, enabling boy children to experience the continuity, connectedness, womanliness in themselves that would make them whole."

Brazelton's (1989) genial book *Families Crisis and Caring* noted that if parents are not supported by the general society, then the society is being self-defeating. Leo Buscaglia (1989) joined the party as only Leo could with his *Papa My Father: A Celebration of Dads.* Streiker's (1989) *Fathering: Old Game, New Rules* shares with the reader his view of the even more newer and more improved U.S. father (p. 36): "Dad needs a new image (or new images) of who he is, what he does, and why he is important. He needs an understanding of himself and his family that takes cognizance of the way things are and yet empowers him to make a difference. He needs to throw away and discard inappropriate images, for not only do current images of father and of the family invalidate all of us, but they are warped by outmoded expectations, unworkable models and mind boggling confusion". Then he asks the, perhaps rhetorical, question (p. 129): "How then does a man get in touch with the tender giving and caring aspects of his own being?" and Streiker (1989, p. 150) proffers the trilogy: "Great fathering requires three things: being there, being aware, and being real. Everything else is dessert."

Pittman (1993) explains masculinity to the reader with his article "Fathers and Sons: What It Takes to Be a Man." We are told that "We know that raising children is the central experience of life, the greatest source of self-awareness the true foundation, of pride and joy, the most eternal bond with a partner. We know that being father is life's fullest expression of masculinity. So why did so many men forego this for so long, and will the current crop of post-patriarchal fathers fare any better?" (p. 52).

For those men who needed a how-to book, Levant and Kelly (1989) were able to supply *Between Father and Child: How to Become the Kind of Father You Want to Be.* The authors are clear in their goal in that they "want to change the terms of the father–child relationship from distant, wary, and respectful to warm, open, intimate, and tender."

It may have some tempering value to remember that the generation to which these people are referring had a divorce rate about half the current one and whose percentage of out-of-wedlock births were less than half of the current percentage. There may be some salutary effect in remembering that the generation to which these people are referring managed to survive a great depression and were on the winning side of World War II.

It is also useful to remember that most of the literature described above was not intended to be seen as outgrowths of the scientific enterprise. The samples of subjects that were tested, if they existed at all, were usually very small and either self-selected or highly nonrandom. Again, the image of the U.S. father is that which is being crafted by the authors. They are sculpting folklore. And as has been presented earlier with examples from advice on how to use time and on how childhood is interpreted, folklore can cover the entire range of worth on any dimension. The image of fathers is not an exception.

There is father the good: "I would give you some violets, but they withered all when my father died" (Shakespeare's *Hamlet*).

There is also father the bad:

> When men abandon the upbringing of their children to their wives, a loss is suffered by everyone, but perhaps most of all by themselves for what they lose is the possibility of growth in themselves for being human which the stimulation of bringing up one's children gives. (Ashley Montagu).

Finally, there is father the ugly: "My father was frightened of his father, I was frightened of my father, and I am damned well going to see to it that my children are frightened of me" (King George V). The bulk of the literature that focused on the U.S. fathers did not attempt to establish behavioral central tendencies on what they were, in fact, doing or even attempting. Image.

During the same time frame, a second very different imagery on the exact same subject, the U.S. father, was being created.

THE IMAGE OF THE
LESS-THAN-GOOD DAD

Pirani (1989) concisely states this alternate image: "Fathers are missing; away at work; separated by divorce from their children. Paternal authority has been eroded, yet paternalism is still in evidence, and under attack by the women's movement. The reliability of male political leaders is at a low point, the spiritual fathers are alienated, the God the Father is a fading concept."

Popenoe (1993) was less lyrical, but more analytical. He wrote: "Recent family decline is more serious than any decline in the past because what is breaking up is the nuclear family, the fundamental unit stripped of relatives and left with two essential functions that cannot be performed better elsewhere: childrearing and the provision to its members of affection and companionship."

As early as 1983, Russell (1983) presented data that indicated that more egalitarian marriages were also more fragile and prone to separation or restructuring (along a more traditional format) than were less egalitarian marriages.

Charlie Lewis and Margaret O'Brien's (1987) edited book *Reassessing Fatherhood: New Observations on Fathers on the Modern Family* also waved a flag of caution. On page one they write "In contrast to much of the literature, this book reflects critically on the 'new father.' Despite the wave of optimism driving contemporary accounts, the evidence for the existence of such a man is much less convincing. As early as the mid-1980s, Charlie Lewis (1986) interpreted his data on fathers thus: "There is no evidence to suggest that father–infant relationships are closer today that they were. We might expect to see differences in the small amount of comparative data that exists, but in effect the figures which Schaffer and Emerson (1964, p. 175) produced 20 years ago are broadly similar to those presented in Chapter 7."

Blankenhorn's (1995) book title is rather straightforward—*Fatherless America: Confronting Our Most Urgent Social Problem*. One of Blankenhorn's working premises is that "fatherlessness is now approaching a rough parity with fatherhood as a defining feature of American childhood." If a critical mass were to be reached and the fatherhood role were to be adopted by a shrinking minority of U.S. men, no one has any clue on the ramifications of such a structural shift in the U.S. culture.

The phrase and specter of the "deadbeat dad" began to filter through the professional and poplar press and media. Cutright (1986) wrote "Child Support and Responsible Male Procreative Behavior." In the 1960s, with freedom and personal liberty given high marks for individual goals and socially sanctioned priorities, divorce was envisioned as a reasonable solution to the problem of adults who no longer wanted to be married to each other. Again, the interface of science and society became in evidence. Our society wanted to know that divorce was not troublesome for the children involved. Accordingly, studies were conducted which, unsurprisingly enough, found no deficits in children of divorce. Studies which suggested that mother-alone families entail the highest risk in terms of social maladaptation and psychological well-being of the child (Bohman, 1971; Kellam, Ensminger, & Turner, 1977) were simply ignored. The conventional wisdom was clear: surely it was better to live in a quiet house with one parent than to live in a noisy, raucous house with two parents who did not like each other. The title of Wallerstein and Kelly's (1980) book is informative: *Surviving the Breakup: How Children and Parents Cope with Divorce.*

By 1989, revisionism was occurring, Wallerstein and Blakeslee's (1989) sequel to the 1980 book was titled *Second Chances: Men, Women and Children a Decade after Divorce: Who Wins, Who Loses.* The authors chronicle children grown to adulthood who were anything but pleased at the prior breakup of their family. The much ballyhooed blended family—mine, yours, ours—was not reported by children to be as nurturing or as stress free as their biological nuclear family (Amato, 1994; Amato & Keith, 1991; Booth & Amato, 1994; Dawson, 1991; Furstenberg, 1987; Hanson, McLanahan, & Thomson, 1996).

Children of divorce, as mentioned earlier, tend to remain with the mother. The father, the noncustodial parent, tends to have very little contact with his children after the dissolution (Blankenhorn, 1994; Furstenberg, Morgan, & Allison, 1987). Again, it is the mother, by more than a 2 to 1 margin, who dominates the petitioning for divorce. What became the focus of media presentations was the noncompliant man, the deadbeat dad, who became noncomplaint after being separated from his children. The woman who initiated the separation of the father from his children received much less scrutiny. The movie *Mrs. Doubtfire* encapsulated the process quite neatly. Seltzer (1991) noted that for most children born outside of marriage or whose parents divorce, the father role is defined as much by omission as by commission. Here, too, the father's behavior is given a negative cast. Less often noted is the mother's behavior. Again, the mother is typically given custody. The father has no right to visit the home of his children. The usual pattern is that the man goes to the child's home, the child enters the motor vehicle of the father, and then they drive away to a destination. The child visits the father. The mother can control such visitations. She can facilitate easy access between the father and his child, or she can block or sabotage such access. Given that the bulk of postdivorce interviews are with the mother, her version of events becomes the only version presented to the reading or viewing audience. When fathers were *also* interviewed, a very different picture of the social chess involved is painted (Braver, Wolchik, Sandler, Fogas, & Zventina, 1991). It became clear that some mothers thwarted visitation between a father and his children with forethought, intent, and skill.

The role of dad the breadwinner was then given a macabre twist. From the mid-1970s to the present, the role of breadwinner as executed by the father was progressively ignored by the academics and the literati as a barometer on any evaluation of the individual man as a father. But as soon as the father is separated from his children via divorce (generally instigated by the mother), his monetary support became *the* evaluative yardstick of his fathering efforts. Regardless of any other service or support or nurturance that he may provide for his children, if he falls behind in his payments of money to his ex-wife, then the man becomes a deadbeat dad.

Below is how the editorial staff of *U.S.A. Today* viewed the situation of the deadbeat dad with the editorial entitled: "Stiff laws nab deadbeats." The editorial begins: "The sight of deadbeat dad kin Jeffrey Nichols nabbed, cuffed, and jailed in New York for ducking $580,000 in child support ought to shake up other scofflaws" (a "scofflaw" is someone who habitually violates the law or fails to answer court summonses). "There are 7 million deadbeat parents, 90% of them dads. If all paid what they are supposed to, their children would have $34 billion more—money that sometimes has to come from the taxpayers instead." Such sentiments resonate with compassion and justice and fairness, and a counterargument seems totally unavailable. But a glimpse of the realities of the process, independent of individuals such as Jeffrey Nichols, may soften the starkness of black and white to various shades of gray.

1. Child support is not given to the children. Child support is given to the ex-wife. As described in Chapter 2, there is zero accountability by the courts on how child support money is actually spent. If child support monies given by the father to his ex-wife are spent by the ex-wife only upon the ex-wife, then the enthusiasm for the father to continue making payments might understandably be muted.
2. Any monies or resources given directly to the child by the father count for zero in the eyes of the court in the accounting of the father's child support payments. Any food, clothing, medications, recreations, and the like which are given to the child by the father have no reality in relationship to the court's mandated child support payments.
3. If the child is spending the summer or a vacation with the father and the child's expenses are totally underwritten by the father, these expenses count for zero when the next month's child support payments are due. The ex-wife is to be paid the child support payments, in full, even though the child is living with the father for an extended period of time.
4. Child support payments have zero deductibility when tax season rolls around.
5. Visitation time and child support payments are totally separate. The court will, on its own inertia, *nab, cuff,* and *jail* fathers who are not making payments at the court's bidding. Any thwarting

of the visitation between father and child by the ex-wife has no parallel legal recourse by which the court will automatically pursue on behalf of the father. The father is on his own.

ABUSE

Over and beyond the deadbeat dad who abandoned his children, economically and emotionally, an additional spectre arose of the physically abusive, violent man. Story after gruesome story after anguished story after incomprehensible story of men hurting and killing women and children has bombarded the U.S. public.

Domestic Violence and Fathers and Nonfathers

Early in the 1970s, the issue of family violence has been brought to public attention. As with any other version of violent, physical aggression, young males are overrepresented in nearly any statistic that is kept and filed. What is of interest to this chapter is the merging of father with nonfather into the more generalized category of "man." The tacit assumption would be that fathers and nonfathers are interchangeable and that the status of father, versus that of nonfather, does not affect the man's behavior. An example of the confluence in terms of husband versus nonhusband occurs in Lindsey's (1994) section on wife battering. The first sentence in that section reads: "Assault by a male social partner accounts for more injury to women than auto accidents, mugging, and rape combined." The only person who can batter his wife is the husband; yet the section begins with the focus on male social partners. (See O'Campo et al., 1995 for an empirical example wherein married women represented 10% of the sample, but 38% of the women reported partner-perpetrated violence.) Lindsey's section on child abuse follows the same pattern ("How physical abuse of children differs"). The first sentence reads: "Currently, if a child is beaten senseless by a parent, with multiple broken limbs, perhaps a concussion, there is no guarantee that the child will be removed and provided any protection whatsoever from the abusive parent." Nowhere in the section is any other abuser but parent referenced. While the sentence quoted above may, by itself, be accurate, the equation of *abuse of children* in the heading with *abuse by parents* in the text may be misleading. The germane question thereby becomes: Are fathers equally likely to abuse their children as nonfathers who are the male social partners to the mothers? The answer seems to be: No, an ongoing presence of a social *and* biological father reduces the chance of harm to his child.

In her review of relevant studies, Lenington found that the presence of a stepparent doubled the risk of abuse to the child. The presence of both parents (71% of the samples) reduced by about half (46% of the reported abuse cases) the chance of child abuse. In a Canadian study, Daly and Wilson (1985) found a similar pattern, with age of the child making a difference. The intact family represented 90% of the families in the sample, but represented only 42% of the child abuse cases in the youngest group (birth to 4 years), 21% for children 5 to 10 years, and 28% for the oldest children (11 to 17 years).

In other words, intact families represented a clear majority (90%) of the family types, but they represented a clear minority (21%–42%) of the instances of child abuse. Single parent (predominantly the mother) families represented 6% of the sample, but 36% of the cases of child abuse for the youngest children, 33% for the middle group, and 34% for the oldest children. Stepparent (usually the stepparent is a male) families were 1% of the sample, yet had 16% of the child abuse cases for the youngest children, 33% of the cases for the middle children, and 30% of the cases for the oldest children. The argument that fathers and nonfathers are equally dangerous to their children seems extremely weak. These data indicate that having a biological and social father in the house is an insurance policy against the child being abused.

Sexual Abuse

A similar pattern emerges if focus is restricted to sexual abuse. Russell's (1986) early study in San Francisco found that stepfathers represented 17% of the sexual abuse cases (47% of the more traumatic episodes) whereas biological fathers represented only 2% of the cases (26% of the more traumatic episodes). Natural fathers are underrepresented in these data and stepfathers are overrepresented. Gordon and Creighton (1988) found similar results in Great Britain: Stepfathers and boyfriends of the mother were more prone to sexually abuse the mother's child than was the child's biological father. Tyler (1986) reported that stepfathers were five times more likely to sexually abuse the mother's child than were the natural fathers.

Accordingly, it appears that any attempt to equate fathers and non-fathers in relationship to child abuse belies the data. Fathers are not just any man when it comes to their own children. That there are villainous men is not being disputed. What is being disputed here is any endeavor that would paint the villainy of some men with the same brush as fathering. The distinction between a father and a mother's social partner—in relation to the father's children—is real and profound and important and often overlooked.

It is now time to switch gears from imagery to some more promiscuous empiricism wherein the U.S. version of fathering *behaviors* (diagnostically separate from the images of the good, bad, and ugly) will be compared to versions of *behaviors* (minus any imagery) found in alternate non-U.S. cultures.

CHAPTER 9

U.S. Fathering
In Search of a Benchmark

. . . mothers are more devoted to their children than fathers: in that they suffer more in giving them birth, and are more certain that they are their own.

ARISTOTLE

You don't have to deserve your mother's love. You have to deserve your father's. He's more particular.

ROBERT FROST

As enthusiasm for evaluating the U.S. father figure built momentum in the 1980s one generalized interest of several researchers has been to track the father's amount and type of nurturing–caretaking behaviors and the scope and intensity of attitudes toward his children. As was described earlier, a typical research method has been to (1) survey fathers, (2) survey mothers, and then (3) compare the surveyed parent's profiles. The results of these studies suggested that fathers, even though quite capable of exhibiting an egalitarian parenting quotient parallel to mothers, had nurturing quotients that were lower than the mothers.

Although this model, which can evaluate fathering with a mother template is certainly valid and can generate answers to a particular class of questions, it is neither the only nor necessarily the most diagnostic and useful model available. An alternative model would be to compare men with other men rather than with women.

In other words, if an analysis or evaluation of U.S. fathering is deemed appropriate, then there are at least two separate routes to follow in order to execute that analysis:

1. Compare U.S. mothers with U.S. fathers.
2. Compare U.S. fathers with other fathers in other subcultures. For examples of studies of non-U.S. fathers, see Block, 1976;

Bozett and Hanson, 1991; Bronstein–Burrows, 1981; Hewlett, 1992; Lamb, 1987; Lynn and Sawrey, 1959; and Ninio and Rinott, 1988. It is the purpose of this chapter to explore the latter route and to compare the U.S. father-to-child relationship with the non-U.S. father-to-child relations.

Accordingly, the generalized question to address is: Are U.S. men in the father role similar or dissimilar to men in the father-role of other cultures?

METHOD

Fathering obviously covers a wide range of behaviors. For this book in general and this chapter in particular, two indices are surveyed to compare U.S. men with non-U.S. men. The first index to fathering is the joint association of men with their children (1) in public areas, which are (2) away from the domicile, and which are (3) equally accessible both to male and females during (4) daylight hours. The two fundamental reasons for this choice follow.

The first is a basic precondition for more elaborate interaction to occur between people is the sheer presence of one person with another. From verbal interactions to affiliative behaviors, the actual, shared physical presence of the actors is required: a necessary, if not sufficient, component for further, more refined, interaction. Given the *de facto* superior political and social power of adults in general and men specifically when compared with that of children across cultures (Levinson & Malone, 1981), the joint association of a man and a child, away from the domicile and during discretionary times for men, during which numerous other activities and associates are available to the men, indicates a willingness of the man to be with his children. Furthermore, the level of association of men with children, away from the domicile, is not a trivial happenstance, but reflects priorities and hierarchies of motivations on the part of a number of people, not the least of whom are the men. In the survey's diagnostic times and places, there is ample opportunity for men *not* to be with their children.

The second reason for this choice is that cross-cultural comparisons need a unit of behavior that is comparable across cultural boundaries. The more precisely a behavior is delineated, the more that behavior may have culturally specific interpretations, hence, a lack of comparability occurs. See Brown (1991), Buss (1989), Ekman (1980), and Fisher (1992), for a discussion and list of human universals. Although association is a coarse unit, the physical association or presence of men with children does have the advantage of being comparable across otherwise disparate social matrices or structures.

The second index is the level of activity from the father to the child (in the context of the level of activity from the mother to the child). The three proxemic examples (from Chapter 3) include: proximity to the child, level of touching from adult to child, and whether the adult can see the child (was the child in the adult's field of vision?).

Association: U.S. Men versus Non-U.S. Men

Two measures of U.S. men versus non-U.S. men were used to define dissimilarity and similarity:

1. The first measurement was the ranking of the percentage of children associating with U.S. men within the 23-culture sample (22 non-U.S. cultures + 1 U.S. culture). If the rank of the U.S. culture was in the middle of the sample, for example, within the ranks 6–17 (inclusive), then the U.S. culture would be defined as similar. If the U.S. rank fell beyond those ranks, in either direction, then the U.S. culture was considered dissimilar. Ranking by the percentage of children in (i) men-only groups, (ii) men-and-women groups, and (iii) total percentage of children with men-only groups plus the percentage of children with men-and-women groups were compared separately. All children (boys plus girls) and boys only and girls only were also analyzed separately. Of course, the sum of the percentages of children in men-only groups + men-and-women groups + women-only groups must equal 100.0%.

2. The second measurement tested for the predictability of the U.S. sample from the non-U.S. sample. Using regression equations, the data from the non-U.S. cultures were used to predict the U.S. levels of man-child association. That is, if the actual percentage of children with men fell within the confidence limits (.01; 2-tailed) of the predicted percentage, then the U.S. culture is defined as similar. If the actual percentage fell beyond the confidence limits, then the U.S. men were defined as dissimilar. All children, boys only and girls only, were analyzed separately.

Note that the scores and ranks for the U.S. sample were developed by the computed averages from the subsamples. Kentucky, California, Nebraska–California, Iowa, Virginia, El Paso (Texas). Each of the subsamples was weighted equally.

Ranks

The percentage of children with each of the three man-child groups (men-only groups, men-and-women groups, total (men-only + men-and-women groups) were ranked across the 23-culture sample (22 non-

U.S. cultures + 1 U.S. culture) for all children. China was not coded for gender of child, therefore the number of cultures for both boys only and girls only was 22 (21 non-U.S. cultures + 1 U.S. culture = 22).

The rankings of the U.S. sample varied from a high of 11 to a low of 15. The mean rank was 12.1. Because all of the ranks were within the middle two quarters, the data suggest that, for this one characteristic (association), the U.S. men were similar to the non-U.S. men. See Table 10.1 for all children, Table 10.2 for boys only, and Table 10.3 for girls only.

Table 9.1. Percentage and Ranks of Associations between Men and Children (Boys and Girls) in 23 Cultures for Men-Only Groups, Men-and-Women Groups, and Total (Men-Only Groups + Men-and-Women Groups)

Culture	Men-only (1) %	Men-only (1) Rank	Men and women (2) %	Men and women (2) Rank	Total 1 and 2 %	Total 1 and 2 Rank
Israel	31.9	1	14.5	23	46.5	18
Iceland	29.0	2	31.4	13	60.4	8
Morocco	28.5	3.5	14.7	22	43.2	20.5
India	28.5	3.5	28.5	17	57.0	12
Brazil (urban)	24.4	5	29.2	15	53.6	14
Taiwan	23.8	6	19.4	19	43.2	20.5
Ireland	22.9	7.5	40.6	7	63.5	5
Japan	22.9	7.5	38.8	9	61.7	7
Brazil (rural)	22.8	9	22.9	18	45.7	19
Kenya	21.9	10	28.9	16	50.8	15
China	21.3	11	58.5	1	79.8	1
Senufo	21.0	12	37.5	10	58.5	10
Hong Kong	20.7	13	47.0	1	67.7	4
Austria	20.5	15	42.4	6	62.9	6
Sri Lanka	20.5	15	14.8	21	35.3	22
United States	*20.5*	*15*	*35.85*	*11*	*56.35*	*13*
Virginia	17.5		39.0		56.5	
Iowa	18.6		34.8		53.4	
El Paso, TX	21.8		33.9		55.7	
Kentucky	30.7		24.6		24.6	
Nebraska and California	18.8		48.0		66.8	
California	15.6		34.8		50.4	
Ivory Coast	17.4	18	15.2	20	32.6	23
London, United Kingdom	17.4	18	40.3	8	57.7	11
Lima, Peru	17.4	18	30.4	14	47.8	17
Spain	16.8	20	51.7	3	68.5	3
Mexico	14.2	21	35.6	12	49.8	16
Paris, France	8.7	22	68.4	1	77.1	2
Karaja	8.3	23	50.9	4	59.2	9

Table 9.2. Percentages and Ranks of Associations between Men and Boys-Only in 22 Cultures for Men-Only Groups, Men-and-Women Groups, and Totals (Men-Only Groups + Men-and-Women Groups)

Culture	Men-only (1) %	Rank	Men and women (2) %	Rank	Total 1 and 2 %	Rank
Israel	40.7	1	15.5	21	56.2	17
Iceland	40.1	2	26.4	15	66.5	6
Morocco	37.5	3	13.6	22	51.1	20
Ivory Coast	36.3	4	15.7	19	52.0	19
Brazil (urban)	35.9	5	25.4	17	61.3	11
India	34.2	6	31.1	31.1	65.3	8
Brazil (rural)	32.7	7	25.6	16	58.3	14
Taiwan	31.4	8	18.4	18	49.8	21
Kenya	30.8	9	26.9	14	57.7	15
Senufo	28.6	10	36.6	10	65.2	9
Ireland	28.4	11	44.7	5	73.1	2
Sri Lanka	27.3	12	15.4	20	42.7	22
*United States**	*24.7*	*13*	*34.2*	*11*	*58.9*	*13*
Virginia	20.9		40.2		61.1	
Iowa	23.2		32.5		55.7	
El Paso, TX	28.7		34.7		63.4	
Kentucky	30.2		26.5		56.7	
California	20.5		36.9		57.4	
London	23.4	14	40.3	7	63.7	10
Lima, Peru	23.1	15	30.7	13	53.8	18
Mexico	22.6	16	36.4	8	59.0	12
Austria	22.4	17	43.1	6	65.5	7
Hong Kong	21.5	18	47.7	4	69.2	4
Spain	20.0	19	48.4	3	68.4	5
Japan	19.7	20	37.7	9	57.4	16
Paris	11.3	21	67.4	1	78.7	1
Karaja	7.1	22	63.0	2	70.1	3

*Gender x adult group was not available for the Nebraska-California sample.

Predictability of U.S. Men from Non-U.S. Men

A correlation coefficient and regression equation were computed between the percentage of children in men-only groups and the percentage of children in men-and-women groups in the non-U.S. sample. For all children the n was 22. For boys only and girls only the n was 21 (the children in China were not coded by gender).

All children. With the correlation coefficient (r_p) of $-.611$ ($p <$ .01; 2-tailed, $n = 22$), the regression equation for all children was

$$Y = (-.2443)(X) + 29.4\%$$

Table 9.3. Percentage and Ranks of Associations between Men and Girls-
Only in 22 Cultures for Men-Only, Men-and-Women Groups, and Totals
(Men-Only Groups + Men-and-Women Groups)

Culture	Men-only (1) %	Men-only (1) Rank	Men and women (2) %	Men and women (2) Rank	Total 1 and 2 %	Total 1 and 2 Rank
Israel	28.2	1	13.2	20	41.4	17
Japan	27.9	2	36.3	7	64.2	4
India	26.6	3	25.5	16	52.1	10
Hong Kong	25.4	4	40.3	4	65.7	3
Iceland	24.3	5	29.7	13	54.0	8
Taiwan	22.0	6	17.6	18	39.6	18
Ireland	21.9	7	36.0	8	57.9	6
Austria	21.7	8	40.0	5	61.7	5
Kenya	18.7	9	26.3	15	45.0	13
Morocco	18.2	10	12.7	21.5	30.9	20
*United States**	*18.1*	*11*	*31.6*	*11*	*49.7*	*11*
Virginia	15.1		36.4		51.5	
Iowa	15.8		34.2		50.0	
El Paso	17.4		31.8		49.2	
Kentucky	31.3		22.4		53.7	
California	11.1		33.9		44.1	
Spain	17.7	12	50.6	2	68.3	2
Senufo	15.6	13	38.5	6	54.1	7
Sri Lanka	13.9	14.5	12.7	21.5	26.6	21
London	13.9	14.5	31.8	10	45.7	12
Lima, Peru	13.3	16	29.2	14	42.5	16
Brazil (rural)	12.9	17.5	21.3	17	34.2	19
Brazil (urban)	12.9	17.5	30.5	12	43.4	14
Ivory Coast	10.6	19	15.5	19	26.1	22
Mexico	9.3	20	33.8	9	43.1	15
Karaja	8.6	21	44.6	3	53.2	9
Paris	6.0	22	69.4	1	75.4	1

*Gender x adult group was not available for the Nebraska-California sample.

where Y = the predicted percentage of children in men-only groups,
and X = the percentage of children in men-and-women groups. Plugging in the U.S. data for the percentage of children in the men-and-
women groups, the equation becomes:

$$20.6 = (-.2443)(35.85\%) + 29.4\%$$

The actual value of the percentage of all child in men-only groups was
20.5%. This actual value of 20.5% was within 0.1% of the predicted
value (20.6%) and within the confidence limits of the predicted value:
17.5% to 23.7%.

Boys-only. For the non-U.S. sample, the correlation coefficient (r_p) between the percentage of boys in the men-only groups and the percentage of boys in the men-and-women groups was $-.862$ ($p < .001$; 2-tailed, $n = 21$). The regression equation was

$$Y = (-.510) \, (X) + 44.6\%$$

where Y = the predicted percentage of boys in men-only groups and X = the percentage of boys in men-and-women groups. Plugging in the U.S. data for the percentage of boys only in the men-and-women groups, the equation becomes

$$27.2\% = (-.510) \, (34.2\%) + 44.6\%$$

The actual value of the percentage of boys in the men-only groups was 24.7% and was 2.5% from the predicted value (27.2%). This value of 24.7% was within the confidence limits of 24.2%–30.2%.

Girls-only. For the non-U.S. sample, the correlation between the percentage of girls in men-only groups and the percentage of girls in the men-and-women groups was $-.275$ (n.s.; $n = 21$). The regression equation was:

$$Y = (-.132) \, (X) + 21.7\%$$

Where Y = the predicted percentage of girls in men-only groups, and X = the percentage of girls in men-and-women groups. Plugging in the U.S. data for the percentage of girls in the men-and-women groups, the equation becomes:

$$17.6\% = (-.132) \, (31.6\%) + 21.7\%$$

The actual value was 18.1% which was 0.5% from the predicted value. The actual value of 18.1% was within the confidence limits of the predicted value: 13.3%–21.7%.

Thus following the definitions and operations of this exercise, non-U.S. man-to-child relationships successfully predicted the U.S. man-to-child relationship vis à vis this one behavioral index. Thus both for compared ranks and for predictability, the U.S. men in the father role were similar to non-U.S. men in the father role.

DISCUSSION

Prior to a brief discussion of the results as a whole, it may be useful to reexamine the nonsignificant relationship ($r_p = -.275$, n.s., $n = 22$) between men-only groups and men-and-women groups for girls only.

As was discussed in Chapter 5, several of the cultures, for example, Morocco, illustrate a tradition of a strong division of labor by gender (see Mackey, 1981 for a discussion). As a consequence of this tradition, males and female are generally not together in public: the genders are somewhat segregated. To compensate for this confounding or mediating variable of strength of division of labor by gender, the proportion of girls (versus boys) per culture in men-only groups was plotted, across cultures, against the percentage of children in men-and-women groups. As the percentage of children in men-and-women groups increased (indicating *less* division of labor by gender), the ratio of girls (versus boys) in men-only groups also increased ($r_p = .500$; $p < .01$; 2-tailed; $n = 21$). The regression equation was

$$Y = (1.395)\,(X) + 19.9\%$$

Where Y = the predicted percentage of girls (versus boys) in men-only groups, and X = the percentage of children (girls + boys) in men-and-women groups. Plugging in the U.S. data for the percentage of children in men-and-women groups, the regression equation becomes:

$$66.6\% = (1.395\,(33.5\%) + 19.9\%$$

The actual value of 66.6% was the same as the predicted value of 66.6% and within the confidence limits of 44.1%–89.1% (.01; 2-tailed).

The U.S. proportion of girls (versus boys) in men-only groups tied at the 9th rank. Again, the U.S. sample of men was typical of men in the non-U.S. sample, and their level of association was accurately predicted by knowledge of men from other cultures.

INTERACTION: TACTILE CONTACT, PERSONAL DISTANCE, VISUAL FIELD INCLUSION

U.S. Men

There were 30 measurements (gender of child, age of child, type of interaction) that were coded across the surveyed cultures. Of the 30 measurements, there were 23 (76.6%) occasions when the U.S.-men results were with the majority of the other surveyed cultures. In seven results (23.3%), the data from the U.S. men were in a minority of the cultures. There were zero (0.0%) occasions when the U.S.-men data were unique or singular. That is, there were no occasions when U.S. men were aberrant from all the other surveyed cultures. See Appendixes 9.1–9.4 for specifics. Consequently, in terms of interactions (along the three coarse-grained dimensions of *proximity, touch, see*), U.S. men were typical, average, and mundane. Neither overly solicitous, nor overly deficient.

U.S. Women

For the 30 categories of measurement, U.S. women were also quite normal. In 22 (73.3%) cases, U.S. women were found with a majority of the other surveyed cultures. In eight (26.7%) instances, the data from U.S. women were found with a minority of the other cultures. There were no (0.0%) examples wherein U.S. women were unique or different from all other cultures.

Accordingly, U.S. parents, mothers *and* fathers, appear more similar than not to the other parents around the world.

SYNOPSIS

The question that this chapter strove to address was whether U.S. men, as a class, in the father role were typical or different from non-U.S. men in the father-role. Within the narrow framework of the behavior sampled and the constraints of definitions and operations, the answer is unambiguous: typical. Other cross-cultural studies on behavioral dimensions may develop dissimilarities, but, on the two dimensions (associations & interactions) examined in this chapter, U.S. men were usual, common, garden variety fathers.

It should be noted that, except for China, in all of the other cultures, women clearly predominated in levels of adult-child association. The U.S. women were no exception to this trend. To the extent that proxemics, in public areas, can be extrapolated to other parenting and fathering behaviors, an anomaly may become potential. The anomaly would arise based on the following argument.

To wit: Evidence in the above exercise, though limited, suggests that U.S. men are performing fathering roles rather typically, rather normally. U.S. men are doing less than U.S. women; yet so are the other men, as a class, in the great majority of the other sampled cultures.

Were the U.S. men to expand their role of father to match that of the mother template, the U.S. men may become typical parents when compared to U.S. women, but they simultaneously become clearly aberrant men—when compared to other non-U.S. men.

It is self-evident that making a judgment on the efficacy, advisability, or social value of such parenting egalitarianism is, of course, not within the scientific domain. However, there may be some advantage in considering carefully potential *sequelae* of any social policy, wherein gender egalitarianism is pursued, which if actually achieved, may create an abnormality within a larger context.

APPENDIX 9.1.

The Relationship between the Age of Child and the Level of Interaction from Adult to Child; by Men and Women Separately in Both Single and Plural Gender Adult Groups: 17 Cultures[a]

	Number of measurements in which there is:												
	An inverse[b] relationship between age and level of interaction[c]				No relationship between age and interaction				A noninverse relationship between age and level of interaction				Total
	Gender group				Gender group				Gender group				
	Single		Plural		Single		Plural		Single		Plural		
Interaction type	Men	Women	Men	Women	Men	Women	Men	Women	Men	Women	Men	Women	
Tactile contact	16*[d]	16*	16*	14*	0	1	1	3	—	—	—	—	67
Personal distance	13*	13*	10*	13*	3	3	7	4	—	1	—	—	67
Visual orientation	10*	11*	5*	5*	5	3	12	9	1	3	—	3	67
Total	39	40	31	32	8	7	20	16	1	4	—	3	201

[a]The Hong Kong sample and the men-only groups in the Karaja had too few cases for analysis.
[b]An inverse relationship occurred when the youngest age bracket (birth - years) was overrepresented in the more active levels of interaction from adult to child.
[c]$p < .05$; X^2, $df = 2$.
[d]Data from the U.S. sample are indicated by an asterisk (*).

APPENDIX 9.2.
Comparison between Men and Women in Relation to the Level of Interaction toward All Children (Boys and Girls): 18 Cultures[a]

Adult groups	Gender of adult responding more actively[b]	Interaction category			Total
		Tactile contact	Personal distance	Visual orientation	
Men-only vs. women-only	Men more active	4	2	4*	10
	Women more active	1	3	0	4
	Neither more active	13*	13*	14	40
	Total	18	18	18	54
Men (with women present) versus women (with men present)	Men more active	1	0	1	2
	Women more active	6	5	5	16
	Neither more active	11*	13*	12*	36
	Total	18	18	18	54

[a]Data from the U.S. sample are indicated by an asterisk (*).
[b]$p < .05$; X^2, $df = 1$.

APPENDIX 9.3.
Comparison between Men and Women in Relation to the Level of Interaction toward Children (Boys and Girls Separately): 18 Cultures[a-b]

Adult group comparison	Gender of adult responding more actively[c]	Interaction category and gender of child						Total
		Tactile contact		Personal distance		Visual orientation		
		Boy	Girl	Boy	Girl	Boy	Girl	
Men-only versus women-only	Men more active	1	4	2	5	1	4*	17
	Women more active	2	0	0	0	1	0	3
	Neither more active	14*	14*	15*	13*	15*	14	85
	Total	17	18	17	18	17	18	105
Men (with women present) versus women (with men present)	Men more active	3*	0	2*	0	1	1	7
	Women more active	0	2	0	5*	3	5	15
	Neither more active	15	16*	16	13	14*	12*	86
	Total	18	18	18	18	18	18	108

[a]Data from the U.S. sample are indicated by an asterisk (*).
[b]The Karaja had insufficient number of boys in the men-only groups for analysis.
[c]$p < .05$; X^2, $df = 1$.

APPENDIX 9.4.
Comparison of Level of Interaction
from Adult (Man or Woman) to Child by
Gender of Child and Composition of Adult
Group: 18 Cultures[a]

Gender of adult and adult group composition	Gender of child receiving more active responses[b]	Interaction category			
		Tactile contact	Personal distance	Visual orientation	Total
Men-only	Girl	4	2	0	6
	Boy	0	0	0	0
	Neither	13*[c]	15*	17*	45
	Total	17	17	17	51
Women-only	Girl	0	3*	0	3
	Boy	0	0	2	2
	Neither	18*	15	16*	49
	Total	18	18	18	54
Men (with women present)	Girl	0	0	1	1
	Boy	2	4*	1	7
	Neither	16*	14	16*	46
	Total	18	18	18	54
Women (with men present)	Girl	1	3*	0	4
	Boy	0	0	0	0
	Neither	17*	15	18*	50
	Total	18	18	18	54

[a]The Karaja had an insufficient number of boys in the men-only groups to allow analysis.
[b]$p < .05$; X^2, $df = 1$
[c]Data from the U.S. are indicated by an asterisk (*).

CHAPTER 10

Fathering in the Breccia

On the Banks of the Rubicon

You can do anything with children if you only play with them.
PRINCE OTTO VON BISMARCK

Many a man spanks his children for things his own father should have spanked out of him.
DONALD ROBERT PERRY (DON) MARQUIS

In the 1990s, the man who is in the father role finds himself in the whirling, howling ecology of the U.S. megatribe. Human males, just as adult males in other species, or human children or human women, tend to avoid unpleasant or noxious stimuli and to approach pleasant and pleasurable stimuli. A whole discipline in learning psychology was based on such learned approach-avoidance gradients and reinforcement schedules (see Dollard & Miller, 1950; cf Seligman and Hager, 1972; Skinner, 1938, 1953, 1971). As the U.S. father views the fathering role within the U.S. culture, what does he see? This chapter examines some of the societal dynamics that surround the status of U.S. father.

THE FATHERING INCENTIVE: A HARD LOOK

Although rarely found in the public forum, an eminently sensible question is, Why would a man *want* to be a father? That is, what is in it for him? Why should he bother—ever? Why would he turn his treasure over to children when he can spend the treasure on himself? This chapter attempts to profile some of the aspects of a fathering incentive.

The question of Why would a man bother to accept the role of father at all? is not without a basis. A high nurturing quotient by males in the mammalian world is unusual. As mentioned in Chapter 5, males of some arboreal primates, tamarins, marmosets, and a species here and there with a unique ecological niche tend to be very solicitous to their own young (Gubernick & Klopfer, 1981; Kleiman, 1977; Mock & Fujioka, 1990). But there are exceptions to the rule: male mammals do not nurture their young. That human males typically do spend time, energy, resources, and emotions on their young should not be taken for granted. Human males are an exception to the zoological world (Lamb, 1987; HRAF #22–#26, 1949; Hewlett, 1992; Mackey, 1985, 1986). Whereas the mother-child relationship is strongly analogous to other mammalian species, it is the human male that is the aberrancy when the frame of reference is zoology. The forces that drive paternalistic behavior in men are argued in this book to be biocultural in character. Those individuals who reject the "bio" part of the biocultural basis of fathering behavior are left with a tabula rasa explanation, a la Margaret Mead, or may simply ignore the issue and take fathering as a behavioral given: a premise that exists, but whose genesis would not be investigated further.

But biology is not destiny. The "cultural" part of the "biocultural" basis of fathering behavior that brings men to their parenting roles is neither magical nor omnipotent. Sufficient social pressure can be brought to bear on men such that being a father becomes too expensive: the negatives outweigh the positives, minuses outweigh pluses. That is, as men adjust the calculus of their motivational priorities, the benefits of being a father outweigh the costs of being a father. Were that to occur, he either eschews or jettisons the duties and responsibilities of fatherhood and, hence, is able to invest his interests in other, less demanding, more rewarding pursuits. The next section profiles what costs and benefits accrue for the father role.

There are three main motivating sets that can push or pull the human condition. The three certainly can, and do, overlap, but they can also be teased apart and studied individually. The three are (1) social motivators, (2) economic motivators, and (3) psychological motivators.

SOCIAL MOTIVATORS FOR FATHERHOOD

By the 1990s, the U.S. father was the recipient of a kaleidoscope of expectations that others—with various social and political agendas— have held for him. The fathers themselves were rarely consulted. Current premises on the motivations to father are deeply embedded in a folklore or mythological matrix that has developed apart from how men behave. This matrix has two main features: (1) men *should* be responsible and *should* be good fathers, and (2) men, quite analogous to women, have a nurturing side and can be, and want to be, warm and caring parents: (cf. Buscaglia, 1989; Garbarino, 1993 inter alios; Osherson, 1986; Pruett, 1987; Sears, 1991). These two features are examined below.

The Way Men "Should" Be

Any number of authors have built arguments predicted on the, often latent, tenet that men should shoulder more responsibility in the nurturance of their children, e.g., Streiker, 1989. Deadbeat dads have become an easy-to-flagellate symbol of dereliction. *Frontline* (5/18/95) presented a documentary on "The Vanishing Father" that primarily focused on fathers who were not keeping up with their child care payments. Part of the presentation included men being led away to jail in handcuffs for failing to make their child-support payments on time. Not a pretty picture, and not one that would serve as a poster for recruiting men into the father role. Nonetheless, after the flagellation is finished, the problem is still squarely there: Why would a man want to absorb more responsibility? The world is full of people who do not relish more work, more responsibility, or more demands being placed upon them. The mere existence of someone's wish for others to do better may not be highly persuasive.

Men as Mothers

Recent literature—some popular, some professional—is replete with the advocacy of men assuming a more nurturing, more motherly parent role. The tacit assumptions are that men can dispense more nurturance than the level that they would normally exhibit and, given the opportunity, become more nurturing and relish that opportunity (e.g., Clary, 1982; Crittenden, 1985; Greene, 1984; Kimball, 1988; Levant & Kelly, 1989; Pirani, 1989; Risman, 1986; cf. Colman & Colman, 1988; Lewis & O'Brien, 1987). Virtually no evidence, beyond the anecdote (Kort & Friedland, 1986; Pruett 1987), is sought or presented to sustain the assumptions. They are givens that probably tell the reader more about the authors than about how fathers actually behave and why they do so.

Social Pressures

What is the social motivation for a man to choose to become a father? Whereas other cultures view childlessness as a condition to be avoided, and social pressures are subtly and not-so-subtly applied to correct the condition (Rosenblatt et al., 1973), the United States is not a good example of a culture where parenthood is a social imperative. Having a child tends to lower adult participation in social events aimed at adults. There are virtually no public and formal sanctions that encourage and reward parenting, and there is no social opprobrium directed at childlessness or at parents who leave the parenting role via divorce. Hence, social incentives, which would meaningfully enhance the entry and constancy of men in the father role seem nonexistent.

ECONOMIC MOTIVATORS
FOR FATHERHOOD

With virtually no exceptions, children in the United Stats are economic costs.[1] Children can be economic "black holes" who absorb huge amounts of money. Wherein children in alternative cultures are net economic benefits to their parents (Aghajanian, 1979, 1988; Bradley, 1984; Nag, White, & Peet, 1978), such is not the case in the United States. Child labor laws and mandatory formal schooling create a situation wherein children consume much more than they produce: the more children, the more the magnitude of the cost to the father. For diverse discussions on the economics of parenthood and childhood, see Adams, Milner, and Schrepf (1984), Arnold et al. (1975), Bulatao et al. (1983), Caldwell (1982), Cochrane (1983), Easterlin and Crimmins (1985), Fawcett (1983), Handwerker (1986), and Ross and Harris (1987). Accordingly, to the extent that a man would rather spend his money on goods and services for himself than for his children, the economics of fatherhood is more of a disincentive than an incentive. An economic basis to recruit men into the U.S. father role is not promising.

PSYCHOLOGICAL INCENTIVES
FOR FATHERHOOD

Having precluded economics and social pressures as important incentives to be a father, psychological reasons, by default, seem the best candidate for an effective incentive. The psychological rubric may include the satisfaction with the status of fatherhood, the satisfaction of doing "fatherly" behaviors, and the satisfaction of loving and being loved by his children. As indicated in Chapter 2, the sampled men, in

[1]The debate concerning the economic incentives to have additional children to receive additional welfare benefits is beyond the focus of interest of this chapter. For a discussion, see Harris (1981).

the main (African American men were aberrant), indicated that psychological satisfaction was their highest priority for becoming a father, but it should be repeated that the men were queried only about their expectations of fatherhood. They were not asked if their expected psychological satisfactions were actualized. Let's review the evidence from Chapter 2 which suggests a down-side or cost to parenting. The evidence consist of five components: birth rates, Ann Landers' survey, surveyed spouses, surveyed fathers, and dysphoria producing aversive events.

Birth Rates

Continuing a decades-long trend, U.S. birth rates have declined to a level below replacement value (2,100 per 1,000 women, or 2.1 children per woman). The subreplacement level was reached in 1972 and has stayed there since that time. Given that there has been no environmental pollution or parasitic epidemic to generate massive sterility, the decline in fertility implies a voluntary reduction of reproduction by men and women. That is, if people have an opportunity to have fewer children, they avail themselves of that opportunity.

Borrowing once again from learning theory, part of the solidification in its niche in academia has been achieved by noting that people will repeat those behaviors which give them satisfaction and pleasure and will avoid those behaviors which cause them discomfort or distress. The decreases in birth rates, i.e. the fewer numbers of children per family, is offered as *prima facie* evidence that rearing children is problematic in generating net psychological rewards. If children were, on balance, more positive than otherwise, stopping at two or less seems at odds with classic (operant or respondent) learning theory. Can ten million pigeons and Norwegian white rats *and* B. F. Skinner all be wrong?

Ann Landers

In 1975, the popular columnist Ann Landers queried her readers: "If you had it to do over again, would you have had children?" She received nearly 10,000 responses, more than 70% of which were in the negative. The majority of the parents indicated a strong dissatisfaction with their parenting experiences (Landers, 1976). Even though the respondents represent sampling problems of the highest order, the sample was an excellent pilot study that certainly asked an interesting question and posited a clearly testable and falsifiable hypothesis. Yet there seems to be no evidence of any follow-up study with much more rigorous sampling techniques.

Surveyed Spouses

A number of studies on marital happiness have converged on the notion that those years of marriage that include young children are the least happy years for the spouses, especially for the wife and mother. Again, there is a strong intuition that, left to their own devices, people will try to maximize their own happiness and minimize their own unhappiness. If unhappiness is aligned with stress, and stress is associated with young children, then fewer children would mean less stress. Americans seem to have opted for less stress rather than more stress.

Surveyed Fathers

Surveyed fathers, when asked to evaluate their children, indicated that latter born children were less appealing their earlier born children. In terms of absolute judgments, even the last born children were evaluated as being loved and wanted, but the comparative trajectory was clearly downward, not upward.

Aversive Events from Children

Patterson's (1980) study indicated two trends in relation to the interaction between normal children and normal mothers. First, rearing normal children provides the mother with high rates of aversive events. Second, normal children rearing may be accompanied by dysphoria (battle fatigue) for the mother.

In addition, if the child is hyperactive or has a behavioral problem, then the frequency and amplitude of the mother–child difficulties escalate. Finally, mothers of socially aggressive children will describe themselves as more deviant than will mothers of normal or of other types of problem children.

These data reflect mother–child interaction. It would take a swashbuckling optimist to assume that a man, a father, would seek out for himself a high "density" of "dysphoric" inducing "aversive events" and risk becoming "deviant." The earlier question can then be repeated: "Why would a man want to enter or to remain in the father role?" Neither aversive events nor dysphoria nor deviancy seem incentives.

A CROSS-CULTURAL PERSPECTIVE

In societies that have not intensively industrialized, fatherhood is a given to their populace. The sequence of events is that (a) the prospective groom indicates to the prospective bride and her kin a promise of resources for her and subsequent children; (b) the bride and her kin make a determination on his prospects; (c) if the groom passes the resource test (and is otherwise covetable); (d) the wedding occurs; (e) children are procreated; and (f) the father shares his time and treasure as a matter of course. But if resources do not appear to be forthcoming, then the man stays celibate. If the promised resources fail to appear on a continuing basis, the man becomes divorced. As the Human Relations Area Files, (1949 #24–#26) illustrate, this sequence occurs independent of ecological circumstances, social structure, or subsistence technique (see Buss 1987, 1994 for an extended discussion).

The question then becomes: In these societies, what is the *glue* which adheres the man to the woman–children dyad? The answer seems to be inertia. As Fox (1980) has noted: "Centuries know more than social scientists." The worldview of the men, as molded, sculpted, refined by generation after generation of ancestors and mercilessly filtered by natural selection for congruence with our core human nature (our motivational systems), take their paternalistic behavior for granted. In a silent, tacit way, these men (read: fathers), provide for their children. If the fathers do not, their children suffer privation. Everything in the society supports the father's worldview, and nothing negates it. His children are the extra hands in the fields or in the kitchen. His children are his walking, talking, breathing, flesh and blood social security cards and his old-age pension.

However, as cultures move to service-oriented economies with a public school system and a strong centralized government, the view of and the need for children change drastically (see Zelizer, 1985 for a discussion). Parenthood becomes much more discretionary. Children become discretionary. The utility of children, over and beyond private, emotional satisfactions, diminishes to zero. Pensions and governments provide for retirement.

To the extent that the automatic linkage between being a father and providing for his children becomes broken, the greater become the chances of the man not entering or remaining with the mother–child dyad. For example, across cultures, divorce is negatively associated with the percentage of the population engaged in small-farm agriculture wherein the family is a functioning economy. The loss of a father directly threatens the entire familial economy (Day & Mackey, 1986). But, if the nuclear family does not function as an economic unit with husbands or fathers and wives or mothers performing complementary labors, then the adhesion of mutual financial interests is lost. If that added ply of adhesion is removed, then alternate centrifugal forces in the form of stresses and strains make marital dissolution that much more likely. Divorce rates increase, and, to the extent that children in a divorce situation would remain with the mother rather than with the father, the man is effectively reduced in performing the role of the ongoing social father.

In addition, across cultures, as women reach economic independence thereby lessening their dependence upon the men for provisioning, the percentage of children born out-of-wedlock increases. Once an out-of-wedlock birth occurs, then, with the power of a definition, the biological father's status and influence as a social father becomes the null set.

Thus, there are two routes that can systematically peel away the man from his children. How these two routes can operate beyond the control of U.S. men can now be examined.

TWIN HORNS OF A DILEMMA: DIVORCE AND ILLEGITIMACY

There seems to be a consensus that, in fact as well as in imagery, the proportion of children in the United States is increasing who are growing up to adulthood without the presence of their biological and social father. This social dynamic has generally, though not exclusively, been evaluated as deleterious to the child. That is, the fatherless child is viewed as experiencing deficits when compared to the child who experiences the ongoing presence of his or her biological or social fathers. The villain is usually portrayed as the father: the deadbeat dad. Let's see how the portrayal measures up against scrutiny.

Illegitimacy

The choice of words is important here. "Illegitimacy" may have shadings of meanings separate from "out-of-wedlock" separate, in turn, from "single-parent birth." "Bastard" will surely conjure up connotations of its own. The reader is invited to select any or of all of the above terms. The attempt here is only to convey the notion that the new mother is not married to the biological father (genitor) of the new infant. The next question germane to this section is *not* what is the role of the genitor in the development of the fertilized egg (zygote). Biology

101 settled that. The next question does become, What is the relationship of the genitor to the continuation of the pregnancy?

To wit: In the *Roe v. Wade* decision by the Supreme Court and all of
the legal machinations and adventures that have ensued, one point
became solidified in our culture: the woman was given sole legal authority as to whether her pregnancy was carried to term. The biological
(sperm) father (genitor) has no legal call on whether he will be a social
father. Framed a little differently, the genitor can be coerced to be a
parent—or not. The gender asymmetry is quite stark.

If the woman finds herself pregnant, then, in our megatribe in the
1990s, she is legally allowed to terminate the pregnancy. The genitor
has no legal leverage in the decision. His wishes or desires or expectations or preferences to be a parent, however intense and well meaning,
count for naught in the legal decision-making process. If the woman
decides that she wishes against being a parent, she can abort the fetus
and not be a parent. When the abortion occurs, she simultaneously
precludes the genitor from being a parent.

Conversely, if the woman finds herself pregnant, then in our megatribe in the 1990s, she is legally allowed to continue the pregnancy to
term—the birth of the child. The genitor has no legal leverage in the
decision. His wishes or desires or expectations or preferences to avoid
parenthood, however intense and well meaning, count for naught in
the legal decision-making process. If the woman decides that she
wishes to be a parent, she simultaneously makes the same decision for
the genitor.

The concept of coercing parenthood onto the woman is unacceptable in the United States in the 1990s. Similarly, the concept of mandat-
ing and coercing an abortion (precluding parenthood) upon the woman
is unacceptable. But, and this is a large but, the man can be forced to be
a parent against any expressed choice on his part. If the woman becomes a parent, so does he. He has no option. He can, however, be
assessed child support for 18 years as a result of the coerced parenthood. Others can decide just how close this scenario comes to taxation
without representation.[2] If the man were to propose marriage to the
woman and she refused him, then the man is, again, without recourse.
He cannot coerce marriage, nor will the government coerce the marriage. Here, too, he has no choice, no option.

Thus with the focus upon out-of-wedlock births, it is a difficult
case to make that it is the men, as social fathers, who become the
determining factor in those children born out-of-wedlock and thereby

---

[2] A Plan B might include a waiver signed by the man in which the man would forego both
rights and responsibilities vis-à-vis his biological child.

grow up in a fatherless household. They had no say-so in the continuance of the pregnancy—only the mother did. They had no say-so in the mother's acceptance or rejection of any overture to marry. Only the mother did. If the mother refuses to marry, then the genitor is never placed in the status of social father. Because he was never in this status, he has no opportunity to leave it. Thus whatever evaluations are made of the U.S. social father, it is awkward to apply those evaluations to genitors who may have been strongly opposed to the existence of their own paternity, but whose opposition was totally irrelevant to the event occurring and had had their offer of "social fatherhood" via marriage to the mother rejected by the woman.

No-Fault Divorce U.S. Style

The thirteenth amendment to the U.S. Constitution (Section 1) states: "Neither slavery nor involuntary servitude, except as a punishment for crime whereof the party shall have been duly convicted, shall exist within the United States, or any place subject to their jurisdiction". At first blush, the Thirteenth Amendment and no-fault divorce have virtually nothing in common. However, at a deeper hue, there is a linkage.

One emotional and evocative image that energized the antislavery forces in the nineteenth century and gave them moral leverage was that of the "slave family" being separated involuntarily at slave auctions. A father was sold to one planter, the mother to a second, and, perhaps, the young children to a third. All of these separations were under the aegis of the state government and thereby were backed up by the manpower and firepower of the local constabulary, and, if that failed, the state militia. This vision of the forced fragmentation of the family generated public outcry, and, one war later, eventuated in the Thirteenth Amendment. Between Abraham Lincoln and Harriet Beecher Stowe, there were to be no more family fragmentations enforced by the power of the state.

Whereas a scenario of involuntary family division under the guise of slavery would be totally denounced by virtually everyone in the civilized world, a less dramatic form of state backed forced family dissolution occurs daily in the United States, but has been given minimal publicity and even less scrutiny. The dynamic, of course, is no-fault divorce in general and "no-fault" divorce involving minor children in particular.

Let's revisit the scenario of no-fault divorce as presented in Chapter 1:

1. All fifty states have some variation upon the themes of no-fault divorce. With minor variations, the fundamental process is thus: if one spouse wants a divorce, the divorce will happen. In terms of the legal apparatus, the wishes of the other spouse are totally irrelevant. Mutual agreement is not necessary, nor is it even solicited.

2. More than twice as many petitions involving minor children are filed by the mother than by the father (one child: mother 64.8% vs. father 27.82%; two children: mother 64.74% vs. father 27.64%; three or more children: mother 65.66% vs. father 27.44% (Mackey, 1993, National Center for Health Statistics, 1989). Hence, because of the gender asymmetry, the scenario will be viewed from the woman's perspective.

3. The woman will file for divorce at the local courthouse. The filing guarantees the eventuation of the divorce.

4. In the great majority of the cases, the court will award custody of the minor children to the woman. The wishes of the father and his children can be totally ignored by the court.

5. When the woman is granted custody of the minor children, she and she alone will make decisions for the child. The father has no legal standing in the matter.

6. The state government will determine the amount of child-support payments that the father must make. The payments may be up to 50% of his disposable income. Any failure to pay punctually can result in a fine, time spent in jail, or both. In the *Frontline* documentary, real fathers with real handcuffs were taken to real jails. These items are not hypotheticals. Again, the father need not have done anything wrong to have those payments mandated.

7. Visitation times are controlled by the ex-wife. The ex-wife's compliance with visitation times are, at best, problematic (Braver, Wolchik, Sandler, Fogas, & Zventina, 1991). It is worth repeating that, while the state monitors the father's child support payments with the threat of sanctions, the wife's compliance is not, *pro forma,* monitored by the state at all.

8. The father is not provided access to his children's home during visitation times. The "visitation" itself is awkward and somewhat misleading. The father picks up the child, and then the child "visits" the father away from the child's home. It is the child who visits the father rather than the reverse.

Thus, the various states have constructed a process in which a parent, usually the father, can be systematically denied association with his own children and is mandated to pay a large portion of his income to the ex-wife. Both the destruction of his family, coerced by the power of the state, and the tax against his income, levied and coerced by the power of the state, have occurred without the parent, usually the father, having done anything wrong or untoward at all. It should be noted that there is no legal mechanism available to the state that is set up to monitor or oversee how the child support funds are actually spent by the ex-wife.[3] The tacit assumption is that the monies are spent to upgrade the child's life, but virtually no research has validated the assumption. The idea of "taxation without representation" is once again very close to being actualized by this process. The notion that a bank account in the child's name, which is funded by the child support payments and from which the noncustodial parent receives a monthly statement, truly does seem to be within the realm of current computer technology. And, perhaps, a notion whose time has arrived.

The current process of no-fault divorce described above has a clear asymmetry. Whereas the father's payment to the ex-wife is closely monitored by the state (and the penalties for tardiness include fines and jail time), the appropriate expenditure of the father's funds for his children is not monitored at all.

Framed a little differently, the nonpetitioning parent, generally the father, without committing any offense, can have his children taken away by the state, and he has absolutely no recourse whatsoever. That is, the destruction of his family is mandated and enforced by the manpower and firepower of the state. Where are you, Harriet Beecher Stowe?

Looking backward in time, the legal destruction of a family through slave auctions is clearly profiled as an awful event; an event awful enough to help spur actions to eradicate slavery. Part of the actions involved one horrific war. However, a contemporary view on divorce in the United States is much more muddied. Family destruction is simply one phenomenon among many available for public attention. *Individual rights, happiness as an entitlement, the primacy of freedom, domestic abuse,* even Murphy Brown—all have adherents who can make their case coherently and persuasively. One can only wonder how our current no-fault system will fare when evaluated in hindsight a century from the present.

---

[3]The anecdotes of "child support" payments being spent by the ex-wife on boyfriend's wardrobes, junkets, and drugs may be apocryphal. Nevertheless, they do point out the total lack of accountability by the woman on spending the funds provided for his children by the father.

Nonetheless, the additional brief for the primacy of a parent—who by all accounts has given no offense—being allowed to remain a de facto parent does seem compelling. At the very least, a two-tiered system would seem minimal.

Tier 1. No-fault divorce involving no minor children.
Tier 2. No-fault divorce that does involve minor children.

At the bare-bones levels, one would surely think that some determination would be made that the children would benefit from the deletion of a parent—usually the father.

Thus the current hue and cry of "family values" and "disintegration of the family" (see Whitehead's 1993 "Dan Quayle was right") has received a large amount of ink and electricity, for example, Blankenhorn, 1995; Popenol, 1996). But, at base, what has happened is the removal of the father from the mother–child dyad. Mothers and their children have essentially stayed together in an intact unit.

The two main routes have led to this abrasion: (1) Single-parent births wherein the woman has eschewed the role of wife, and government—local, state, and federal—is available for both the latent and manifest replacement of the traditional role of the father as a provider. Along this route, the man has no options on whether the conception is carried to term and on whether the wife will accept any proposal of marriage. (2) The wife, displeased with the role of wife, jettisons the husband, hence her status as wife. When children are involved, she can force him to jettison the role of father. He has no option on whether the divorce will occur. The government can assure that both jettisons are successful.

Thus for the main driving forces on fatherlessness, the man has extremely little room to maneuver to minimize their occurrences.

MEN AFTER DIVORCE

What, then, of the men after a divorce has occurred? The divorced father's stereotype includes: the deadbeat dad, lack of visitations (as we noted, however, the term "visitation" is a bit of a misnomer: it is the child who does the visiting, not the father) (Braver et al. 1991; Furstenburg, 1987; Seltzer et al., 1991) a lack of accountability, and lack of child support (Lindsey, 1994; Seltzer, 1991; Weitzman, 1985; *Frontline*, 1995). These are images that others have for the divorced father, but how does he see himself? A reasonable way to find out how the divorced man views himself is to ask him.

Accordingly, a study was designed to determine (1) what divorced fathers experience as their hierarchy of problems and (2) how accurately their fellow citizens are able to perceive how divorced fathers view themselves. It should be emphasized that this study is concerned only with the attitudes and perceptions and not with the actual behaviors of the divorced fathers. Here, too, the linkage between reported attitudes and behaviors can be tenuous. Consequently, this inquiry will focus directly on the reported experiential domain. The correspondence between the subjects' stated subjective reality and their deeds is beyond the scope of the study.

Literature on Divorced Fathers

Factors which lead to divorce have been covered extensively (e.g., Cherlin & Mccarthy, 1985; see Day & Mackey, 1981, for a bibliographic overview; Glenn & Supancic, 1984; Mackey, 1980). The consequences of divorce for the man, however, have received far less attention. There are, nonetheless, several studies germane to this inquiry.

Hetherington, Cox, and Cox's (1979) survey of divorced men revealed that finances, occupational problems, running the household, social relationships, the ex-spouse, self-concept, and their children all contribute to the problems of divorced men. Spanier and Caso (1979) found that relationships with their children were a concern for divorced fathers. White and Bloom's (1981) data listed, in rank order, loneliness, social integration, reintegration of sexuality, finances, and homemaking as sources of problems.

Greif's (1985) survey of custodial fathers indicated that social relationships, frustration with the legal system, and balancing work with home obligations were problem areas. Koch and Lowery (1984) also found that the legal system was troublesome for the divorced men. Social networks (Daniels-Mohring & Berge, 1984), the ex-spouse (Kitson, 1982), and finances and social networks (Bloom Caldwell, 1981; Gersatl, Riessman, & Rosenfeld, 1985) were found to be problem areas for divorced men. The widely reported analysis of divorce by Weitzman (1985) presents a strong indictment against divorced fathers for being uncaring toward their children and for being derelict in child support. According to Weitzman, the lack of mandated child support of that time was due to the lack of enforcement of court-ordered child support (cf Hoffman 1977). See Jacobs (1982) and Arditti (1990) for extensive reviews of the literature on divorced fathers.

From these studies on divorced fathers, three questions are generated:

1. How does the divorced father rank his problems?
2. How do other men (not divorced fathers) and women rank the problems of divorced fathers?
3. Are the rankings of these three groups similar or different?

METHOD

Definitions

Divorced fathers were defined as those men who had previously been legally married and divorced and who had fathered at least one child during that legal marriage. The general public (the men and women) consisted of adult males and females in any of the following marital statuses: (1) single, never married, (2) married, (3) widowed, (4) divorced, and (5) married, but previously divorced.

Questionnaire

A problem perception questionnaire (PPQ) consisting of 10 items was developed. Each item was a potential problem area for divorced fathers. The selected problems were culled from a literature review and included (a) relationship with parents, (b) loss of self-image and low self-esteem, (c) housework and domestic chores, (d) finances and money, (e) relationship with children, (f) establishing and maintaining legal rights, (g) relationship with ex-spouse, (h) social isolation, (i) relationship with in-laws, and (j) a tenth option, *other,* which allowed the respondent to list a problem not appearing in the other nine categories. Note that, because less than 1% of the respondents filled in the *other* category, only the nine itemized categories will be discussed.

Subjects

Divorced fathers ($n = 37$) were found via a nonprobability sampling, for example, through the "snowball" method. Questionnaires were first handed out to divorced fathers who were known by the researcher. These men then gave the researcher information leading to other divorced fathers and so on.

Data were similarly gathered from the general population, both men and women. Coworkers, friends, relatives, factory workers, and college studies were all eventually sampled. In this manner 142 women and 81 nondivorced men were surveyed. The sample was not strictly random; however, it was certainly eclectic.

Procedure

The questionnaires that listed the problem items were given to the subjects. The problem items were neither numbered nor lettered to avoid any possible influence that one or more of the number's connotations may have in the subjects' ranking of the items. The presentation of the problem items were reversed in half the questionnaires to avoid any ordering effect.

All subjects were asked to rank the items as first, second, third, eight, ninth and tenth in importance as being troublesome or problems for the divorced fathers. For this study, only items ranked in the top three were analyzed. It may be dubious to consider any item ranked fourth or beyond as a real problem. Responses were immediately put into a sealed envelope. Anonymity of response was guaranteed and was complete.

RESULTS

How Does the Divorced Father Rank His Problems?

The results from the rankings by the divorced fathers are presented in Table 10.1. *Finances* was the item ranked most frequently in the top

Table 10.1. Distribution in Percent and by Rank of the Top Three Problems Faced by Divorced Fathers as Reported by Divorced Fathers ($n = 37$).

Problem	Percentage (in the top three)	Rank
Finances	64.9	1
Children	59.5	2
Ex-spouse	54.1	3
Low self-image	45.9	4
Social isolation	27.0	5
Legal rights	18.9	6
Parents	8.1	7.5
In-laws	8.1	7.5
Housework	2.7	9
Other	<1.0	10

three problems: 64.9% of the divorced fathers ranked finances as being in the top three. *Children* was second at 59.5%. The only other item to be selected by half or more of the men was *relationship with the ex-spouse:* 54.1% of the men ranked it in the top three. The one item that most targeted the man's psychoemotional life was ranked fourth (*low self-esteem/loss of self-image:* 45.9%). *Social isolation/Loneliness* was fifth (27.0%). *Legal rights* was sixth (18.9%) followed by *Relationships with Parents* and *in-laws* (tied for seventh at 8.1%). Only one divorced father selected *housework/domestic chores* as one of the top three problems (ranked ninth at 2.7%). The distribution of these nine items was not random ($X^2 = 54.24$; $df = 8$; $p < .001$ [$C = .77$]) and reflected patterned responses from the divorced fathers.

How Do Other Men (Not Divorced Fathers) and Women Rank the Divorced Fathers' Problems?

Both women and nondivorced men were not guessing randomly. Their guesses—which is probably better denoted as empathy—was patterned ($X^2 = 166.81$ and 111.37 respectively, $df = 8$; $p < .01$). See Table 10.2. The question now becomes: how accurate was their empathy?

Are the Rankings of the Three Groups Similar or Different?

The set of rankings from the three samples was not random ($X^2 = 21.69$; $df = 8$; $p < .01$; Friedman's two-way analysis of variance). In

Table 10.2. Distribution in Percent and by Rank of the Top Three Problems Faced by Divorced Fathers as Reported by Divorced Fathers and Perceived by Women and by Other Men

Problem	Divorced fathers		Women		Other men	
	%	Rank	%	Rank	%	Rank
Finances	64.9	1	44.8	3	49.3	3
Children	59.5	2	66.7	1	70.4	1
Ex-spouse	54.1	3	61.9	2	60.5	2
Low self-image	45.9	4	33.3	5	38.3	4
Social isolation	27.0	5	38.1	4	35.8	5
Legal rights	18.9	6	18.1	7	7.4	8
Parents	8.1	7.5	2.9	9	4.9	9
In-laws	8.1	7.5	12.4	8	17.3	6
Housework	2.7	9	24.8	6	12.3	7

Table 10.3. Correlations (r_p) among the Three
Samples: Divorced Fathers, Other Men,
and Women

Compared samples	Correlation (r_p)
Divorced fathers vs. women	0.851[a]
Divorced fathers vs. other men	0.909[b]
Women vs. other men	0.961[b]

[a] $p < .05$; 2-tailed
[b] $p < .01$; 2-tailed

addition, each of the three correlations (by rank) taken separately was also significant (divorced men vs. nondivorced men; [r_s = .909, $p < .01$; 2-tailed]; divorced men vs. women [r_s = .851; $p < .05$; 1-tailed]; nondivorced men vs. women [r_s = .961; $p < .01$; 2-tailed]). See Table 10.3.

DISCUSSION

Problem Hierarchy of the Divorced Fathers

The results suggest that the three most salient problems faced by divorced fathers, as a class, were, in rank order, *finances, children,* and *ex-spouses.* These three items are those that were also deeply involved in their former nuclear families. Seen from a slightly different angle, the former nuclear family was the most highly cathected set of problems: more so than the psychoemotional state of the men, which seemed intermediate, and more so than the outside or social world of the men, which seemed least bothersome.

While caution is always advisable when bridging the gap from self-reports on attitudes to actual behavior, these data provide inferential evidence that the divorced fathers had *not* severed their emotional ties to their children after the divorce, and, from the divorced fathers' perspective, had not become emotionally aloof and detached.

The divorced father's ego was secondary to the first group of problems, but had precedence over the "network" items (social isolation, parents, in-laws, and the legal system). *Housework/domestic chores,* with perhaps floating thresholds for *acceptable hygiene,* was not an important problem with the sampled men.

These data lend more support to the image of a high level of paternalistic interest by U.S. men, as suggested by Bailey (1992, 1994), Booth and Edwards (1980), Mackey (1985), and Pedersen (1980) and lend less support to the image of paternalistic psychoeconomic desertion by U.S. men as suggested by Weitzman (1985).

Comparison of the other two samples (nondivorced men and women) with the divorced men indicated that they had a good "feel" for the problems that the divorced father was experiencing. The two most divergent samples, divorced fathers and women, illustrate an interesting pair of disconnects: *finances* and *housework.* Most divorced fathers (64.9%) indicated that money was a primary problem for them, but less than half (44.8%) of the women so identified finances as a primary problem of the divorced fathers.

Given the importance that cash has in our monetarized economy (see Hollingshead 1949, 1975, for clear examples; cf Caldwell, 1982), any systematic discrepancy between the genders on the importance of finances would surely lead to unfulfilled expectations followed by misunderstandings and resentments. When the divorced couple's children are entered into the calculus of expectations, the resentment can only be exacerbated.

A diminutive 2.7% of the divorced fathers experienced *housework/domestic* chores as a primary problem, whereas nearly a quarter (24.8%) of the women anticipated that those men would find *housework* of some moment. These findings support Pleck's (1985) suggestion that a source of domestic friction is the gap between wives' expectations of husbands' household involvement and their husbands' actual involvement (cf.Hochschild, 1989; Shelton, 1992; Deutsch, Lussier, & Servis, 1993).

SUMMARY

Let the obvious be stated that divorced fathers, as a class, are quite human and thereby vulnerable to human emotions—the pleasant ones to experience plus the ones that are less pleasant to experience. They, too, will have idiosyncratic problems as well as common problems inherent in any social process such as the divorce process.

An ex-father who is the noncustodial parent is still an ongoing father and must deal with the psychological, emotional, and resource needs of his children through their mother. This indirect route of his relationship with his children places him in a complex, delicate, and emotionally charged position. Given that the Ramboesque, Clint Eastwood, John Wayne myth structure for U.S. men is still not only a role model but also a role reflection, for sizable proportions of men in the United States, strong, silent men will not gratuitously articulate their own frustration, vulnerabilities, and anxieties. Their muteness can easily be equated with insensitivity or detachment. Nonetheless, an un-voiced disappointment can be just as vexing as a voiced one.

One does not have to be garrulous to be annoyed.

THE AFRICAN AMERICAN
SAMPLE REVISITED

In Chapter 2, an anomaly cropped up, and this section will exam-ine that anomaly. Whereas Chinese American and Hispanic and Cauca-sian men expressed the anticipation of *love and emotional satisfaction* as a primary rationale to be fathers, the African American sample of men did not. Their primary stated reason was that children were *wanted by the wife.* Men became fathers to satisfy or to mollify the wife.

The Chinese American and Hispanic and Caucasian women were each predictive of their men's rationales to be fathers as well as the other two ethnic groups of men. The African American sample of wom-en did not predict the men's priorities for becoming fathers. The Afri-can American women's primary expectation of what their men would indicate was that the children were accidents. There was a unique disconnect between the genders.

The question of how this anomaly occurred comes to the fore. Two possibilities, which are not mutually exclusive, may provide an expla-nation: a racial and a cultural explanation.

A Racial Hypothesis

A major problem in using race to analyze behavior in the African American community is that there is a large infusion of non-Sub-Saharan African genes into the taxon African American. But, for the moment, let's assume that all the ancestors of African Americans can be traced to sub-Saharan Africa: 100%. With such racial purity assumed, it seems reasonable that the motivational differences as tapped by the gameboard is expected to parallel the behavioral differences in the cross-cultural data as catalogued in Chapter 4.

Virginia versus Sub-Saharan Africa

To test this possibility, data from Kenya, the Ivory Coast, the Senufo, and the African American subsample from Virginia (the only subsample that coded for *race*) were examined in comparison to each other and to the other non-Sub-Saharan African cultures. The mean percentage of children in men-only groups for the three sub-Saharan samples was 20.1% (sd = 2.4%). The Virginian African American percentage for children in the men-only group was 13.8%, only two-thirds of the sub-Saharan African sample. The mean percentage of children in the men-and-women groups in the sub-Saharan Africa sample was 27.2% (sd = 11.2%). This figure of 27.2% was virtually the same as in the Virginia African American sample of 27.4% of children in the men-and-women groups.

Sub-Saharan African American Sample versus Non-Sub-Saharan African Sample

The mean percentage for children in the men-only groups from the sub-Saharan African American sample (Virginian African Americans + Ivory Coast + Kenya + the Senufo) was 18.5%. The mean percentage for children in the men-only groups from the non-sub-Saharan African sample was 21.1% (n = 20). Less than 3% separated the two samples.

The percentage of children (boys and girls) in men-and-women groups for the sub-Saharan African sample was 27.25%. The percentage of children (boys and girls) in the men-and-women groups from the non-sub-Saharan African sample was 35.8%. Accordingly, there may be some depression of the index in the men-and-women groups. But the percentage from the sub-Saharan African sample was well within a standard deviation (14.9%) from the mean of the non-sub-Saharan African sample men of 35.8%. In the overall data base, the sub-Saharan African sample is not an outlier. Its men and women groups may indicate a low average score, but the average part, not the low, is the better interpretation.

Given the reality of a racial admixture in the Virginia African American subsample, if there were racial differences separating sub-Saharan African subsample from the non-sub-Saharan African subsample, then the Virginia African American subsample is expected to be intermediate between the other two. But such was not the case. The percentage of children in the men-only groups from the Virginia subsample was 13.8%: a figure which was below the sub-Saharan subsample of 20.1%. The figure was not intermediate. The percentage of children in the men-and-women groups from the Virginia subsample (27.4%) was essentially the same as from the sub-Saharan subsample (27.2%).

If these behavioral data are used as a benchmark, any racial explanation on the anomalous motivators to be fathers seems very weak and without corroborating predictive validity. Similarly, the notion that there is a generalized set of traditions or cultures or worldviews from sub-Saharan Africa that explain the gameboard data suffers via the same analysis. The percentage of children in the men-only groups from the Virginia subsample was lower than the sub-Saharan African subsample. One does not predict the other.

Therefore, if a racial explanation is not promising and if a generalized culture that has been transferred from sub-Saharan Africa is equally unpromising, then the differential found in the *motivation to father* data must originate from an alternative locale and that locale would most reasonably be from within the United States.

The Removal of the African American Father

Aligned with this microstudy on the motivation to become a father is the overall, more global pattern of the African American family structure. In short, their father is gone. Garfinkel and McLanahan (1986) estimate that only 15% of the current African American children will remain with their two parents from their birth to adulthood (18 years). In 1991, nearly two-thirds (68%) of the African American children were born to single parents (read: mothers). Compare this figure to 60% in 1985 and to 55% in 1980 and to 38% in 1970 (U.S. Bureau of the Census, 1994). If death, separation, divorce, and desertion are all included, then the figure exceeds the 80% mark. With the deletion of the father, any effective communication between the two genders that may have existed also seems to have been dissolved.

TRANSFIGURATION OR COUP D'ETAT

If racial characteristics are not germane here, and if a generalized cultural motif spanning two continents is likewise not germane, then by process of elimination, the most likely candidate to explain both the (a) lack of consonance of adult African Americans to each other and to other ethnic groups and (b) the normality of out-of-wedlock births is the evaluation of the African American father by the African American community. If the father is viewed as irrelevant or redundant or dispensable, then he will be treated as such and—thanks to a fair amount of research on the development of *self-image* (Cooley, 1964; Mead, 1934; Merton, 1957; Rosenthal & Jacobson, 1968; Snyder, Tanke, & Berscheid, 1995)—he will act how he is treated or how he is expected to behave. See *Newsweek* (1993) for a cover story on just such a dynamic: "A world without fathers: the struggle to save the Black family".

An interesting derivative of African American experience in the last quarter century is the question of generalizability. Are African American fathers like the miner's canary? Do they signal what is about to happen? Are African American men simply aberrant people? If so, then what are the characteristics of that aberrancy? How could the aberrancy be reversed? How can men from other groups be immunized to prevent a comparable aberrancy from arising? Or it may be that no such aberrancy exists and the basic difference between different groups of fathers is a difference in timing only. As fathers (in whatever referent group that can be imagined) are systematically sliced away from their children, is there a critical mass which, if reached, simply tells growing boys that fatherhood may entail more costs than benefits and that such an adventure is not worth the effort?

To wit: If a man follows a traditional father template, then he is vulnerable to the charge of exploiting the domesticity of the wife or mother. He is a troglodyte in a patriarch's clothing. While the father may consider his breadwinning role as crucial to fulfilling the father role, he will have a sparse number of theoreticians agreeing with him. Father the provider is "non-chic". If he does decide to accept the mother template as a proper model to fathering, he will jeopardize his earning capacity and career trajectory. Childless coworkers and traditional fathers will have a lot more energy and time at their discretion to outcompete him in the office or workshop (Barnett, Marshall, & Pleck). Wives who may have been annoyed at his lack of enthusiasm for laundry may well be virulently irate at his underachieving paycheck. Looking through the eyes of young boys growing up, one wonders at the incentives and disincentives they perceive in a future as a father. Depending on how these boys, growing to manhood, perform the social calculus, the African American model may be unique or may be a harbinger. The constant reference by the academics and the literati to a "new, improved father" may be a bull's-eye that is right on the target or such a reference may be more ironic than they suppose.

CHAPTER 11

Electra and Lady Macbeth

It is only rarely that one can see in a boy the promise of a man, but one can almost always see in a little girl the threat of a woman.

ALEXANDER DUMAS

To bear many children is considered not only a religious bless-ing but also an investment.

INDIRA GHANDI

The relationship between the two genders has generated an enormous amount of literature from, at least, the Greeks (*Lysistrata* [Aristophanes circa 400 B.C.]) through Shakespeare (*Romeo & Juliet; Macbeth* circa 1600) to U.S. popular culture (*Men Are from Mars, Women Are from Venus* (Gray, 1994), *You Just Don't Understand* (Tannen, 1990). This chapter attempts to analyze how one facet of the otherwise multi-dimensional, multifascinating, multifaceted relationship between men and women may impact on fatherhood.

Current models or paradigms of the gender interrelationships, also known as war between the sexes, vary from an inflexible tabula rasa (Skinner, 1953, 1971; Mead, 1935, 1949) to the phenomenologic (Bernard, 1982), to the sociobiological and biocultural (Symons, 1979; Buss, 1989, 1994; Cashdan, 1993; Fisher, 1992). This biocultural chapter's starting point is behavioral tendencies and biases that can be and are encoded in the human genetic material, and that anything as impor-tant as mating strategies can be, has been, and is affected, in a nontrivial way, by Darwinian selection of the motivational systems (endocrine system, neural system) that would support and direct and energize reproductive behavior.

In her book *The Sex Contract,* Fisher (1983) cleanly encapsulates the crux of the human mating system. In gist, as australopithecines evolved into early *Homo,* a behavioral *contract* emerged that proved to be inordinately successful for humans and has essentially vanquished competing or alternative forms of organizing a society. Fisher argues that, for their part of the contract, men had (and have) agreed to protect and provision a woman and his young children. The protection is not totally exclusive. Men will protect and defend their extended family or entire tribe in organized armies if called upon. Similarly, a systematic food sharing has been ritualized in many, if not all, societies. Rarely can a hunter claim a large kill for his own (Coon, 1971; Lee, 1982). But, within these contexts, a man provides singular attention to the woman he has been married and to the legitimate children that he had fathered in terms of protection and provisioning (see HRAF 1949, #22–26, Ridley, 1993).

For her part, the woman is expected to offer her sexual favors exclusively to the man (to whom she is married). Unofficially, of course, trysts, dalliances and affairs with nonhusbands do occur and, undoubtedly, had occurred in the distant past. Nonetheless, (1) female monogamy is a very strong consistency across cultures (Divale & Harris, 1976; Van den Berghe, 1979) and (2) the double standard, wherein wives' extramarital affairs are more proscribed than are husbands' extramarital affairs, is also predictable across cultures (Broude, 1980; Schlegel, 1972).

The timing of our ancestor's transition from precultural pair-bonding to the cultural marriage is and will remain unknown. Certainly this chapter cannot address the timing feature. However, whether the zoological term "pair-bonding" or the cultural term "marriage" is used, the end result is the same: within the behavioral domain, a man singularly protects and provisions his own wife and children, and a woman offers relative sexual exclusivity to that man, her husband. Said a little differently, one gender becomes inextricably intertwined with the other. One gender becomes an integral part of the other gender's environment—an environment to which the gender must adapt or both genders go extinct. See Dawkins (1976) *Selfish Gene* and *Extended Phenotype* (1982) for discussions, and see Barkow (1980, 1989), Durham (1979, 1990) and Boyd and Richerson (1985) for theoretical discussions on coevolution. In the next section, a dynamic to the contract is examined.

EMERGENCE OF THE SEX CONTRACT

With "Lucy" (*Australopithecus afarensis*) as a convenient benchmark, it seems reasonable to infer that emergent *Homo* was fully bipedal, that is, terrestrial, at least moderately sexually dimorphic, and, for a primate, fairly large (Hall, 1985; Johnson & White, 1980; Leakey & Lewin, 1992; Lovejoy, 1981). In the transition from *Australopithecus* to

Homo, a number of variables were probably operating simultaneously and in synchronous feedback loops: hidden ovulation, continuous receptivity, rudimentary language, continuing encephalization, a shift in the foreskin from an attachment to the base of the penis to an attachment to the distal end of the penis. Teasing out cause and effect from effect and cause from correlation is daunting at best. Nonetheless, it seems very reasonable to infer that paternal caregiving and provisioning was becoming aligned with pair-bonding (and perhaps early components of a cultural marriage ritual). That is, the "sex contract" was being forged. In addition, a general consensus is that early *Homo* was social and lived in bands with plural men and plural women.

If other nonhuman primates are reviewed to develop convergences or analogues or homologues to our human mating system, then it is contrast, more than comparison, which is the more salient. For example, after a bit of a shaky start (cf. Washburn & Devore, 1961), primatologists quickly noticed that it is adult females and their offspring that form a core to many of the social terrestrial primates. The adult females and their young remain together and give continuity to the troop across generations. Young males migrate to other troops to begin the tussle to integrate themselves into the new troop's hierarchy and then to compete with other males for the females (Hrdy, 1977, 1981; Jolly, 1972; Kawai, 1958; Packer, Collins, Sindimwo, & Goodall, 1995; inter alios; see Small, 1984 for a review; cf. De Waal, 1983, 1995; Goodall, 1986).

In contrast to the nonhuman primate affinity for matrilines, the majority (70.9%) of known human cultures are patrilocal in character wherein the bride moves into the domicile of the groom's kin. Matrilocality, an analogue to the terrestrial primate model, accounts for only 11.3% of known cultures. Alternate domicile forms (e.g., avunculocal, bilocal, neolocal) account for the remaining percentages: 17.8% (Divale & Harris, 1976).

A second contrast is that, by and large, adult male primates do not procure food and then return to the adult females and their young to give away that food. The adult males may allow a shared feeding from the same feeding source, or may relinquish food to a begging female, for example, the chimpanzee (Goodall, 1986; Teleki, 1973). However, adult males leaving the perimeter of the troop, then obtaining food, and then giving the food to adult females and thence to the young is not a primate trait.

As mentioned previously, such food provisioning is a cultural constant (HRAF 149; #22–26; Hewlett, 1992); and its potential is often a prerequisite for marriage, and its omission is often a cause for divorce, for example, the Yanomamo (Chagnon, 1977, China (Chance, 1984), Tibet (Ekvall, 1968), the Tiwi (Hart & Pilling, 1960), the Dani of New

Guinea (Heider, 1979), Japan (Norbeck, 1976), the Yuqui (Stearman, 1989). While not a primate characteristic, food sharing by adult men is, however, paralleled by canids: wolves (Mech, 1966; Mowat, 1963; Murie, 1944), coyotes (Dobie, 1949; McMahan, 1976; Ryden, 1974; Young & Jackson, 1951), jackals (Lawick & Lawick-Goodall, 1971; Moehlman, 1980), and hunting dogs (Kuhme, 1965). See King (1980), Mackey (1976), and Thompson (1978) for discussions. For example, the adult male wolf will catch prey, return to the den, and give the food to the mother wolf and her or his pups for their consumption (Mech, 1970).

As hunting and scavenging became a greater part of *Homo's* subsistence lifestyle, a canid characteristic (Bunn & Kroll, 1986; Mackey, 1987; Potts, 1988; cf Schaller & Lowther, 1969; Shipman, 1986), the pressures for division of labor intensified: men would hunt and women would not (Murdock, 1937; Murdock & Provost, 1973; Lee & Devore, 1967; Ingold, Riches, & Woodburn, 1988, cf Zihlman & Tanner, 1978). Simultaneously, additional pressures arose for the development of some sort of systematic accommodation or contract within each gender's mating strategy. Fisher's conceptualization of the *Sex Contract* seems elegant and parsimonious.

Nevertheless, as with any other social exchange, the dual problems of "how to successfully cheat" or "how to successfully renege" plus "how to counter the cheating and reneging" must necessarily arise. (see Dawkins, 1976, 1982; Hamilton, 1964; Waddington, 1975; Haldane, 1932, 1971; and Maynard Smith, 1964, 1975] for theoretical discussions on evolutionarily stable strategies and how some new genes can succeed in a gene pool whereas others cannot). The depiction of the male advantage of "love'em and leave'em (impregnated)" has a rich heritage in popular folklore (e.g., *Playboy* 1953–1995) and academic literature (Buss, 1987, 1994; Buss & Schmitt, 1993; Cashdan, 1993). The female strategy of cuckoldry or of having a nonhusband contributing his genes to the conceptus and having the husband rear that child has also enjoyed a long literary tradition (Chaucer's *Canterbury Tales;* Gangstad & Simpson, 1990). Counterstrategies to prevent or blunt or thwart cheating and reneging have received somewhat less interest but are no less interesting or complex.

To wit: If a wife reneges on her part of the bargain and has sexual intercourse with men not her husband, then the husband has two main, not mutually exclusive, remedial counters to her illicit behavior.

1. Because, over the millennia, women selected mates who were physically more powerful than themselves, the husband was capable of physically punishing, coercing, or cloistering the offending wife.

2. The man could simply abandon her and *her* children (due to her extramarital sexual activity, she had cast doubt on *his* paternity, i.e., he may not be abandoning his children, and his best strategy was to "cut bait" and begin anew with a more faithful mate). The fate of an isolated woman–child dyad, especially in a climate with a winter season, would tend to be dire, if not lethal. Ethnographic literature and folklore are replete with incidents and tales of the misfortunes wrought upon adulteresses.

What is less clear is the manner and means by which the construction of the contract would have made available to the woman any counters to the reneging by the husband on his terms to the union. That is, if a man was less than enthusiastic about generating and capturing resources or was less than enthusiastic about sharing his time or treasure or energy with the wife and her children, then what counter would emerge for the woman to emend the errant husband?

What were *not* available for sanctions against the offending man included the following:

1. *Physical coercion.* An attempt at physical coercion would be a poor strategy. Her upper body strength would be no match for his. Men, in general, have a clear and substantial advantage in upper body strength, and the woman's husband, in particular, was probably selected by her to be superior to her in size, weight, and muscularity. Because weapon making is a male-only event (Murdock, 1937; Murdock & Provost, 1973), his arsenal would be superior to hers.

2. *Female alliances.* An attempt to develop group pressure, that is, a female alliance would be unlikely to succeed. Unlike some primate groups wherein an alliance of adult females would successfully intimidate a wayward male (Hrdy, 1981), it would be the woman who would more likely be isolated within the kin group and alliances of the offending man. She would be outmanned in several senses.

3. *Abandon the husband.* Any abandonment of the husband would be equivalent to her being abandoned. His provisioning and protection could no longer be remedied. She had separated herself from him. By her leaving, those two items would be precluded from rectification by her own choice. Again, winter in a preagrarian era would magnify the dangers of her leaving (see Calvin, 1990 for a discussion on winter and human evolution).

4. *Threats to the child(ren).* Any threat to the health and well-being of the husband's children would be counter productive. They are her children also. Systematic filicide (killing one's own child) would efficiently remove descendants of the perpetrators, and thereby, eliminate the basal tendencies for filicide, in the form of genetic alleles, from

future generations (cf. Daly & Wilson, 1987). That is, women who kill their own children minimize their chances of becoming grandmothers.

5. *Conscious, official, as a matter of principle, withholding of sexual intimacy.* The willful, deliberate refusal of the woman to copulate with the errant husband does have the advantage of making a rational point in a rational way: quid pro quo, tit-for-tat, a symmetrical negation of the key clauses of the initial contract. Nonetheless, the risks are clear: physical coercion is still an option for the husband plus the husband's counter-counter of his abandonment is still viable: if no sex, then no children; hence the man loses nothing by jettisoning the woman. In other words, if the wife refuses to copulate at the present, then future children become impossible. His better strategy for additional copulations (and potential grandchildren) becomes to bid the functionally sterile current wife an adieu and to seek a more compliant woman.

While each of the above counters by the woman to the reneging husband is potential and surely must have occurred sporadically across the millennia, it seems unlikely that any of them would be effective over generations, and thus none of them would become systematic or normative across the species. The dynamics offered by this chapter as a candidate for a systematic reaction to a husband's failing to fulfill his terms of the sex contract is a psychoemotional shutdown.

PSYCHOEMOTIONAL SHUTDOWN AS A FEMALE COUNTER

In a world without governmental agencies to act as surrogate providers and protectors, and such is surely the world of early *Homo,* a threat to the food supply or to physical health or to the degrading of material well-being would generate stress and anxiety. The greater the ability to plan or to imagine what the future may resemble, the greater would be the potential for stress if that future presaged privation or danger. That is, the less someone can contemplate what the future might be, the less that someone would worry about the future. On the flip side, the better the sheer ability to anticipate coming events, the more that a threatening, ominous future would create anxiety in that someone.

Because (1) archaic *Homo's* forebrain grew rapidly (in a geological time frame) and (2) current *Homo's* quiver of abilities includes the capability to foresee future potentials, a woman of emerging *Homo* would be increasingly able to recognize a disadvantageous domestic situation and how that situation, if extrapolated into the future, would worsen her chances for longevity.

Accordingly, a classic approach-avoidance conflict would have occurred for her. The status quo was unacceptable for her. Plus, previous
attempts to modulate or upgrade her husband's behavior through conventional social interchanges had failed, and the future was portending
more of the disadvantaged condition.

What was she to do?

I argue in this chapter that the genetic material positively selected
over the millennia was the material that blueprinted a neurohormonal,
for example, motivational, system in females that was increasingly vulnerable (compared to the males) to respond to social stress with a
depressive reaction. That is, if the behavioral options for the wife were
systematically eliminated, then the most effective counterstrategy was
to have a psychoemotional shutdown: an involuntary attack of the
"blues" or an attack of "depression. The definition of depression by the
Diagnostic and Statistical Manual of Mental Disorders, Fourth Edition
(DSM-IV; American Psychiatric Press, 1994) is instructive:

> The essential feature of a Major Depressive episode is a period of at least 2
> weeks during which there is either depressed mood or the loss of interest or
> pleasure in nearly all activities. . . . The individual must also experience at
> least four additional symptoms drawn from a list that includes changes in
> appetite or weight, sleep, and psychomotor activity; decreased energy; feel-
> ings or worthlessness or guilt; difficulty thinking, concentrating or making
> decisions; or recurrent thoughts of death or suicidal ideation, plans or at-
> tempts. . . . The episode must be accompanied by clinically significant dis-
> tress or impairment in social, occupational, or other important areas of
> functioning. . .
>
> The mood in a Major Depressive episode is often described by the per-
> son as depressed, sad, hopeless, discouraged, or "down in the dumps". . . .
> In some individuals who complain of feeling "blah," having no feelings, or
> feeling anxious, the presence of a depressed mood can be inferred from the
> person's facial expression and demeanor" (pp. 320–321).

According to the DSM-IV, the essential feature of a chronically
depressed mood (dysthymic disorder) is that it occurs for

> most of the day more days than not for at least two years. Individuals with
> Dysthymic Disorder describe their mood as sad or "down in the dumps". . . .
> During periods of depressed mood, at least two of the following additional
> symptoms are present: poor appetite or overeating, insomnia or hypersom-
> nia, low energy or fatigue, low self-esteem, poor concentration or difficult
> making decisions and feelings of hopelessness. Individuals may note the
> prominent presence of low interest and self-criticism, often seeing them-
> selves as uninteresting or incapable" (pp. 345–346).

In other words, the affected individual is immobilized. Effective
social behavior is minimized. The individual shuts down.

The advantages of depression as a counter to a reneging man are
threefold:

1. The depression is not a willful, defiant, challenge to the husband. The condition is beyond the conscious control of the wife:
   it is not her fault. Thereby, the depression would be less prone
   to elicit retaliatory activities against the wife.
2. The sexual attractiveness quotient of a depressed woman is lowered. This loss of her sexual attraction is important to a husband, and it is to his advantage for the depression to be lifted.
3. Although his children, as well as hers, may not experience a
   life-threatening situation, their ability to flourish in the absence
   of a functional mother is suboptimal, if not sublethal. Enhanced
   parenting duties would then accrue ad hoc to other members of
   the group, including the father. The other members of the group,
   including the father, would not relish these added responsibilities, and this added ply of duty would spur them to have
   the wife resume her normal psychology and hence assume her
   normal responsibilities. The adjustments needed to return her
   to this normalcy would not go unheeded.

In essence, a psychoemotional shutdown changes the wife's behavior. It lowers her activity level. Her mood shift and depression is noted
by others in her immediate familial and social circles. Whether the
cultural traditions label or otherwise characterize the putative shutdown as a mental illness (Laing, 1967; cf. Szasz, 1961), or a super-
natural possession (Chagnon, 1977), or the result of a hex (Newman,
1982) is irrelevant. The wife is immobilized and the immobilization is
dysfunctional to those around her. During the depressive episode, both
the wife and the husband, plus any additional family members who are
proximate, have the opportunity to reassess, reprioritize, and reinte-
grate expectations of themselves and others. De facto, for as social a
being as *Homo sapiens,* there is little difficulty for humans to establish
linkages between one person's poor role performance and another person's adverse reaction to that poor performance. Both the personalized
pressures from the husband upon himself and the social pressures
upon the husband by others to shape-up would be forthcoming.

It would be immaterial whether it was a maternal aunt or a grizzled
uncle or a shaman, or a minister, or an existential-phenomenological
psychotherapist who would serve as the catalyst, the sequence would
be invariant:

1. The husband operates below the wife's expectations and is immune from her entreaties to improve.
2. The wife becomes heavily stressed because of his dereliction of
   his part of the sex contract.

3. The wife reacts with a variation on the theme of depression. She shuts down.
4. The wife's lowered activity level creates dysfunction within the family.
5. Pressure is then exerted on the husband to upgrade his performance.
6. The husband makes a readjustment (or at least says that he will. Given that males and females have two rather separate, if overlapping, reproductive strategies, it would be expected that, for any one stratagem, there would emerge a counterstratagem: in this instance "lying").
7. The stress is ameliorated.
8. The depression lifts.

It should be noted that, currently, most depression for most people will lift in a relatively short amount of time whether clinical treatment is provided or not. (APA, 1994; see Eysenck, 1952 for a discussion). This short-lived quality of depressive episodes would be expected to have a long history.

HYPOTHESIS

Even though the preceding argument is relatively easy to configure, its validity is quite another matter. The preceding argument might qualify for the Kiplingesque were it not for its testability. Once the argument becomes a hypothesis that can be falsified, then that which intimates the Kiplingesque is transduced to the Popperesque (Popper, 1959, 1962). Fortunately, the argument does lend itself to being testable. To wit: (1) if the woman's psychoemotional apparatus is prewired to react to stress more with a depressive reaction than alternatives such as aggression, and (2) if the woman's psychoemotional apparatus is constituted to be activated at a lower threshold than a man's, then it would be expected that the prevalence of women with a depressive episode would exceed that of men.

Hence the hypothesis is offered that "Women, compared to men, are overrepresented in indices of depression."

DATA

For the United States, records of individuals with reported bouts of depression do indicate that women, compared with men, are overrepresented in cases of reported depression. For the nine samples surveyed, all had females overrepresented with an average of a two to one ratio. Note the large gap between married men and married women, for example, the gap expands from a normative 2 to 1 ratio, to more than 4 to 1 if the marriage is more amicable, and 3 to 1 (at a much higher baseline) if the marriage is less amicable (Bromberger & Castello, 1992). Because this exercise is more concerned with the maintenance of the contract—marriage—than the recruitment into the contract—courting—then these ratios are especially illustrative (see Table 11.1). Accordingly, with the United States as the frame of reference, the hypothesis is supported.

Of additional interest is that the preponderance of the first episodes of depression occurs at adolescence or young adulthood. That is, the onset typically comes after puberty and before menopause. The onset is timed with prime mating and family formation intervals (Bromberger & Costello, 1992; Leon, Klerman, & Wickramaratne, 1993; Sorenson, Rutter, & Aneshensel, 1991). Additional conditions that would serve the same dynamics within the female counterstrategy include (i) seasonal affective disorder (SAD; DSM-IV, 1994; Rosenthal, 1993; Weissman & Klerman, 1995), (ii) histrionic personality disorder (DSM-IV, 1994) and (iii) attempted suicides (rather than completed suicides) (Rogers, 1990; see Bespali de Consens, 1995 and Le-Peng & Wing-Foo, 1995 for data from Uruguay and Singapore, respectively,

Table 11.1. Incidences of Depressive Reactions by Gender

	Gender		Ratio of Female/Male
Study	Male	Female	
Leon et al. (1993) : (relative risk)	1.00	1.82	1.82
Radloff (1975) Mean score on the Beck Depression Inventory			
Employed	7.05	9.01	1.28
Housewives	—	10.30	1.46
Bromberger & Costello (1992)			
Separated or divorced (%)	4.4	6.3	1.43
Single (%)	2.4	3.9	1.625
Married and gets along with spouse (%)	0.6	2.9	4.83
Married and does not get along with spouse (%)	14.9	45.5	3.05
Mean			2.73
DSM-IV (1994) (%)	5–12	10–25	2.0–2.08
Stein et al. (1988) (%)	1.6	2.5	1.56
Mean (unweighted)			2.12

which parallel the U.S. trends). For the United States, women are over represented in all three of these conditions. Placing these three conditions in the context of the Munchausen syndrome by proxy in which most known perpetrators are female (Kahn & Goldman, 1991) and "repressed memories" wherein 92% of the cases are adult females (False Memory Syndrome Foundation, 1994, cf *Frontline Divided Memories* 4/12/95) would seem like an interesting endeavor.

These data are from the United States. The United States may have a unique cultural matrix that eventuates in increased expectations of a gender (female) and an age bracket (postadolescence) that isolates young women as a type of individual most vulnerable to exhibit depression and to be officially recorded has having had a depressive episode. That is, the higher rates of recorded depression are an artefact of a society's particulate history and ecology interacting with a specific gender: the female (see Bromberger & Matthews, 1994 for just such an example that emphasizes this point) and these gender dimorphic rates have virtually nothing to do with inherent gender differences.

Accordingly, cross-cultural data were sought which, despite problems in definition and conceptualizations, offer comparability to the U.S. data (see Al-issa, 1995 and Murphy, 1976 for discussions on cross-cultural comparability.). The Cross-National Collaborative Group (1992) did conduct such a cross-cultural study.

Consonant with the cross-cultural method on fathering that was presented in Chapter 4, the fundamental precept utilized in evaluating the cross-cultural data on depression is that if cultures are *varied* and if the genotype is held *constant* (all subjects are *Homo sapiens*) and if a consistent/constant behavior is found in the otherwise disparate, distinct cultures, then the consistency or constant is better explained by a second consistent or constant than by a variable (see Buss, 1989, 1994; Eibl-Eibesfeldt, 1975; Ekman, 1973; Fisher, 1992; Mackey, 1985 for examples of this experimental design).

The Cross-National Collaborative Group surveyed ten nations— the United States, Canada, Puerto Rico, Germany, Italy, Lebanon, New Zealand, Taiwan, South Korea, and France. In all of the ten nations studied, women were overrepresented in illustrating depressive reactions ($p < .001$; 05^{10}) (Weissman et al., 1994, see Weissman & Klerman, 1995, for a discussion). Similar results of an overrepresentation of females afflicted with depression were found in India (Varma & Chakrabarti, 1995), Israel (Bilu, 1995), Turkey (Tuncer, 1995), Jamaica (Wedenoja, 1995), Iberia (Seva & Fernandez-Doctor, 1995), Native Americans (Somervell, Manson, & Shore, 1995), the Maori (Durie, 1995), and Great Britain (Cochrane, 1995). Furthermore, whereas gender was a clear marker for depression, so, was age. The 16 to 25 year bracket was overrepresented in the probands. (note that there were no interaction effects between age and gender). Again, the 16 to 25 year bracket is consistent with the age bracket wherein initial courting and family formation are most likely to occur for the female, and the suitor or husband can be tested for his level of susceptibility to her counter of depression in its many variations.

SUMMARY

It bears repeating that for any emotion to exist there must be a neurohormonal base that must also exist to create it. Similarly, no neural or hormonal system is going to exist unless genetic material acts as a blueprint or a recipe to direct their construction. Said differently, the basis for depression, an emotion, must be coded in the human genotype.

This chapter argues that, for incipient, of not inchoate *Homo,* the great benefit of having two parents (one mother, one father) who nurture their (his + her) offspring must offset two costs: (1) the man has to forego time, energy, and treasure in the nurturance of his children rather than concentrate on conceiving more of them, and (2) the woman is wedged into a dependency wherein her provisions and protection are at least partially dependent on a man who is not a consanguine kin. It should be emphasized that, during a long winter, any gathering skills of nonexistent vegetable matter would be of minimal importance.

The resultant sexual contract exchanged the man's provisioning and protecting of the woman and his or her children in exchange for her sexual exclusivity (i.e., enhanced paternal certainty). The man's options for countering the women's reneging on the contract are overt, clear, direct, and manifest. As proffered here, the woman's options—a psychoemotional shutdown—are less clear, more indirect, more covert, and more subtle, but not necessarily less effective.

A final note: irrational, that is emotional, responses that are used to correct felt inequities are not guaranteed to be effective. They are a strategic-tactical attempt to achieve a particular end. Sometimes they work; sometimes not. Sometimes they are applied adroitly with impeccable timing, sometimes clumsily and ill-timed. However, the bases for the emotions, just as with any other behavior, will exist because in the past the emotions and the emotional responses on balance created more descendants for their owners than would have been otherwise achieved. Within this context, Lady Macbeth, a woman who worked hard to garner resources through her husband, the Thane, would loom as an exemplar. Electra, a woman who nobly waited and waited and waited for the chance to avenge the death of her father becomes error variance.

Let's assume that the above dynamics have a grain of validity. The analysis is essentially of a husband and wife relationship. The excellent question here is: What does an analysis of a husband and wife relationship have to do with parenthood?

An answer: There are three perspectives involved in the family in question.

- The man's perspective: husband/father
- The woman's perspective: wife/mother
- The child's perspective

If a wife reneges on her part of the sex contract, then the man, as husband, will become agitated. The man, as father, has no quarrel with the woman, as a mother. Sexual exclusivity to a husband has nothing to do with the mother–child relationship. The sexual adventures of a woman has nothing to do with mothering. Sexual promiscuity between adult men and adult women has no direct contact with mothering. In addition, sexual activity between mothers and children is the null set. Incest taboos between mothers and children seem to be redundant. Such reported sexual activity hovers around the zero mark (see Weinberg, 1955; Seemanova, 1971; Willner, 1975; Justice & Justice, 1979, and DeYoung [1982] for prevalances).

If a man reneges on his part of the sex contact, the woman, as wife, feels threatened at the marginal loss of provisioning and resources. The woman, as mother, would see the same danger to her children. That is, a felt loss of resources for herself as wife is also a loss of resources for her children. Here the evaluations of the father role and the husband role are merged. This merging of spouse and parenting roles does not occur for the woman's two roles of wife and mother. In terms of the sex contract, wife and mother can be evaluated separately.

From the young child's perspective, the man has only one role: "father," and the affiliative: child-to-father bond is separate from the man's level of provisioning and securing resources.

There is no evidence that the young children's affection for their father is directly proportional to the fathers' access to resources. The wife or mother may be irritated or frustrated at the man for his, either apparent or real, violation of the sex contract, but the children would not be.

In other societies, there are social and economic pressures in abundance that can be brought to bear to resolve such dissension informally.

Again, if the family is an economic unit, then divorce rates are very low.

However, in the contemporary United States, where most families are not an economic unit of production (e.g., a small farm) and divorce rates are comparatively very high, the institution of no-fault divorce changes the familial calculus.

If the woman feels the man has reneged on his half of the sex contract and has cheated her (and, by extension, from *her* perspective, has cheated her children), then she can jettison the man (husband and, by extension, the father). Government (local, state, or federal) is in the position to take up the economic and provisioning slack, if needed.

Other societies with high divorce rates tend to be matrilineal (goods and services are passed down the female line) and matrilocal (married couples reside with the bride's kin). When divorces occur, the man leaves with virtually nothing. The children and the property belong to the woman and her kin. In these societies, the mother's brother (the *avunculus*) has a structurally important relationship to the mother's children. A constancy of an adult male figure is embedded in the society's framework. Mother's husbands may come and go, but her brother, the child's uncle, is constant.

United States society is not so structured. We are neolocal (couples live separate from either the wife's or the husband's kin), and we are bilineal (inheritance is passed to both genders). Once the father is jettisoned, there is no structured replacement. In terms of a father figure, each mother-child dyad operates on an ad hoc basis. In the United States, the children of divorce who were not feeling betrayed have lost a father because the wife found fault, real or apparent, in the husband.

Thus this chapter argues that the very basis of the husband and wife relationship, the sex contract, systematically places children at risk of losing their father when women follow their *natural tendencies* in the context of a government that becomes a competitor to the father's traditional role of provider: breadwinner. The less the women's need to depend on the man for resources, and the less the man's ability to compete with government, the greater number of children will be at risk of losing their fathers.

CHAPTER 12

The U.S. Father

A Tragedy of the Commons?

He that hath wife and children hath given hostages to fortune;
for they are impediments to great enterprises, either of virtue
or mischief.

FRANCIS BACON

There are times when parenthood seems nothing but feeding
the mouth that bites you.

PETER DE VRIES

Garrett Hardin (1968), a man who is the epitome of a curmudgeon, wrote an essay entitled "The Tragedy of the Commons" in *Science.* In gist, the essay, almost in allegory form, is thus:

A commons or meadow belongs to the group. It is a commons for any and all who would want to use it. One person, Citizen Smith, decides to raise cattle on the commons. He can do this because the commons belongs to him as much as to anyone else. The cattle grow fat and sassy and then are marketed. The proceeds of their sale goes for profit and more cattle for Citizen Smith. A neighbor notices the process and decides to participate. More cattle are brought to the commons to eat the grass, to fatten, and to be sold for profit and more cows. A second neighbor, then a third, and a fourth, and so on all begin to use the commons for cattle and profit.

With so many cattle and a finite amount of grass on the commons, it becomes clear to Citizen Smith that unless cattle are withheld from the commons, the grass will be gone, and the commons will be useless for grazing. The commons will be destroyed.

However, Citizen Smith realizes that if he withheld his cattle from the commons, he would lose his investment and the commons will be destroyed regardless of whether he withholds his cattle. Therefore, his best strategy is put into the commons as many cattle as he can before the commons is totally gone, as assuredly it will be. All of Citizen Smith's fellow citizens, equally astute, come to the same conclusion. More cattle are inserted and the commons is destroyed. The destruction will come to pass even though all who were concerned with it had conceptualized exactly how the process worked and all of its consequences.

Hardin explains that there are occasions wherein individual freedom or liberty is maximized, and the group or society as a whole is threatened with destruction. If everyone, from Citizen Smith on down, exercised to the hilt his or her individual liberty to heap cows on the commons, then the grass is gone and replaced by a quagmire of mud and "cowpies." The commons cannot support any cows for anyone. To prevent a quagmire, an enforceable rule or tradition must be imposed that theoretically applies to everyone. Individual freedom and liberty are reduced for the good of the group. Maximal gain per individual is prevented for the benefit of the commonweal.

Examples abound in our megatribe: Federal laws, state laws, local laws and ordinances all include examples of "don't" and "can'ts": homicide, driving speeds and directions and parking. If there is a rampant disregard for the laws, then anarchy will occur. The laws apply to everyone equally, even though some individuals tend to be more equal than others. Religions operate similarly as their individual members forego personal license for the greater glory of the flock. The local United Way makes the same appeal. The mandate for taxes to support the public school system has the same rationale. With Hardin's offering as a background, let's look at fathering.

INDIVIDUAL LIBERTY AND
SOCIETAL VIABILITY

For personal liberty to be maximized, two necessary, but not sufficient, preconditions that must be met include (1) a maximum amount of unclaimed, discretionary time available per citizen and (2) a maximum amount of resources per citizen for use with his or her discretionary time doing discretionary behaviors. The closer to 24 hours per day that a person is free to choose how, where, and with whom his or her 24-hour day is spent and his or her resources are utilized, the more freedom that person has. At the 24-hour per day mark with infinite resources, absolute freedom is reached.

On the one hand, while these two conditions seem faultless goals for which to strive, and with the individual as the focus, over the short term, there is little to dispel the aura. On the other hand, at the societal level, over the long term, a complex problem arises. Society is an abstraction referring to an aggregation of individuals who live out each life one at a time and who are anything but abstract. Each individual is a flesh-and-blood mortal. For a society to survive as an intact, cohesive entity, there must be a continuous supply of these flesh-and-blood mortals who will replace those individuals, their ancestors, who have followed the "dust to dust" axiom. Currently and in the foreseeable future, the only means of replenishing a society's population is by women having babies. There is, without qualification, no substitute mechanism. Perhaps because the statement is so over-the-head-with-a-2-$\times$-4 obvious and without any analogues, the causal nature of such a phenomenon is prone to be overlooked. Just as the Chinese aphorism tells that the fish would be the last to discover the ocean, the pervasive presence of motherhood—everyone has a mother—may help to mask its influence on sequelae of perceptions, attitudes, and behaviors. Nonetheless, despite its usually low analytical profile, the consequence in any qualitative or quantitative variation on the theme of women having children will affect quickly and deeply the rest of the entire social structure.

If a society is to survive intact at even a steady population level, the women of that society must average two and a fraction births. The two babies replace one mother and one father. The fraction replaces those children who die before reaching reproductive age and because there is an excess of births to sons (about 52%) rather than to daughters (about 48%; that is, the number of females is the determining factor in population growth or stasis; see Wattenberg, 1987 for a discussion). If more than two and a fraction births per woman occur, then the population grows. If two or less children per woman are born, then the population will decline and over time can reach oblivion. For example, a one child per family average is socially maladaptive. While the familial trio may bring joy, satisfaction and contentment to each individual of the family, a society based on one child per woman cannot survive intact. In only ten generations, a society averaging one child per family would only be one-tenth of one percent of its original size ($100 \times (.5)^{10} = .00098 = .098\%$). From the societal perspective, at least two children per female (per family if monogamy predominates) is the minimum requirement.

It should be remembered that there are no guarantees, nor have there ever been guarantees, of the longevity of any society. From Sodom to Carthage to Rome to Tasmania, societies can easily come and can just as easily go. Ozymandias may have made his enemies despair, but not in perpetuity. There is no evidence of a demographic "thermostat" which will automatically respond to dysfunctional population levels.

At this juncture, the always legitimate question may be asked: So

What? If we can assume that all of the above is true, then where is the problem of men having their freedom curtailed (the same argument also applies to women, but the focus here is on men).

If a man in the United States were to follow an economic, highly rational strategy and demonstrate economic wisdom, then this rational man should follow the scenario described below:

1. I wish to maximize my discretionary time and money.
2. I also wish to retire and to receive Social Security support and any governmental assistance that might be available to me. In my retirement I want an efficient, well-run society within which I am safe and secure and can shop and live leisurely in comfort, enjoy recreational facilities, and be confident that effective medical treatment is available.
3. If I eschew raising any children of my own, then I need not expend time and money rearing them; yet I can be supported by the children (grown to adulthood) of other individuals. Those soon-to-be adults can be guarantees of social security pension payments plus will operate the institutions of the society that I have every intention of enjoying. My retirement IRA and social security receipts are not based on the number of children that I raised and funded. If I did have children, the quality of my children, grown to maturity, is also irrelevant to how the overall society performs and what services would be available to me.

Clearly, if there are a number of such rational individuals who pursue such a strategy, then the continuity of such groups would have a very finite longevity: the more the number of such people, the greater the vulnerability of the group, and the quicker that group is absorbed or displaced by competing groups.

In what can be loosely labeled "traditional" American society, men, as a class, have been socialized in preparation for the traditional roles of breadwinner and provider and protector of hearth and home. Over the eons, men have voluntarily, with various levels of enthusiasm, allocated the necessary time and resources required in providing for the needs of their children. That they were at least minimally successful is attested to by the current population level of 260 million plus citizens. One advantage to this option of having men voluntarily provide for their children is the increased probability of the continuation of a stable, effective society. Other advantages would be in the proportion to (i) the number of men (and women) who were competent and satisfied in their parenting roles and (ii) the number of children with a satisfactory childhood. However, the point of interest here is that the assumption of the parental role has always been voluntary with no formal, legal, or official rewards or incentives. Any benefits derived from the parental roles were informal, emotional, and personal.

The United States, like other cultures, has continued to rely on what amounts to the goodwill and altruism of individuals both to procreate and rear children with very little or no reciprocity from society. that is, the commons. Such have been the dynamics for the millennia and theoretically they can extend into the future indefinitely. Nevertheless, relatively recent social developments (the 1960s is always a convenient benchmark) make such extrapolations tenuous.

With the increase in the proportion of out-of-wedlock births and with the high rate of no-fault divorce, the percentage of children being denied and deprived of an ongoing social father is high and appears to be going higher. For there to be a reversal of these trends, there will have to be some shifting of priorities. Incentives will have to be increased and disincentives decreased.

INCENTIVES

If a family or clan or dynasty, or an isolated rustic, picturesque village wishes for longevity over the centuries, then that social group is simply going to have to average plural children per female. If the mavens of psycho-social-emotional cognitive development of children are more right than wrong, then any enhancement of the quality of U.S. childhood will requires an ongoing social father.

The question asked earlier in this book is still with us: What is in it for the man? What fathering incentives does our U.S. megatribe offer to men so that they want to enter into and remain in the fathering role? Children are very expensive to nurture. Children are an economic vacuum cleaner. They are a severe wear and tear on the nerves. They are emotionally draining. In exchange for a man's time, energy, and treasure spent to rear the sine qua non of any country—a citizenry—the men are offered _____ (try to imagine how the blank could be filled).

The idea of "Well, virtue is its own reward" is appealing, but not particularly analytical. Let's go through the drill:

1. The man has zero legal standing on whether a conception of his will be brought to term. He is about as legally relevant as the potted plant found in any shopping mall.
2. No-fault divorce can systematically deprive him of his children, totally independent of whatever he may be or may have been or have done or have aspired.

3. If he achieves a marriage and avoids divorce, then the ratchet is
    further tightened. He will view himself as a breadwinner, a pro-
    vider. Were he to excel at this, he is vulnerable to the charge of
    exploiting his wife. He has abandoned his fair share of domes-
    tic chores to devote himself to a mere career to generate income
    for his children: prima facie evidence of a cold, distant patri-
    archical male chauvinist you-know-what. Were he to sacrifice
    career for family, he will be surpassed economically by child-
    less men, childless women, and fathers who adopt a traditional
    breadwinner role. Now, he finds two strains of stress (i) the
    wife complains of a comparative lack of resources and (ii) the
    breadwinner role that buttresses his image of himself is sacri-
    ficed (Again, nontraditional marriages seem to be extremely
    fragile in structure and difficult to maintain; Williams & Radin,
    1993; MacDermid, Huston, & McHale, 1990; Russell, 1983.). The
    phrase "damned if he does and damned if he doesn't" seems
    apropos.

The heretofore linkage between men and access to women in
an ongoing relationship was marriage. Women no longer require the
link.

So, why should the man bother? There are no economic incentives
to fatherhood. There are no social incentives. Children are a major
impediment to unfettered social activity.

The remaining domain is the psychological. Yet his main emotional pillar of being a breadwinner has been discarded by the literati and
academics as a part of fathering. He is asked to be a second mother. Men
are simply not very good as mothers. They are an inept, poor substitute.
Men, however, are rather competent fathers. But the reasons for them to
continue being so have been consistently eroded.

The collision between the two polar fathering types seems inevitable. The traditional father versus no father at all, that is, the state: a state
that is a more reliable provider and requires far less debate and negotia-
tion to develop priorities.

The men who tenaciously hold onto the traditional father role are
outmatched. The state collects *their* taxes to fund and to maintain fatherless children. The state is a much easier partner with whom the
woman can negotiate. The state requires no negotiations, no reciprocity, no demands, and no expectations.

The higher the proportion of fatherless children, the lower the
proportion of fathered children, and the more taxes fathers pay with
less money for their own children. The luxury of fatherhood may end
up being a hobby for the wealthy. Well, what to do?

A MODEST PROPOSAL

It is not unreasonable to assume that current U.S. men would enter in and remain in the father role primarily for psychological rather than for social or economic reasons. I argued at the beginning of the book for an independent man-to-child affiliative bond that is partially dependent upon the genetic material common to *Homo sapiens*. That is, men are envisioned to be "built" to be fond of their children. This putative bond, at whatever level of penetrance, would certainly be enhanced by a universal trait in that men enjoy and take pride in the accomplishments of their growing children. That his efforts are partially responsible for his children's flourishing would increase his joy and the pride. The notion that he makes a difference in the success of his children is an important glue to adhere him to his children. It also seems reasonable that this glue is the more likely candidate considered in any attempt to maximize the ongoing presence of men with their children.

Thus, it is modestly proposed here that governmental agencies decide with some specificity what all children need to succeed in the United States circa 1995. The governmental agencies can then make available to all children those resources that they will need to succeed. The public school analogue is very appropriate here. All children are afforded access to the public school system. If parents choose not to avail their children of the public school system but send them to a private school, then they are allowed to do so. Parents could utilize the resources from the governmental agencies or not: their choice. However, if a father can add to or supplement the opportunities and goods and services available to his children from the government, then that supplement should be allowed to occur without penalty. The idea that the government should be a systematic competitor with the father as a provider to his children is an idea that has created a good deal of mischief. It may be time to put away the mischief. With the competition between the father and the government dissolved, then no sliding scales need be brought to bear. Fathers can be allowed to make a difference in the life chances of their children with no penalty. The thought is that fathers can and do take pride and joy in provisioning of their children, and, with that added ply of satisfaction, more of them may decide to stick around.

TRAGEDY OF THE COMMONS: ANOTHER UNEXPECTED CONSEQUENCE

In the man's calculus of how he will spend his life—his time and resources—he may opt to forego fatherhood for less demanding, less costly, alternatives. His enhanced freedom, great for an individual, may prove deleterious to the social group in the form of fewer children being born: too few to provide continuity of his tribe. Such is one variation upon the theme of "The Tragedy of the Commons". There is another example: fatherlessness and violent crime.

Young Males and Violent Crime

Recently, violent crime in the United States has received increased exposure in the popular media: news magazines, television specials, and radio talk shows. The exposure has taken two forms: (1) the depiction of high rates of violent, sometimes very violent, crime, especially those perpetrated by young males, and (2) the response by the media and politicians to the violent crime.

Rates of Violent Crime

The difficulties in assembling national data on violent crime are formidable and interpretations are normally strewn with qualifications. Nevertheless, there is a general agreement that violent crime has escalated substantially within the last few years. For example, from 1987 to 1990, murder was up 13.2%, aggravated assault 21%, and the total violent crime rate 21% (U.S. Bureau of the Census, 1992). For the same time periods, arrests of minors for aggravated assault was 6% higher and arrests of minors for murder and non-negligent manslaughter was 46% higher.

Media Responses

Such escalation might generate public reaction, and indeed, it did. A major theme interlaced in the various responses was the assumed relationship between unemployment, a lack of jobs for men, and the genesis of violent crime. Commentators in the various media have sided themselves with the angels and have denounced violent crime. Many of them have aligned the recent outbreak of violent crime with the lack of jobs for men. Both national and local outlets have addressed the topic. For example, on *This Week with David Brinkley* (1994), the then-governor, Mario Cuomo, spoke on the causal nature of unemployment on violent crime. Clarence Page from *The McLaughlin Group* (1994) and Jesse Jackson (quoted in the *Chicago Tribune* (1994) expounded upon the notion that, if violent crime is to be reduced, a

necessary, if not sufficient precondition for its reduction is the development of jobs for young men. News magazines, for example, *U.S. News &
World Report* (Minorbrook 1994) and editorial comments both in national newspapers, for example, the *Washington Post* (Pearson-West
1994), as well as in local newspapers, for example, the *Waco Tribune*
(1994), all voiced the assumption that a lack of employment is causally
linked to violent crimes: more men unemployed, more violent crime.
The nature of the putative linkage was rarely specified, just assumed. For example, a story from the Los Angeles Time Service (Stolberg, 1994) which was discussing a theory on the potential biological
underpinning to different levels of aggression noted in passing that the
". . . work challenges long held assumptions that social and environmental factors—poverty, *joblessness,* discrimination, lack of education—are the sole causes of crime and violence" (italics added).

In sum, the argument is made, in many forms, that if more jobs
were available, then the rates of violent crime would be attenuated.
Usually no evidence is presented to substantiate the argument. The
assertion is simply made.

It may be noted that scholarly work does not, in the main, sustain
such a linkage (Bacon, Child, & Barry, 1963; Freeman, 1975; Gillespie,
1975; see Wilson & Herrnstein, 1985 for a review, cf. Blau & Blau 1982).

Fatherlessness and Violent Crime

Another facet of America circa 1995 that has been aligned with
violent crime is that of the disruption of the U.S. family unit: men have
been systematically peeled away from the mother–child dyad. In other
words, if a responsible adult male role model is unavailable to young
boys, those boys become more prone to engage in violent behavior. That
is, there is a tendency for delinquents to come from fatherless homes
(Adams, Milner, & Schrepf, 1984; Anderson, 1968; Chilton & Markle,
1972; Monahan, 1972; Mosher, 1969; Robins & Hill, 1966; Stevenson &
Black, 1988). See Mischel (1961a) and (1961b) for a theoretical orientation on the putative linkage. See Wilson & Herrnstein (1985) and Draper and Harpending (1982) for reviews of the literature.

Not unlike the case with the unemployment-causes-violent-crime
argument or model, the lack-of-appropriate-role-model argument, can
be made in an anecdotal or idiographic mode. It can also be subject to
empirical or normative corroboration.

The empirical route seems like an interesting path to follow. The
relative accuracy of these two sentiments in the current United States is
testable. This section of the chapter will analyze the relationships

among the three indices—violent crime, unemployment rates for men, and fatherlessness—across the 50 states, hence a normative model, and then examine the U.S. data within a cross-cultural context.

Method

Out-of-wedlock births, by state, were obtained from the *Vital Statistics of the U.S.* (U.S. Bureau of the Census, 1992 p. 62). Unemployment rates for men, by states, were obtained from the Dept. of Labor (U.S. Bureau of the Census, 1992 p. 384). Rates of violent crime, by states, were obtained from the FBI (U.S. Bureau of the Census, 1992 p. 181).

Results

The rates of unemployment for men, by state, were not significantly related to violent rates, by state (r_p = .187, n.s.). Consequently, at this level of analysis, changes in the rates of violent crime were independent of variations in unemployment rates in men. See Table 12.1.

Across the 50 states, violent crime rates were significantly related to the percent of all births born to unwed mothers (r_p = .655; p < .001; 2-tailed). As the percentage of out-of-wedlock births increased so did rates of violent crime. Over 40% (r_p^2 = (.655)^2 = .429) of the differences in violent crime rates can be attributed to differences in the levels of out-of-wedlock births. See Table 12.1. (Note that if the District of Columbia is added to the sample, the correlation increases to .825, p < .001; 2-tailed).

Table 12.1. Rates of Illegitimacy, Violent Crime, and Male Unemployment across States

State	Rates of illegitimacy[a]	Rates of violent crime[b]	Rates of male unemployment[c]
Maine	21.8	143	8.6
New Hampshire	15.7	132	7.8
Vermont	19.8	127	7.7
Massachusetts	23.8	736	10.1
Rhode Island	24.9	432	9.3
Connecticut	26.3	554	7.2
New York	31.9	1,181	7.8
New Jersey	24.1	648	7.3

(continued)

Table 12.1. (*Continued*)

State	Rates of illegitimacy[a]	Rates of violent crime[b]	Rates of male unemployment[c]
Pennsylvania	27.9	431	7.5
Ohio	28.0	506	6.8
Indiana	23.8	474	6.3
Illinois	30.9	967	7.7
Michigan	24.5	790	9.7
Wisconsin	23.4	265	5.9
Minnesota	19.5	306	6.1
Iowa	19.4	300	5.0
Missouri	27.1	715	6.9
North Dakota	16.9	74	4.3
South Dakota	21.8	163	3.3
Nebraska	19.3	330	2.9
Kansas	19.6	448	4.4
Delaware	29.1	655	7.2
Maryland	28.9	919	5.9
Virginia	25.2	351	5.7
West Virginia	23.5	169	11.5
North Carolina	27.7	624	5.8
South Carolina	31.6	977	6.4
Georgia	31.7	756	4.8
Florida	30.2	1,244	7.1
Kentucky	22.6	390	7.4
Tennessee	29.1	670	6.7
Alabama	29.8	709	6.8
Mississippi	39.4	340	8.3
Arkansas	27.7	532	7.2
Louisiana	35.3	898	6.6
Oklahoma	23.8	547	7.1
Texas	19.6	761	6.5
Montana	21.7	159	7.4
Idaho	16.1	276	6.3
Wyoming	18.5	301	5.2
Colorado	20.5	526	5.1
New Mexico	34.5	780	7.2
Arizona	30.8	652	6.2
Utah	12.7	284	4.8
Nevada	23.5	601	6.1
Washington	23.4	502	7.1
California	30.0	1,045	7.9
Alaska	24.6	525	9.9
Hawaii	23.8	281	2.7
District of Columbia	64.3	2,458	7.8

[a]Births to unmarried women, percentage of total births (1989).
[b]Offenses known to the police per 100,000 population (1990).
[c]Percentage of male civilian labor force (1991).
Source: U.S. Bureau of the Census (1992).

To check for the extent if any overlap in the three social indixes, the percentage of unemployment for men was partialled from the correlation coefficient between violent crime rates and percent of all births to unwed mothers. The correlation between violent crime rates and out-of-wedlock rates was still significant (r_p = .640; p < .001; 2-tailed). That is, violent crime rates were strongly associated with percent of births to unwed mothers independent of unemployment rates for men.

Arguably, this connection between unwed mothers and violent crime may be a phenomenon highly specific to the U.S. megatribe, that is, a quirk. To see if the linkage between violent crime and births to unwed mothers was unique to the cultural matrix of the United States a similar analysis was conducted across cultures.

A CROSS-CULTURAL PERSPECTIVE

Method

As was mentioned in Chapter 3, any cross-cultural analysis is hampered by the problems of meaningful units of analysis. Analysis on rates of crime is often problematic because of the lack of consonance among countries in the definitions and reporting of various crime. However, one crime, murder, is universally accepted as a crime with reasonably concordant definitions (Archer & Garnter, 1984; Daly & Wilson, 1988). Accordingly, rates of murder in the United States (U.S. Bureau of the Census, 1992 p. 181) were correlated with illegitimacy rates in the United States and compared to similar figures generated by cross-cultural data (Smith-Morris 1991; United Nations, 1992). Note that the United Nations defines "illegitimacy" in the following manner.

> Legitimate refers to persons born of parents who were married at the time of birth in accordance with the laws of the country or areas. Illegitimate refers to children of parents who, according to national law, were not married at the time of birth, regardless of whether these children have been recognized or legitimized after birth (United Nations, 1992, p. 104).

Results

The United States. The relationship, across the 50 states, between murder rates and illegitimacy rates was significant (r_p = .749; p < .001; 2-tailed). As illegitimacy rates increased, so did murder rates. Over half ($[r_p]^2$ = $(.749)^2$ = .561 = 56.1%) of the variance in murder rates can be attributed to differences in illegitimacy rates. See Table

12-2. If the District of Columbia is included, the correlation coefficient increases to .8565; p < .001; 2-tailed).

Cross-cultural data. There were usable data from the U.N. source for 45 countries in which both murder and illegitimacy rates were reported to the satisfaction of the United Nations. See Table 12.2. The relationship was significant (r_p = .429, p < .01; 2-tailed).[1]

SUMMARY

At the level of the state, no evidence was found to substantiate the assertion that an increase of employment for men would impact upon violent crime rates in the United States. A more finely grained analysis may pick up a significant relation, but at the state level, folklore was not sustained.

Before the results of the relationship between violent crime and illegitimacy are discussed, several caveats and qualifications need to be presented.

1. Problems in the reporting of (violent) crime are legion.
2. If the focus is cross-cultural, the legionary problems are intensified.
3. Rates of unemployment are always predicated upon people who are seriously looking for employment. Those individuals who are able to work, but not actually seeing active employment, are not counted as unemployed. Thus, to the extent that the levels of labor force dropouts vary across states, the unemployment rates would be similarly distorted.

On the other hand, each of the above sources of error variance would tend to lessen or lower any index of association that was being computed. In spite of large amounts of noise in the system significance was still reached, suggesting that the relationship between violent crime and rates of illegitimacy is more real than apparent. With the

---

[1]The two rates, for illegitimacy (6.7) and for murder (38.7), were also available for the Philippines. However, the Philippines' murder rate of 38.7 was over 8.5 standard deviations (sd = 4.09) over the sample mean of 3.62. Accordingly, the Philippines was enough of an outlier to be excluded from the sample. If rankings were used to generate the correlation coefficient (r_s) and if the Philippines are included in the sample, then the relationship between illegitimacy and murder rates is significant (r_s = .889, p < .01, two-tailed, n = 45). If the Philippines are not included in the sample, the correlation, based on ranks, is still significant (r_s = .896, p < .01; two-tailed, n = 44).

Table 12.2. Rates of Illegitimacy and Murder across the United States ($n = 50$); and across Nations ($n = 44$)

State	Rates of illegitimacy[a]	Murder rates[b]	State	Rates of illegitimacy[a]	Murder rates[b]	State	Rates of illegitimacy[a]	Murder rates[b]
Maine	21.8	2.4	New Hampshire	15.7	1.9	Vermont	19.8	2.3
Massachusetts	23.8	4.0	Rhode Island	24.9	4.8	Connecticut	26.3	5.1
New York	31.9	14.5	New Jersey	24.1	5.6	Pennsylvania	27.9	6.7
Ohio	28.0	6.1	Indiana	23.8	6.2	Illinois	30.9	10.3
Michigan	24.5	10.4	Wisconsin	23.4	4.6	Minnesota	19.5	2.7
Iowa	19.4	1.9	Missouri	27.1	8.8	North Dakota	16.9	0.8
South Dakota	21.8	2.0	Nebraska	19.3	2.7	Kansas	19.6	4.0
Delaware	29.1	5.0	Maryland	28.9	11.5	Virginia	25.2	8.8
West Virginia	23.5	5.7	North Carolina	27.7	10.7	South Carolina	31.6	11.2
Georgia	31.7	11.2	Florida	30.2	10.7	Kentucky	22.6	7.2
Tennessee	29.1	10.5	Alabama	29.8	11.6	Mississippi	39.4	12.2
Arkansas	27.7	10.3	Louisiana	35.3	17.2	Oklahoma	23.8	8.0
Texas	19.6	14.1	Montana	21.7	4.9	Idaho	16.1	2.7
Wyoming	18.5	4.9	Colorado	20.5	4.2	New Mexico	34.5	9.2
Arizona	30.8	7.7	Utah	12.7	3.0	Nevada	23.5	9.7
Washington	23.4	4.9	Oregon	25.3	3.8	California	30.0	11.9
Alaska	24.6	7.5	Hawaii	23.8	4.0	District of Columbia	(64.3)	(77.8)

Country	Rates of illegitimacy[a]	Murder rates[b]	Country	Rates of illegitimacy[a]	Murder rates[b]	Country	Rates of illegitimacy[a]	Murder rates[b]
Australia	15.5	4.2	Austria	22.4	1.3	Belgium	5.7	3.1
Canada	16.9	2.2	Denmark	43.0	1.25	Finland	16.4	1.1
France	19.6	4.05	West Germany	9.4	1.5	Greece	1.8	0.85
Ireland	7.8	0.5	Italy	4.4	1.5	Japan	1.0	1.2
Luxembourg	8.7	7.0	Netherlands	8.3	1.2	New Zealand	24.9	2.9
Norway	25.8	0.9	Portugal	12.4	3.0	Spain	3.9	2.3
Sweden	46.4	1.7	Switzerland	5.6	0.9	United Kingdom	19.2	1.3
United States	21.0	8.6	Hungary	9.2	2.3	Yugoslavia	8.4	5.4
Brunei	0.4	1.9	Fiji	17.3	2.0	Hong Kong	5.5	1.2
South Korea	0.5	1.3	Sri Lanka	5.4	18.9	Mauritius	26.0	2.4
Cyprus	0.4	1.7	Israel	1.0	1.7	Malta	1.2	1.8
Tunisia	0.3	0.7	Argentina	32.5	0.2	Bahamas	62.1	12.2
Barbados	73.1	4.0	Chile	31.8	5.6	Costa Rica	37.2	4.0
Jamaica	84.3	18.0	Mexico	27.5	7.4	Panama	71.9	4.6
Peru	42.6	1.2	Venezuela	53.9	8.4			

[a]Births to unmarried women, percentage of total births.
[b]Offenses known to authorities per 10,000 population.
Sources: Smith-Morris, 1990; United Nations, 1992; U.S. Bureau of the Census.

above qualifications squarely ensconced in the background, some interesting patterns emerged in the foreground.

Violent crime (including murder) is associated with single-parent births: that parent is the mother, not the father. The association is fairly robust. With murder rates as a vehicle, the United States exemplified a cross-cultural phenomenon. If the father is systematically abraded from the mother-child dyad, then violent crime is expected to be under pressure to increase.

Several points are germane here.

1. Neither the single mothers nor the babies are committing the crimes. Violent crime is predominantly committed by men, especially young men (U.S. Bureau of the Census, 1992 p. 173).
2. Family structure is almost totally immune from penal codes, law enforcement, and the legal institution. Marriages cannot be coerced. Abortions cannot be coerced. Abstinence cannot be coerced. Use of contraceptives cannot be coerced. Men cannot be coerced into the role of social father. All of these items are, to one degree or another, related to illegitimacy, and none can be modified by acts of governance. The long arm of the law does not reach so far. Illegitimacy is quite beyond the long arm of the law.
3. The United States does not appear to be reflecting an idiosyncratic or deviant relationship. The patterns appears across cultural boundaries: an increase in unmarried mothers is aligned with an increase in violent crime.
4. The hoary chestnut, "correlation does not demonstrate causality" is, as always, in force (of course, its lesser known parallel cousin—perhaps a filbert—is also available, "correlation does not preclude causation"). In this instance, it seems clear that illegitimacy is not causing violent crime. Nor is violent crime, by men, causing out-of-wedlock births. The divining of the causal links which *do* serve to mesh single parenthood with violent crime is well beyond the scope of this chapter, book, and author. There is this nagging feeling that perhaps Freud (1987; see Fox, 1987, for a complementary conjecture) was on to something when he constructed the Oedipus Complex. What that *something* may be will probably remain a nag.
5. Lastly, the relationship between biological, but not social, fathers and those who commit crimes appears to be unknown and only barely knowable. Hence the concatenation between elevated rates of illegitimacy and violent crimes is similarly unknown, but probably more knowable. The specialists interested

in child development and those sociologists interested in marriage and the family and those criminologists interested in crime and criminals seem to have a splendid knot to untangle.

SYNOPSIS

A series of choice points have made themselves available to the United States as the 21st century looms on the ever-approaching horizon. Will the United States make an attempt to maximize incentives and minimize disincentives (rather than the reverse) for growing boys to enter into the role of social father and for already grown men to stay in that role? Raising an incompetent and dependent child to a competent, independent adult is not easy. Costs abound for the caretaker. Moral indignation that intones the mantra of *be more responsible* is not convincing to the target. Whereas the deletion of social father from one's *resume* may potentially be great for any given individual, such deletions, if done en masse, might well be lethal for the commonweal.

Violent men are one of the problems with which any organized society must deal. The addition of a father seems to tamp down violence within any given society. The erasing of fathers is associated with increased rates of violent crime. To the extent U.S. fathers are systematically removed from the fathering role, the more the United States ought to expect violent crime from young men to occur.

Because there are no viable societies with any length of history that have had men, as a class, avoid the role of social father, no one has any idea on the competitive quotient that fatherless societies have versus fathered societies. We just do not know. A real experiment is currently being conducted. The next chapter looks at some plausabilities.

CHAPTER 13

The Commons Will Not Stay Fallow

Tis a happy thing to be the father unto many sons.
WILLIAM SHAKESPEARE

Common morality now treats childbearing as an aberration.
There are practically no good reasons left for exercising one's
fertility.
GERMAINE GREER

If the two U.S. trends—(i) middle class attainment via education and upwardly mobility plus (ii) below replacement fertility by the middle class—were to continue, then one could theorize that the United States would become a depopulated geographical land mass. Because an additional birth is an option, but death is a guarantee, the possibility of a tribe, mega or micro, which does not replenish its quite mortal citizenry, becoming extinct is quite real (e.g., the Shakers). If a tribe does erase itself, then it is possible that the land that it occupied would become empty of people. Empty land remaining empty is a logical category, but a terrible bet for an empirical category. There are many people in the world who would be delighted to move into otherwise unpeopled land. If one group will not sustain itself on the land, then there are surely other groups that would be most delighted at the opportunity. The question becomes: Which groups? Who would they be? Part of the answer entails some understanding of that mainstay of demography: the *demographic transition.*

DEMOGRAPHIC TRANSITION AND CULTURAL EVOLUTION

At its most fundamental level, the demographic transition is a sequential shift, over time, in birthrates and death rates: (1) a pattern of high birthrates and high death rates in an intact social group is (2) followed by one of falling death rates with birthrates remaining high, which in turn, is (3) succeeded by low birthrates and low death rates. (See Davis, 1945; Bogue, 1969; Nam, 1968; and Berelson, 1978 for a discussion and a historical over-view of the origin and development of the concept of the "demographic transition". See Low, 1994 for a current usage of the phenomenon.)

The demographic transition has enjoyed both descriptive as well as predictive successes. Indeed, a number of countries and geographic areas have been noted as exemplars illustrating the pattern. Depending on the author(s), the demographic transition has been interpreted as a theory, a principle, a rule, a law, or a trend.

Nonetheless, however the demographic transition may be interpreted, its existence and impact are subject to a rather remorseless constraint. For an intact social group—whether a family, a tribe, or a nation—to remain extant over generations, the members of that group must procreate at a level to replace, at a minimum, the preceding generation. If, for any social group, the number of births consistently falls below the number of deaths, then that social group will be replaced by an alternate social group that has a cultural calculus consistently replacing the preceding generation. See the *Human Relations Area Files* (HRAF, 1949), the *Ethnographic Atlas* (Murdock, 1957), and the World Ethnographic Sample (Murdock, 1967) for a long litany of cultures eliminated from the world's community of intact groups. Currently threatened tribes include indigenous peoples of the Amazon region plus attempts at genocide in the former Yugoslavia, and in Rwanda. This chapter analyzes the demographic transition in relationship to how its dynamics may apply to contemporary countries and to the relative viability of their cultural mosaics.

Cultural Evolution

The term cultural evolution refers to changes over time of expectations and behaviors in an intact, cohesive social group. See Harris (1979) for examples and Harris (1974a) for a historical perspective on cultural evolutionary theorists. See Barkow (1980, 1989), Durham (1979, 1990), and Boyd and Richerson (1985) for discussions on the feedback loops of biocultural evolution. The inherent flexibility and malleability of cultural rules and expectations allow the referent culture to adjust and readjust the behaviors of its members to changing ecologies, environments, and threatening neighbors. This adaptability of a culture to shifts in its milieu helps the culture remain extant.

However, there is no guarantee of societal viability. Facets of the demographic transition indicate two such expectations or rules which, in fact, have been incorporated into and shared by a number of groups across the globe:

1. If the premature deaths of kin can be prevented, they will be.
2. If women have greater freedom and autonomy in controlling their reproductive histories, then they will avail themselves of that enhanced freedom and autonomy and have fewer children.

Decline in Death Rates

There is a strong intuition in the notion that if a family can prevent the death of one of their children, then the family will very often do so. Infanticide, especially female infanticide (Dickemann 1979; Divale & Harris, 1976; Hausfater & Hrdy, 1984) is a real event and makes a sweeping generalization problematic (Rohner & Rohner, 1982; cf. Turnbull, 1972). Nonetheless, as medical technology and the control of disease advance, it would surprise no one that the advances would be embraced and utilized. Thus death rates, especially those of infant mortality, would be expected to drop in proportion to the availability and effectiveness of the advances.

Decline in Birthrates

Any similar imperative in the decline in birthrates is less intuitive than death rates. There is no a priori reason why a voluntary reduction in conceptions and births follows any advances in contraceptive technology. Nevertheless, such a decline has occurred in a number of countries. For various discussions on the variables aligned with changes in fertility, see Arnold et al. (1975), Cochrane (1983), Fawcett (1983), Handwerker (1986), Easterlin and Crimmins (1985), and Bulatao et al. (1983). The next section reviews the relative generalizability of the demographic transition.

A CROSS-NATIONAL AND CROSS-CULTURAL REVIEW

In 1972, the United States dropped below replacement value (less than 2,100 children born per 1,000 females [assuming low infant mortality]; U.S. Bureau of the Census, 1994). Hence, it is reasonable to assume that the United States achieved the third phase of the demographic transition: low birthrates and low death rates. If so, this date is a good benchmark wherein both ideologies and contraceptive technologies subtending lowered birthrates were developed enough and solidified enough to be available for sharing with the world's community of nations. That is, if knowledge and technology is available in Peoria, then they are also available in Tokyo, Brussels, Cairo, Berlin, Lima, Melbourne, Calgary, and Pretoria.

Accordingly, the demographics of nations from the 1970s and the 1990s will be examined. The interval from 1970 to 1990 entails a complete generation, and, if the demographic transition were an "invariant" cultural norm or rule or principle, then the declines in birthrates and death rates would have occurred across our "global, internet-linked village," or world.

METHOD

The relevant demographics from five regions were surveyed (United Nations 1973, 1993) in the two time frames: Europe (27 countries), South America (12 countries, East Asia (11 countries), sub-Saharan Africa (29 countries), and the swathe of Moslem nations across North Africa and the Middle East (9 countries). Different nations have their censuses taken at different times. The nearest censuses to 1970–1990 became the scores of record.

Europe is the home of the demographic transition and can serve as a baseline or benchmark for the other areas. East Asia and South America have been modernizing their free-market economy and are a good and reasonable test for the predictability of the theory. The swathe of the Moslem world across northern Africa and the Middle east tilt in the direction of the patriarchal: a patriarchy that does not optimize women's reproductive options. Sub-Saharan Africa is a tropical landmass of some size, and, due to lack of a winter, may have generated different ecological (read: selective) pressures on the indigenous peoples (see Miller, 1993; Rushton, 1985, 1995; and Calvin, 1990 for discussions). See Table 13.1, for a list of the countries.

RESULTS

Birthrates

In four regions, the Moslem swathe, Europe, East Asia, and South American, the crude birthrates (number of births per 1,000 population)

Table 13.1. List of Countries from the Five Surveyed Areas

Europe ($n = 27$)

Albania	Germany	Netherlands
Austria	(German Democratic Republic)	Norway
Belgium	(German Federal Republic)	Poland
Czechoslovakia	Greece	Portugal
Czech Republic/ Slovakia	Hungary	Rumania
Denmark	Iceland	Spain
Finland	Ireland	Sweden
France	Italy	Switzerland
	Luxembourg	United Kingdom
	Malta	Yugoslavia

Sub-Saharan Africa ($n = 29$

Angola	Gambia	Sierra Leone
Botswana	Ivory Coast	Somalia
Burundi	Kenya	Swaziland
Cameroon	Liberia	Tanzania
Central African Republic	Malawi	Togo
Chad	Mozambique	Uganda
Congo	Niger	Zaire
Dahomey/Benin	Nigeria	Zambia
Equatorial Guinea	Rwanda	Zanzibar
Gabon	Senegal	

Muslim North Africa and Middle East ($n = 9$)

Algeria	Iraq	Saudi Arabia
Egypt	Libya	Tunisia
Iran	Morocco	Yemen

South America ($n = 12$)

Argentina	Columbia	Peru
Bolivia	Ecuador	Suriname
Brazil	Guyana	Uruguay
Chile	Paraguay	Venezuela

East Asia ($n = 11$)

Burma	Khmer Rep./Cambodia	Mongolia
China	Korea (People's Dem. Rep.)	Singapore
Hong Kong	Korea (Rep. of Korea)	Thailand
Japan	Laos	

decreased from 1970 to 1990. In sub-Saharan Africa, the birthrates had no significant change from 1970 to 1990. See Table 13.2.

Death Rates

In all five regions the crude death rates (number of deaths per 1,000 population) decreased. See Table 13.3.

Table 13.2. A Comparison of Mean Birthrates (Number of Births per 1,000 Population) between the 1970s and the 1990s for the Five Areas

Geographic area/Number of countries	Birthrates		Difference, 1970s–1990s	$p <$ *
	1970	1990		
Sub-Saharan Africa ($n = 29$)	46.2	46.0	0.2	n.s.
Muslim Swathe ($n = 9$)	46.1	37.5	8.6	.05
Europe ($n = 27$)	17.6	13.4	4.2	.01
South America ($n = 12$)	37.35	24.9	12.5	.01
East Asia ($n = 11$)	34.7	24.7	10.0	.01

*t-test for repeated measures, two tailed.

Percentage of Natural Increase (per Annum)

Europe, South America and East Asia all had a reduction in their percentage of natural increase (birthrates minus death rates = natural increase). The percentage for the Moslem swathe was unchanged. Sub-Saharan Africa had an *increase* in its rate. See Table 13.4.

DISCUSSION

Europe, South America, and East Asia exemplify the dynamics of the demographic transition. However, as of 1990, the Moslem swathe and sub-Saharan Africa do not.

From these available data, it is argued that either the demographic transition is specific to a particular type of generalized cultural mosaic or that it is adopted at different times by different mosaics, that is, the

Table 13.3. A Comparison of Mean Death Rates (Number of Deaths per 1,000 Population) between the 1970s and the 1990s for the Five Areas

Geographic area/Number of countries	Death rates		Difference, 1970s–1990s	$p <$ *
	1970	1990		
Sub-Saharan Africa ($n = 29$)	22.9	17.2	5.7	.01
Muslim Swathe ($n = 9$)	17.5	8.2	9.3	.01
Europe ($n = 27$)	10.4	9.8	0.6	.05
South America ($n = 12$)	9.9	6.6	3.3	.01
East Asia ($n = 11$)	11.5	8.6	2.9	.05

*t-tests repeated measures, two tailed.

Table 13.4. Comparison of Mean Rates of Natural Increase in Percent *per Year* between the 1970s and the 1990s for the Five Areas

Geographic area/Number of countries	Percent natural increase		Difference, 1970s–1990s	$p < $ *
	1970s	1990s		
Sub-Saharan Africa ($n = 29$)	2.33	2.88	+.55	.01
Muslim swathe ($n = 9$)	2.86	2.93	+.07	n.s.
Europe ($n = 27$)	0.72	0.36	−.36	.01
South America ($n = 12$)	2.745	1.830	−.915	.01
East Asia ($n = 11$)	2.32	1.61	−.71	.01

*t-tests for repeated measures; two tailed.

Moslem swathe and sub-Saharan Africa will eventually align themselves with other areas. The latter, of course, is the tacit assumption girding theorists' discussion. In either event, there is clearly some contemporary biocultural item or items that separate the Moslem swathe and sub-Saharan Africa from Europe, South America, and East Asia. The following section offers a plausible, if partial, exposition to address the disparity. Five interrelated points are germane to these data:

- The biocultural character of the human condition
- An increased access to freedom and autonomy
- The individual versus the commonweal
- The value of children
- Feedback loops

Biocultural Character of the Human Condition

The biocultural charter of the human condition is certainly in evidence for this exercise. Birthrates as well as death rates reflect biological processes that are clearly changed by the form and content of different cultural mosaics. Secularized, industrialized societies have, in the main, lowered both their birthrates and death rates. Moslem patriarchical societies have lowered their death rates, but have maintained a high percentage of natural increase. Agrarian sub-Saharan Africa has maintained high birthrates and raised their rate of natural increase. It is of interest to note that all of these patterns occur within the same species and within the same time frame. Humans are a marvel. The extent that the cultural segment (fundamentalist Islamic ideology is a good candidate) is the dynamic driving the demographics versus the extent that the "bio" segment would be the flywheel ("*r*" versus "*K*" selection is an interesting candidate (see MacArthur & Wilson, 1967; Rushton, 1985, 1995 for discussions) is unknown, and hence, well beyond the scope of this exercise. Nonetheless, the ever present, ever ongoing *nature-and-nurture* quagmire is still circling over the horizon to await any attempt at a clean, unambiguous analysis. It is probably salutary just to note the existence of the biocultural character and then to leave the matter.

Access to Increased Autonomy

As a generalized notion, it is reasonable to assume that, as mentioned in Chapter 1, if people are afforded enhanced access to more freedom and autonomy, then they will grasp such enhanced access firmly with both hands. Accordingly, when women in several areas of the planet (e.g., Europe, South America, East Asia) had the opportunity to control their reproductive histories, they did just that: birthrates dropped. As was also pointed out in Chapter 1, two other trends emerged that were aligned with this biocultural phenomenon of choosing fewer births: (i) women were able to increase their proportion in tertiary college educational institutions and (ii) women were able to increase their wage earnings in comparison to men (Smith-Morris, 1990; United Nations, 1993). See Table 13.5. In each of the surveyed countries in which women's economic plus educational levels could be compared to the men's, the birthrates (mean = 13.2, *sd* 1.78; Iceland high at 16.9; n = 12) were well below the mean both for the Muslim swathe (37.5) and for sub-Saharan Africa (46.0).

While these egalitarian trends have ideological popularity in many quarters, the end result of such trends may be less. A worldview of enhanced reproductive freedom cum gender equity is not demographically competitive with societies wherein such freedom is not available. To the extent that a cultural mosaic avoids the European pattern (0.4% natural increase per annum), but emulates the sub-Saharan African or the Muslim swathe pattern (2.9% natural increase per annum), then the more competitive, over time, that mosaic is. Said differently, if entry into educational or occupation hierarchies is not available to women, then these life chances are precluded from impacting upon reproductive options. The upshot of these two separate modes of framing a society—enhanced access to autonomy versus restricted access to autonomy—is that one is more competitive over generations and thus better to propagate itself, and the other is less competitive over generations and thus more vulnerable to be replaced with an alternate, more competitive system.

Table 13.5. Birthrates by Economic Parity for Women: Percentage of Female Tertiary Students Plus Ratio of Female to Male Wage Earnings, Circa 1990 ($n = 12$)

Country	Birthrates	Percentage female tertiary students	Ratio of female to male earnings
Denmark	12.5	50	.84
France	13.2	51	.81
Germany	11.0	41	.73
Iceland	16.9	54	.90
Japan	10.3	37	.52
Luxembourg	12.1	34	.66
Netherlands	12.8	42	.76
Switzerland	13.0	32	.67
United Kingdom	14.0	46	.695
Czech/Slovakia	13.0	42	.68
Hong Kong	12.3	35	.77
South Korea	15.7	30	.48
Mean	13.1	41.2	.71
sd	1.8	7.9	.12

Sources: Smith-Morris (1990) and United Nations (1993).

The Individual versus the Commonweal

As profiled in the previous chapter, Hardin's (1968) *Tragedy of the Commons* is applicable to this wider context. If women (or men), one at a time, opt for reduced fertility in favor of alternative forms of investments of time, energy, and resources, then they may better maximize their own lifestyles and life chances. Yet, if women (or men), one at a time, do systematically opt for reduced fertility levels below replacement value, then their referent social group constricts in size per family and is superseded or replaced by cultural formulas wherein freedom and autonomy in family size is more circumscribed, but the continuity, over generations, of their populace or tribe is more secure. 'Tis a knotty problem.

The Value of Children

In addition to the psychoemotional value that children generate for their kin, the child can also be analyzed within the dismal science of economics. Phrased bluntly, when children become net economic benefits, they appear—birthrates are high. When children become economic net costs, they disappear—birthrates fall (Aghajanian, 1979, 1988;

Bradley, 1984; Day & Mackey, 1986); See Zelizer (1985) for a discussion. A ripple or incidental effect of larger family size is that the population within which the individual family is operating expands demographically. Therefore, a culture whose rules eventuates in its children generating net economic benefits tend to have a demographic advantage compared to culture wherein children are net economic costs.

Feedback Loops

Cultural systems tend to have feed-back loops. The rules or expectations governing culturally *appropriate* behaviors shift over generations to solve the problems inherent in maintaining intact social groups: for example, obtaining food and water, preventing internal turmoil and dissension, procreating and socializing the next generation, and preventing external intrusions by competing groups. Those rules and expectations that enhance the maintenance of the group tend to be solidified in the group's cosmology or worldview, while those rules and expectations, which lessen the viability of the group, tend to be ignored, altered, or discarded. For this exercise, the cultural rules that result in the bearing of children will feedback to maintain and reinforce whatever those rules were. Conversely, if cultural rules or expectations result in a fertility pattern below replacement value, then either their rules are changed or the referent society is replaced, or absorbed, or eradicated.

In other words, if one were curious about what the fathers will be like down the road of time, then the ability to count to three (thank you: Ernie, Bert and Big Bird) serves as a coarse, but useful, barometer. Those groups with three-or-more children per woman have a better, if not excellent, chance to have their version of father existing in the 23rd century. Those groups with less than two children per woman will have very few examples of their version of fathering to be found in the 23rd century.

SUMMARY

Whatever else the demographic transition may be able to predict or explain, the demographic transition may also turn out to be an index or omen of cultural hari-kari. That is, the more that a group parallels the classic definition of the demographic transition, the more clearly it signals its own vulnerability of being replaced. It is conceivable that the fate of the demographic transition is one of a footnote in the human chronicles: a minor blip of only a few centuries in duration with little long-term impact on the thousands of years of the humans' past and the humans' future. The concept of temporocentrism is clearly relevant here. There may also a tint of ethnocentrism in evidence. Cultural imperialism of the scholarly variety may be afoot on this one: if it happened in Europe and its extensions, then—by golly—the rest of the known world really ought to follow suit. The Moslem swathe and Sub-Saharan Africa may have found a trump card of their own and decide not to follow suit.

Ceteris paribus, the less that a group follows the trajectory of the demographic transition to its final stage, the greater the chances that it would be self-sustaining. A trade-off for an increased ply of survivability is the simultaneous reduction of the autonomy and freedom of the group's women who would chose to enter into educational and occupational hierarchies. Such reduced access—in the past, in the present, and highly likely in the future—has been challenged from several quarters, and energetic efforts have been introduced to redress the reduction and to increase the opportunities. How the various forces—synergized, confrontational, complementary, competitive, cooperative, covert, overt, formal, informal, direct, and indirect—play out over the next millennia or so should keep politicians and social scientists busy and intrigued for the duration.

CHAPTER 14

Troglyodyte or Semiconductor

Dad in the Twenty-First Century

There has been a succession of women's revolutions in America. But watch out for the revolt of the father, if he should get fed up with feeding others, and get bored with being used, and lay down his tools, and walk off to consult his soul.

MAX LERNER

If you can't say anything nice, then don't say anything at all.

THUMPER'S FATHER

This chapter looks at fathering as a generalized developmental state in the man's life and examines how that putative stage meshes with the U.S. cultural mosaic of the twenty-first century. Developmental stage is used here in the sense of an interval of time in which a set of motivations are more easily organized and triggered than at other times. The concepts of "imprinting" and "critical or sensitive period" are relevant here (Hess, 1964; Lorenz, 1958, 1965). Puberty is a good example of such a stage. After the mad rush of hormones have finished their appointed tasks, the postpubescent's sense of romance is better enabled to be initiated and maintained than during his or her prepubescence. Prior to puberty, the other gender is often a source of disdain directed at a class of people, or near people, who can be dismissed without a second or third thought. After puberty, the other gender is a lot more attractive. If my memory serves me correctly, in high school the only thing more important than which females were in a classroom was whether the classroom was on fire or not.

The question becomes, Are the sets of motivations that initiate and maintain fathering behaviors of the same quality as those motivations of postpubescent attraction of the other gender? For two main reasons, men have received little attention in the behavioral sciences. These reasons include: (1) ethics (any attempt to have controlled studies with randomly assigned and enforced *men who are fathers* versus *men who are not fathers* with the two groups matched for I.Q., SES, family background, etc. were pulled from funding immediately and given enormously bad publicity by local and national media almost as quickly) and (2) logistics (adult males are unreliable subjects by the behavioral sciences, not just for fathering, but across the board. After males leave their heavily studied sophomore year in college, they tend to disappear as subjects. The same problem is the case in family therapy. They just do not show up (Crowder, 1995).

Major theorists in the analysis of human development include Freud, Piaget, Kohlberg, and Erikson. They too faced the same problems in dealing with postcollege adults and heavily based their cosmology on the young child. The, not unreasonable, assumption was that as the sapling is bent so grows the tree. If the child's family, experiences, constitution, and personality were known, then reasonable hypotheses could be made about the child's future adulthood. See Freud (1964), Piaget (1966), Kohlberg (1981), and Erikson (1985) for examples. A usually latent or tacit assumption was that a form of imprinting was occurring. Early experiences during a sensitive or critical period of time organized a system that was important to the normative development of the individuals. See Bolhuis and Horn (1992), Bornstein (1989), Cook (1993), and Leland (1994) for recent data and theory. Once the system was organized it was difficult to unorganize, that is,organization would inhibit reorganization.

Freud's analysis of personality and psychosexual development essentially stops at puberty; a time prior to any emergence of fathering behaviors. The person's personality had been *set* by that time and, for ill or will, that person's personality would remain where it was set unless some traumatic event or psychoanalytic therapy or both intervened. Freud's *Oedipus Complex* analyzed the young boy's reaction to the perceived image of the father and how he may react to the boy's competition for the wife's or mother's affections. What the father was actually doing (the father's psychodynamics in relationship to his son) was not a focus of Freud's thesis. Jung's (1955, 1969) version of the young, immatue human becoming its older, more mature version would certainly include an archetype of *the father figure,* but why or how that archetype would be there and what its characteristics would be are not wholly synthesized. Jung's constructs are givens or premises that he built upon with great erudition and complexity. Accordingly, these constructs are not useful to this discussion. Piaget's theory of cognitive development also extends to puberty—"formal operations"—

and does not advance further into human maturity. As formal operations occurs (12 to 14 years of age), the person develops adult forms of thinking and analysis (or not, there is no guarantee that everyone achieves formal operations). Kohlberg's theories on moral development (essentially of the male) also assumes a crystallization of moral codes by puberty and continuity from then on. Erikson's scheme of psychosocial personality development emphasizes different stages into adulthood beyond puberty.

Empirical evidence that corroborates Erikson's scheme is problematic, especially for those stages beyond college-aged students (Maddi, 1980). His stage of "generativity" versus "stagnation" most overlaps with the advent and performance of fathering behaviors. Of this stage, Erikson (1950) writes:

> . . . primarily the interest in establishing and guiding the next generation or whatever in a given case may become the absorbing object of a parental kind of responsibility. Where this enrichment fails, a regression from generativity to an obsessive need for pseudo intimacy, punctuated by moments of mutual repulsion, takes place, often with a pervading sense . . . of individual stagnation and interpersonal impoverishment.

Again, the idea of being motivated to be a father is an assumption or premise that is asserted and then discussed. How or why generativity exists and what forms it takes and why were not the foci of interest of Erikson and thereby understandably enough were not examined in depth.

Indeed, for these major players in personality development, if fathers were included, their existence was a given without any particular rhyme or reason. To these theorists, the fathers *are,* once their existence is established, then the ramifications on the child by the good, the bad, and the ugly versions of fathers could be thought about as they affected the unfolding of the child's personality.

Less molar or overarching studies on, primarily, U.S. fathers, tend to focus (1) on the adjustments, usually marital adjustments, from childlessness to the father of an infant and (2) on the match between expectations on parenting and what actual eventuates with the arrival of the infant. The unsurprising conclusion is that the more unrealistic the expectations, the more dislocation, followed by dissatisfaction, is likely to occur (Belsky & Rovine, 1990; Crockenberg, 1986; Osofsky & Osofsky, 1984; Wallace & Gotlib, 1990).

Introductory Developmental Psychology textbooks, because of an intense competition of the marketplace, are often a bellweather that reflects the community at large. That is, there is a shamanistic quality to these books, that is, the authors and editors and publishers anticipate what their audience wants (and, perhaps, needs to have validated). The

books tend to reflect, with the aura of science, the conventional wisdom of the time. Two trends are evident as these types of books are
perused in their treatment of U.S. fathers.

First, U.S. fathers are compared to U.S. mothers (again, this route is
one valid way to evaluate fathers, but not the exclusive one. U.S. fathers could certainly be compared to other non-U.S. fathers). Second,
fathering is, almost magically, transduced into being measured by marital dissatisfaction. It is as if a taboo would be violated if the man were
examined as a person: an adult male evaluating himself and what he is
to do with his role of father.

Hurlock's (1980, 5th ed.) text has five paragraphs devoted to *Adjustment to Parenthood* and writes, "While both husband and wife
must make marked adjustments in the patterns of their lives when they
become parents, mothers with professional training and experience
often suffer extremely severe crisis shock when they realize that they
must give up a role that was highly important to them in favor of one for
which they feel inadequate and which, in the eyes of the social group as
well as in the eyes of their husbands, has less prestige than the role they
were forced to abandon because they were unable to get adequate help
with the care of their babies.

Even though most men do not have to change their roles radically
when they become parents, many fathers show a disenchantment with
the parental role by becoming less sexually responsive to their wives,
worrying about economic pressures or developing feelings of resentment as being 'tied down' or excluded from the mother-child relationship. These unfavorable attitudes can and often do play havoc with
men's attitudes toward parenthood and their marital adjustments"
(p. 310). These two paragraphs ended the section; the next section was
on "voluntary childlessness."

Papalia and Olds (1992) in their section "Parenthood as a Developmental Experience," proffer, "Fathers treasure and are emotionally
committed to their children, but they enjoy looking after them less than
mothers do. Although fathers generally believe they should be involved
in their children's lives, most are not nearly as involved as mothers are"
(p. 421).

Santrock (1995) states, "It is much easier for working parents to
cope with changing family circumstances and day-care issues when the
father and mother equitably share child-rearing responsibilities. Mothers feel less stress and have more positive attitudes toward their husbands when they are supportive partners" (p. 449).

Craig (1992) nots that "although they share some concerns, fathers
and others also display different reactions to the arrival of the first
child. Women characteristically adjust their lifestyles to give priority to

their parenting and family roles. Men, *on the other hand,* more often intensify their work efforts to become better or more stable providers" (p. 476). (italics added). Again, as in the larger society, breadwinning is not viewed as a parenting role. An increased intensity to providing is not interpreted as an adjustment. Providing is not evaluated as a priority for a parent, also known as father.

INDICES OF FATHERING

Even though there are certainly large areas in the domain of fathering yet to be discovered and analyzed, some interesting facets can be inferred. Five very separate, disparate lines of evidence on the normative development of fatherhood are profiled below. These lines of evidence include: (i) universality of fathering, (ii) the Swedish adventure into gender equality, (iii) rates of violent crime, (iv) family violence, and (v) divorce rates.

Universality of Fathering

The sheer omnipresence of men accepting the father role across wildly different religious, economic, ecological, and subsistence cultural mosaics is perhaps the strongest evidence for the notion that fathering is built into the human adult male. This constancy gives additional credence to Lorenz's dictum that we should look for what we take for granted. What we take for granted is more likely to be a cause and less likely to be an effect. It is worth repeating that across societies, men, by all accounts, have the physical and political and economic power to avoid fathering if, as a class, they would decide to do just that. That men, as a class, have decided not to eschew—but to adopt—fathering, tells us much about men.

The Swedish Adventure

As introduced in Chapter 7, Sweden initiated a social experiment in equalizing gender roles that would include parenting roles. Swedish fathers and mothers were to be equal parents based on the mother template. (see Lamb & Levine, 1983 for a discussion). If the goal of parental equality is to be used to evaluate the Swedish program, then the program has, to date, failed. Lamb, who helped spur enthusiasm of parental equality in his book *The Role of the Father in Child Development* (1976) evaluated the Swedish program with an article (1982) entitled; "Why Swedish Fathers Aren't Liberated." He wrote, "Few Swedish men have taken advantage of the legal provisions encouraging paternity leave. And in the homes of those who have, the policy seems to have had surprisingly little impact on styles of child-rearing" (p. 74). The program was initiated in 1974 and, by 1977, only 9.7% of the eligible men availed themselves of the program (Lamb & Levine, 1983). Of those men who did take one or more days of paternity leave, only half (52.9%) or one in twenty (5.1% = 9.7% × 52.9%) used 30 or more days of paid paternity leave. How those 30 or more days were actually spent is unknown. During the thirty or more days taken for paternity leave, the amount of additional time the men spent with their children, compared to those who did not take the leave, is not known.

A study by Haas (1990) provides some interesting insights. In the study only couples were studied (over 40% of the Swedish children are born to single-parent mothers and were not included to be studied). The couples had given birth to a child in 1984, the couple had lived together before the baby was born and were still living together in 1986, and both of the couples had been employed outside the home before the child was born.

In all, 721 qualified couples were contacted and 319 (44%) agreed to participate. Of the 319 fathers who agreed to be in the survey, 234 (73.4%) took *no* leave. At a 100% salary compensation and job security guaranteed, nearly three in four fathers did not accept the idea of gender equality in parenting. There were 85 fathers who did take some leave (26.6%). Haas reported that the modal pattern was that the man would take leave for a short amount of time (under two months) during the middle of the year-long parental leave interval. The woman thus stayed with the child for about five or six months, returned to work for the two months when the man stayed with the child, and then she returned to the childcare to finish up the rest of the allocated leave. The man returned to his job when the woman left hers.

Haas did examine time spent with the child. Fathers who took *no* leave spent 10.48 hours in childcare during a non-workday. Fathers who did take leave spent 10.58 hours in childcare during a non-workday. There was no difference between the two groups. Fathers who took *no* leave spent 3.17 hours of childcare during a workday. Fathers who did take leave spend 3.09 hours of child care during a workday. Again, there was no difference between the two groups.

The demographics of Sweden in the 1990s are interesting. Sweden has completed the demographic transition. They have a low crude birthrate (about 12) and a low crude death rate (about 11). Hence, were a man to take paternity leave, he would be spending time with a child rather than with a number of children. A condition of one infant and one adult seems like a maximal opportunity for men to adopt a mother-template parenting style. The Swedish men just did not make that adoption. A reasonable interpretation of the data suggests that Swedish fathers are not appropriate Swedish mothers. Whether Swedish fathers are appropriate Swedish fathers is an entirely different question. The Swedish data by themselves do not address that quesion. Other countries' fathers need to be surveyed to begin to answer that question. In sum, to the extent that Swedish fathers can be viewed as representing men in general, the Swedish experiment may offer an insight into fathering. That insight would include the notion that men are not very good mothers. Expectations that are predicated on the assumption that the two genders are interchangeable modular parents are probably expectations which are going to be unfulfilled.

Rates of Violent Crime

Violent crime is a young man's phenomenon. In his book, *Criminal Behavior: A Psychosocial Approach* (4th ed.), Bartol (1995) notes: "With monotonous regularity, national statistics from all sources continue to underscore the fact that about half of all those arrested for violent crime are between the ages of twenty and twenty-nine" (p. 219). These youths are male: at least 85% of the arrests for violent crime are males (U.S. Department of Justice, 1993). But, as the young men lose their youth, but keep the male, they, for lack of a better phrase, do "settle down." The level of impetuousness and impulsiveness decrease (see Wilson & Herrnstein, 1985 for a discussion). Although empirical substantiation may be virtually impossible, for all the world, the decrease in violence looks like an end of a developmental phase built into the developing male. High energy and lack of judgment on the far-reaching consequences of their actions seem to be replaced with lower energy and more cautious judgment. As a class, more mature men, both in age and level of responsibility, get jobs, get married, and raise children. Up to the 20th century, the behaviors are highly predictable, if mundane. Most men will be employed (i.e., secure resources): between 1940 and 1970 over 90% of the men 25 years to 64 years were in the labor force (U.S. Bureau of the Census, 1975). Most men will get married. In 1990, over 95% of the men 50 to 54 years of age had "ever married" (U.S. Bureau of the Census, 1994). Most men will raise children (share their resources) (U.S. Bureau of the Census 1975, 1994). There is no reason to believe such a prosaic pattern would not continue unless disincentives are ratcheted up and incentives are ratcheted down.

Intrafamilial Violence

The thoroughly unpleasant topic of within-family violence also sheds some light on how men view the world. An unlikely litmus paper here is intrafamilial homicide. To wit: as Daly and Wilson (1987) explain, "Most murdered relatives are spouses, and a substantial proportion of the remainder are relatives by marriage too." In their (1982) study, Daly and Wilson found that only 6% of all victims in solved homicides were blood relatives. Hence, at most, only 6% of homicides could be biological parent to child filicide. Fathers are loathe to hurt their own children. To the extent that the man may not believe his paternity of a child born to his wife, the maximum of 6% would be similarly lowered.

In much of the literature surrounding family violence, there is a merger of biological and social father, with boyfriend, with stepparent. Nonetheless, the distinction seems to be more real than merely apparent. Violence toward the child is much more likely to occur if the biological and social father is replaced with any other man. (Gil, 1970; Johnson, 1974; see Lenington, 1981 for a review). See Hausfater and Hrdy (1984) for an extended discussion on infanticide. Although Gilder (1974, 1993) is typically prescient and insightful on many issues, his analysis on the taming of the barbarian (the young male) might have missed. While it is true that married men have better social indixes than Gilder's "naked nomads" (also known as unmarried or single men), these married men also tend to have children. As influential as a woman may be on civilizing young men, a better candidate for domestication may be the man's children. In the hurly-burly and swirling ecology known as the family, it is the child who is at the lesser risk of the temper and aggression of the young man. The spouse is at the greater risk. For learning theorists, it should be noted that the spouse is associated with a powerful reinforcer: sex. The spouse, theoretically, should be valued as a source or reinforcer of pleasure. The husband, when aggressing against the source of pleasure risks losing access to that source. Again, theoretically, the child—at first and second blush—seems to offer nothing of intrinsic value to the man, to the father. Yet, yet, and yet again, the child has been relatively immunized from aggression by the ongoing biological and social father. Although being situated in harm's way may seem like an odd barometer for domestication, it does have the advantage of being a double-blind study. Neither the police records nor the individuals involved would be aware of the hypothesis being tested. Experimenter bias would be minimized.

An unhappy choice seems available to the U.S. commonweal. The individual freedom to change marriage partners is strongly aligned with the physical vulnerability to young children with the mother's new male consort. Restricting the individual liberty of exchanging partners strikes at a fundamental core of Americana. Individual freedom is a good thing. Yet, child abuse is universally condemned. Currently, the priority of freedom is in evidence. The social choice is whether or not to keep that priority as paramount.

Drawing the unpleasantness to a close, boyfriends and stepfathers compared to biological fathers are also more likely to commit "incest" (sexual abuse). See Russell (1986) Gordon and Creighton (1988) and Tyler (1986).

What is learned from the above is that biological and social fathers seem to be built with some safeguards against hurting their own young children. As was noted earlier, young men can be aggressive and dangerous beings. However, when their own children are involved, they tend to tamp down the violence directed at their own children. Not reduce it to zero, but to lower the level.

Divorce Rates

As was noted in Chapter 5, when children are involved in a marriage, the fathers tend to *decrease* their petitions for divorce, but mothers tend to *increase* their petitions for divorce. A reasonable interpretation of this dynamic is that, in general, men are more pleased with their children than with their wives. Said differently, men value fatherhood more than spousehood. It is easier for a man to leave a wife than his child.

SYNOPSIS

To encapsulate what these five markers about men can reveal to us, it is suggested that men, as they career toward middle age, will readily adopt the father role which should not be confused with the mother role. Men will provide for their children, be protective of their children, and be reluctant to leave them. These conclusions seem fairly well grounded with data.

With a dash more speculation tossed in, it is suggested here that the man's motivational system (blueprinted from their genes which, by the by, were selected by women who became mothers of those genes and subsequently created fathers and sons) is primed to emit fathering behaviors. As with any other interplay between genes and environment, the environment must provide cues or stimuli to which the organism is (built to be) sensitive. These cues or stimuli can then trigger the motivations which, in turn, trigger the behaviors. In the case of fathering, the trigger is the child. The ongoing presence of the man (father) with his child (son or daughter) bonds the man to the child—the father to his son or daughter. The emotions are real, intense, and long lasting. The idea of imprinting seems extremely relevant. If the trigger is not available, then there is no reason for the motivations to be activated and no reason for fathering behaviors to occur. If no trigger is pulled, then no imprinting would have the chance to occur.

SUMMARY

Fox's 1978 observation that "centuries know more than social scientists" seems quite germane. Over multiple generations, if left to their own devices, cultural groups, whether tiny isolated villages or mega-tribes, will probably invent or reinvent fathers. What fathers do for their children seems highly valuable to them and, by extension, to the viability of their group. No long-term substitutes seem forthcoming. Effective and efficient cultural traditions slowly accrete, and their origins become lost in time and space. How or why the traditions arose in the first place and what problems they addressed in the form of solutions via shared expectations is not something citizens or natives dwell upon extensively.

Nonetheless, if the assumption arises that our ancestors were peoples who were less clever and less able than ourselves, then short-term mischief can be created and then institutionalized. Fathering in the past is correlated with descendants. Our existence is prima facie evidence that past fathering was correlated with producing descendants. Because the axiom that "correlation does not prove causation" is ever yet an eternal verity, there is a logical category that states: In spite of fathers, the human condition muddled on and flourished. But again, the omnipresence of fathers across the world's community of cultures makes that argument problematic. Surely, if fathers were part of the problem—if not *the* problem—rather than a part of the solution, then some clever tribes would have been clever enough to have eliminated fathers, and these superior, unfettered tribes would have displaced those tribes handicapped by fathers. Such is not the case, fathers are everywhere. Occam's Razor would suggest that they have been useful. There may be some utility in examining what our forebears did correctly before any wholesale mischief is committed that is irreversible for a very long, long time. The two-pronged father abrading machine: *single-parent births* and *no-fault divorce* have systematically separated men from the opportunity to be triggered into ongoing fathering behaviors. No current social forces are in effect that have the capacity to reverse the trajectory of reducing father-child bonding. Social planners and policy makers may reach a consensus that fathers, at base, are supernhumerary parents. It may be argued that, at best, fathers are optional alternatives to other ways of organizing a society. Extensive, free, 24-hour day care plus a government commitment to providing for children may be the route our megatribe chooses to go. There are certainly advocates who would develop such a system, and, equally certainly, benefits can be envisioned from such a system. On the other hand, there may be wisdom in at least thinking about the costs of such a fatherless system before too much mischief is achieved. One can never be too sure that the next "snark" would not be a "boojum."

References

Adams, P. L., Milner, J. R., & Schrepf, N. A. (1984). *Fatherless children*. New York: Wiley.

Adams, R. N. (1960). An inquiry into the nature of the family. In G. E. Dole & R. L. Carneiro (Eds.), *Essays in the science of culture in honor of Leslie A. White* (pp. 30–49). New York: Thomas Y. Crowell.

Aghajanian, A. (1979). Economic contribution of children and fertility in rural Iran: An overview. *Journal of South Asian and Middle Eastern Studies 3*, 21–30.

Aghajanian, A. (1988). The value of children in rural and urban Iran: A pilot study. *Journal of Comparative Family Studies 19*, 85–98.

Alderton, D. (1994). *Foxes, wolves and wild dogs of the world*. New York: Facts on File.

Allen, D. L. (1979). *Wolves of Minong: Their vital role in a wild community*. Boston: Houghton Mifflin.

Al-lssa, I. (Ed.). (1995). *Handbook of culture and mental illness: An international perspective*. Madison, CT: International Universities Press.

Amato, P. R. (1989). Who cares for children in public places? *Journal of Marriage and the Family 51*, 981–990.

Amato, P. R. (1994). Father-child relations, mother-child relations and offspring psychological well-being in early adulthood. *Journal of Marriage and the Family 56*, 1031–1042.

Amato, P. R., & B. Keith (1991). Parental divorce and adult well-being: a meta-analysis. *Journal of Marriage and the Family 53*, 43–58.

American Psychiatric Association (1994). *Diagnostic and statistical manual of mental disorders* (4th ed.). Washington, DC: Author.

Anderson, R. E. (1968). Where's dad? Paternal deprivation and delinquency. *Archives of General Psychiatry 18*, 641–649.

Arditti, J. A. (1990). Non-custodial fathers: An overview of policy and resources: literature and resource review essay. *Family Relations 39*, 460–465.

Archer, D., & R. Gartner. (1984). Homicide in 110 nations. In L. I. Shelly (Ed.), *Readings in comparative criminology*. Carbondale, IL: Southern Illinois University Press.

Arens, W. (1979). *The man eating myth: Anthropology and anthropophagy*. New York: Oxford University Press.

Aristophanes. (1969). *Lysistrata* (D. Parker Trans.). Ann Arbor, MI: University of Michigan Press.

Arnold, F., Bulatao, R. A., Buupakdi, C., Chung, B. J., Fawcett, J. T., Iritani, T., Lee, K. J., & Wu, T. (1975). *The value of children: A cross-national study*. Honolulu, HI: East–West Population.

Bacon, M. K., Child, I. L., & Barry, H. (1963). A cross-cultural study of correlates of crime. *Social Psychology, 66*, 291–300.

Bailey, W. T. (1992). Psychological development in men: Generativity and involvement with young children. *Psychological Reports, 71*, 929–930.

Bailey, W. T. (1994). Fathers involvement and responding to infants: "More" may not be "better." *Psychological Reports, 74*, 92–94.

Barkow, J. (1980). Biological evolution of culturally patterned behavior. I. J. Lockard (Ed.), *The evolution of human social behavior*, (pp. 277–290). New York: Elsevier.

Barkow, (1989). *Darwin sex and status*. Toronto: University of Toronto Press.

Barnett, R. C., Marshall, N. L., & Pleck, J. H. (1992). Men's multiple role and their relationship to men's psychological distress. *Journal of Marriage and the Family 54*, 358–367.

Barnett, R. C., & Baruch, G. K. (1988). Correlates of fathers' participation in family work. In *Fatherhood today: Men's changing role in the family*, pp. 66–78. P. Bronstein & C. P. Cowan (Eds.). New York: Wiley.

Barry, H., Bacon, M. K., & Child, I. L. (1957). A cross-cultural survey of some sex differences in socialization. *The Journal of Abnormal and Social Psychology, 55*, 327–332.

Barry, H., Child, I. L., & Bacon, M. K. (1959). Relation of child training to subsistence economy. *American Anthropologist 61*, 51–63.

Barry, H., & Paxson, L. (1971). Infancy and early childhood: Cross-cultural codes 2. *Ethnology, 10*, 466–509.

Barry, H. L., Josephson, L., Lauer, E., & Marshall, C. (1977). Agents and techniques for child training: Cross-cultural codes 6. *Ethnology, 16*, 191–230.

Bartol, C. R. (1995). *Criminal behavior: A psychosocial approach* (4th ed.). Englewood Cliffs, NJ: Prentice Hall.

Bartz, K. W. (1978, July). Selected childrearing tasks and problems of mothers and fathers. *The Family Coordinator*, 209–215.

Baruch, G. K., & Barnett, R. C. (1986). Consequences of father's participation in family work: Parents' role strain and well-being. *Journal of Personality and Social Psychology, 5*, 983–992.

Bateson, G. (1972). Metalogue: Why do things get in a muddle? In *Steps to an ecology of mind.* (pp. 3–8). New York: Ballantine.

Bednarik, K. (1970). *The male in crisis.* New York: Knopf.

Belsky, J., & Rovine, M. (1990). Patterns of marital change across the transition to parenthood: Pregnancy to three years postpartum. *Journal of Marriage and the Family, 52*, 5–19.

Benedict, R. (1959); (orig. 1934). *Patterns of Culture* New York: New American Library.

Benedict, R. (1946). *The chrysanthemum and the sword* Boston: Houghton Mifflin.

Berelsen, B. (1978). Prospects and programs for fertility reduction: What? Where? *Population and Development Review, 4*, 579–616.

Berman, P. W., & Pedersen, F. A. (Eds.). (1987). *Men's transitions to parenthood: Longitudinal studies of early family experiences.* Hillsdale, NJ: Erlbaum.

Bernard, J. (1982). *The future of marriage* New Haven, CT: Yale University Press.

Bespali de Consens, Y. (1995). Uruguay: Subcultures under apparent cultural uniformity. In I. Al-lssa (Ed.), *Handbook of culture and mental illness: An international perspective*, (pp. 239–248). Madison, CT: International Universities Press.

Biller, H. B. (1968). A multiaspect investigation of masculine development in kindergarten-age boys. *Genetic Psychology Monographs, 78*, 89–137.

Biller, H. B. (1971). *Father, child, and sex role* Lexington, MA: Heath Lexington Books.

Biller, H. B. (1974). *Paternal deprivation* Lexington, MA: Heath Lexington Books.

Biller, H. B., & Meredith, D. (1975). *Father power* (pp. 1–9). New York: Anchor Books.

Biller, H. B., & Solomon, R. S. (1986). *Child maltreatment and paternal deprivation: A manifesto for research, prevention and treatment* (p. 306). Lexington, MA: Lexington Books.

Bilu, Y. (1995). Culture and mental illness among Jews in Israel. In I. Al-lssa (Ed.), *Handbook of Culture and Mental illness: An international perspective* (pp. 129–146). Madison, CT: International Universities Press.

Bird, C. (1976). *Enterprising women* New York: Norton.

Blakely, M. K. (1984). Fathering *Ms., 13,* 86–87.

Blakemore, J. E. O. (1981). Age and sex differences in interaction with a human infant. *Child Development 52,* 386–388.

Blankenhorn, D. (1995). *Fatherless America: Confronting our most urgent social problem.* New York: Basic Books.

Blau, J. R., & Blau, P. M. (1982). The cost of inequality: Metropolitan structure and violent crime. *American Sociological Review, 47,* 114–129.

Block, J. H. (1976). Issues, problems and pitfalls in assessing sex differences: A critical review of the psychology of sex differences. *Merrill-Palmer Quarterly, 22,* 283–308.

Bloom, B. L., & Caldwell, R. A. (1981). Sex differences in adjustment during the process of marital separation. *Journal of Marriage and the Family, 41,* 693–701.

Bogue, D. J. (1969). *Principles of demography.* New York: Wiley.

Bohman, M. (1971). A comparative study of adopted children, foster children, and children in their natural environment born after undesired pregnancies. *Acta Paediatrica Scandinavica, Supp. 221:* 1–38.

Bolhuis, J. J., & Horn, G. (1992). Generalization of learned preferences in filial imprinting. *Animal Behaviour, 44,* 185–187.

Booth, A., & Amato, P. R. (1994). Parental gender role nontraditionalism and offspring outcomes. *Journals of Marriage and the Family, 56,* 865–877.

Booth, A., & Edwards, J. N. (1980). Father: The invisible parent. *Sex Roles, 6,* 445–456.

Bornstein, M. H. (1989). Sensitive periods in development: Structural characteristics and casual interpretations. *Psychological Bulletin, 105,* 179–197.

Boyd, R., & Richerson, P. J. (1988). *Culture and the evolutionary process.* Chicago: University of Chicago Press.

Bozett, F. W., & Hanson, S.M.H. (Eds.). (1991). *Fatherhood and families in cultural context.* New York: Springer.

Bradley, C. (1984). The sexual division of labor and the value of children. *Behavior Science Research, 19,* 159–185.

Braver, S. H., Wolchik, S. A., Sandler, I. N., Fogas, B. S., & Zvetina, D. (1991). Frequency of visitation by divorced fathers: Differences in reports by fathers and mothers. *American Journal of Orthopsychiatry, 61,* 448–454.

Brazelton, T. B. (1989). *Families crisis and caring.* New York: Addison-Wesley.

Brenton, M. (1966). *The American male.* Greenwich, CT: Fawcett.

Bridges, L. J., Connell, J. P., & Belsky, J. (1988). Similarities and differences in infant-mother and infant-father interaction in the strange situation: A component process analysis. *Developmental Psychology, 24,* 92–100.

Bromberger, J. T., & Costello, E. J. (1992). Epidemiology of depression for clinicians. *Social Work 37,* 120–125.

Bromberger, J. T., & Matthews, K. A. (1994). Employment status and depressive symptoms in middle-aged women: A longitudinal investigation. *American Journal of Public Health 84,* 202–206.

Bronstein, P., & Cowan, C. P. (Eds.). (1988). *Fatherhood today: Men's changing role in the family.* New York: Wiley.

Bronstein-Burrows, P. (1981). Patterns of parent behavior: A cross-cultural study. *Merrill-Palmer Quarterly 27,* 129–143.

Broude, G. J. (1980). Extramarital sex norms in cross-cultural perspective. *Behavior Science Research 15,* 181–218.

Brown, D. E. (1991). *Human universals.* New York: McGraw-Hill.

Brown, J. K. (1970). A note on the division of labor. *American Anthropologist 72,* 1073–1078.

Brunham, R. C., Homes, K. K., & Embree, J. E. (1990). Sexually transmitted diseases in pregnancy. In K. K. Holmes, P. Mardh, P. F. Sparling, & P. J. Wiesner, (Eds.), *Sexually transmitted diseases* (pp. 771–802). New York: McGraw-Hill.

Bryson, R., Bryson, J. B., & Johnson, M. F. (1978). Family size, satisfaction, and productivity. In J. B. Bryson & R. Bryson (Eds.), *Dual-career couples* (pp. 67–77). New York: Human Sciences Press.

Bulatao, R. A., Lee, R. D., Hollerbach, P. E., & Bongaarts, J. (1983). *Determinants of fertility in developing countries* (Vols, I & II). New York: Academic Press.

Bumpass, L. L. (1990). What's happening to the family? Interactions between demographic and institutional change. *Demography 27,* 483–498.

Bumpass, L., & Sweet, J. (1986). *National survey of family and households.* Madison, WI: Wisconsin Center for Demographic Studies.

Bunn, H. T., & Kroll, E. M. (1986). Systematic butchery by plio/pleistocene hominids at Olduvai Gorge, Tanzania. *Current Anthropology 27,* 431–452.

Buscaglia, L. (1989). *Papa my father: A celebration of dads* New York: William Morrow.

Buss, D. (1984). Evolutionary biology and personality psychology: Toward a conception of human nature and individual differences. *American Psychologist 39,* 1135–1147.

Buss, D. (1987). Sex differences in human mate selection criteria: An evolutionary perspective. In C. Crawford, D. Krebs, & M. Smith (Eds.), *Sociobiology and psychology: Ideas, issues, and applications* (pp. 335–352). Hillsdale, NJ: Erlbaum.

Buss, D. (1989). Sex differences in human mate preferences: evolutionary hypotheses tested in 37 cultures. *Behavioral and brain sciences 12,* 1–49.

Buss, D. (1994). *Evolution of desire: Strategies of human mating.* New York: Basic Books.

Buss, D., & Schmitt, D. P. (1993). Sexual strategies theory: An evolutionary perspective on human mating. *Psychological Review 100,* 204–232.

Calasanti, T. M., & Bailey, C. A. (1991). Gender inequality and division of household labor in the United States and Sweden: A socialist–feminist approach. *Social Problem 38,* 34–53.

Caldwell, J. C. (1982). *Theory of fertility decline* New York: Academic Press.

Calvin, W. H. (1990). *The ascent of mind* New York: Bantam.

Campbell, J. (1991). *The Masks of God* New York: Viking Penguin.

Cashdan, E. (1993). Attracting mates: Effects of paternal investment on mate attraction strategies. *Ethology & Sociobiology 14,* 1–24.

Chagnon, N. (1977). *Yanomamo.* New York: Holt, Rinehart and Winston.

Chance, N. (1984). *China's urban villages.* New York: Holt, Rinehart and Winston.

Chaucer, G. (1960). *Canterbury Tales* (trans. V. F. Hopper). Great Neck, NY: Barron's.

Cherlin, A. (1988). *The changing American family and public policy.* Washington, DC: The Urban Institute Press.

Cherlin, A., & McCarthy, J. (1985). Remarried couple households: Data from the June 1980 current population survey. *Journal of Marriage and the Family 47,* 23–30.

Chesler, P. (1986). *Mothers on trial.* San Diego: McGraw-Hill.

Chilton, R. J., & Markle, G. E. (1972). Family disruption, delinquent conduct, and the effects of subclassification. *American Sociological Review 47,* 114–129.

Clarke-Stewart, K. A. (1978). And Daddy makes three: The father's impact on mother and young child. *Child Development 49,* 466–478.

Clary, M. (1982). *Daddy's home: The personal story of a modern father who opted to raise the baby and master the craft of motherhood.* New York: Seaview Books.

Cochrane, R. (1995). Mental health among minorities and immigrants in Britain. In I. Allssa (Ed.), *Handbook of mental illness: An international perspective* (pp. 347–360). Madison, CT: International Universities Press.

Cochrane, S. H. (1983). Effects of education and urbanization on fertility. In R. A. Bulatao, R. D. Lee, P. E. Hollerbach, & J. Bongaarts, (Eds.) *Determinants in developing countries* (pp. 587–613). New York: Academic Press.

Colman, A., & Colman, L. (1988). *The father: Mythology and changing roles.* Wilmette, IL: Chiron Pub.

Coltrane, S., & Ishii-Kuntz, M. (1992). Men's housework: A life-course perspective *Journal of Marriage and the Family 54,* 43–57.

Cook, S. E. (1993). Retention of primary preferences after secondary filial imprinting. *Animal Behaviour 46,* 405–407.

Cooley, C. H. (1964). *Human nature and the social order* New York: Schocken.

Coolsen, P. (1993). Half full or half empty: Family in society: *The Journal of Contemporary Human Services 74,* 3.

Coon, C. S. (1971). *The hunting peoples.* Harmondsworth, UK: Penguin.

Coverman, S., & Sheley, J. F. (1986). Change in men's housework and child-care time, 1965–1975. *Journal of Marriage and the Family 48,* 413–422.

Craig, G. J. (1992). *Human Development* (6th ed.). Englewood Cliffs, NJ: Prentice Hall.

Crittenden, R. (1985 August). Two cheers for the "New Fathers." *McCalls,* 142.

Crockenberg, S., & McCluskey, K. (1986). Change in maternal behavior during the baby's first year of life. *Child Development 57,* 746–753.

Cross-National Collaborative Group. (1992). The changing rate of major depression: Cross-national comparisons. *JAMA 268,* 3098–3105.

Crowder, A. (1995). *Opening the door: A treatment model for therapy with male survivors of sexual abuse* New York: Brunner/Mazel.

Cuomo, M. (1993, November 14). *This week with David Brinkley.*

Cutright, P. (1986). Child support and responsible male procreative behavior. *Sociological Focus 19,* 27–45.

Daly, M., & Wilson, M. I. (1982). Homicide and kinship. *American Anthropologist 84,* 372–378.

Daly, M., & Wilson, M. I. (1985). Child abuse and others risks of not living with both parents. *Ethology and Sociobiology 6,* 197–210.

Daly, M., & Wilson, M. I. (1987). Evolutionary psychology and family violence. In C. Crawford, M. Smith, & D. Krebs (Eds.), *Sociobiology and psychology: Ideas, issues and applications* (pp. 293–310). Hillsdale, NJ: Erlbaum.

Daly, M., & Wilson, M. I. (1988). *Homicide.* New York: Aldine De Gruyter.

Daniels-Mohring, D., & Berger, M. (1984). Social network changes and the adjustment to divorce. *Journal of Divorce 8,* 17–32.

Davis, K. (1945). The world demographic transition. *Annals of the American Academy of Political and Social Sciences 237,* 1–11.

Dawson, D. A. (1991). Family structure and children's health and well-being: Data from the 1988 National Health Interview Survey on Child Health. *Journal of Marriage and the Family 53,* 573–582.

Dawkins, R. (1976). *The selfish gene.* Oxford, UK: Oxford University Press.

Dawkins, R. (1982). *The extended phenotype.* Oxford, UK: W. H. Freeman.

Day, R. D., & Mackey, W. C. (1981). Redivorce following remarriage: A re-evaluation. *Journal of Divorce 4,* 39–48.

Day, R., & Mackey, W. C. (1986). Children as resources: A cultural analysis. *Family Perspective 20*, 251–264.

Day, R., & Mackey, W. C. (1986). The role image of the American father: An examination of a media myth. *Journal of Comparative Family Studies 17*, 371–388.

Deag, J., & Crook, J. H. (1970). Social behavior and agonistic buffering in the wild Barbary macaque (*Macaca sylvana L.*) *Folia Primat. 15*, 183–200.

Demos, J. (1986). *Past, present, and personal: The family and the life course in American history* New York: Oxford University Press.

Deutsch, F. M., Lussier, J. B. & Servis, L. J. (1993). Husbands at home: Predictors of paternal participation in childcare and housework. *Journal of Personality and Social Psychology 65*, 1154–1166.

De Waal, F.B.M. (1983). *Chimpanzee politics* New York: Harper and Row.

De Waal, F.B.M. (1995). Bonobo sex and society. *Scientific American 272*, 82–88.

DeYoung, M. (1982). *The sexual victimization of children.* Jefferson, NC: McFarland and Co.

Dickemann, M. (1979). Female infancticide, reproductive strategies and social stratification: A preliminary model. In N. Chagnon & W. Irons (Eds.), *Evolutionary biology and human social behavior: An anthropological perspective* pp. (21–367). North Scituate, MA: Duxbury Press.

Divale, W., & Harris, M. (1976). Population, warfare, and the male supremacist complex. *American Anthropologist 78*, 521–538.

Division of STD/HIV Prevention (1990). *Division of STD/HIV Prevention Annual Report* Atlanta: U.S. Dept. of Health & Human Services, Public Health Service, Centers for Disease Control.

Dobie, J. F. (1949). *The voice of the coyote.* Boston: Little, Brown, & Co.

Dodson, F. (1974). *How to fathers: The first truly comprehensive guide for fathers that every mother should read!* Los Angeles: Nash.

Dollard, J., & Miller, N. E. (1950). *Personality and Psychotherapy: An analysis in terms of learning, thinking and culture* New York: McGraw-Hill.

Douglas, M. (1978). *Purity and danger: An analysis of concepts of pollution and danger* New York: Routledge & Kegan.

Draper, P., & Harpending, H. (1982). Father absence and reproductive strategy: An evolutionary perspective. *Journal of Anthropological Research 38*, 255–272.

Durham, W. H. (1979). Toward a coevolutionary theory of human biology and culture. In N. Chagnon & W. Irons (Eds.), *Evolutionary biology and human social behavior* (pp. 39–58). North Scituate, MA: Duxbury Press.

Durham, W. H. (1990). Advances in evolutionary culture theory. *Annual Review of Anthropology 19*, 187–210.

Durie, M. H. (1995). Mental health patterns for the New Zealand Maori. In I. Al-lssa (Ed.) *Handbook of culture and mental illness: An international perspective* (pp. 331–364). Madison, CT: International Universities Press.

Earls, F. (1976). The fathers (not the mothers): their importance and influence with infants and young children. *Psychiatry 39*, 209–224.

Easterlin, R. A., & Crimmins, E. M. (1985). *The fertility revolution: A supply-demand analysis.* Chicago: University of Chicago Press.

Eibl-Eibesfeldt, I. (1975). *Ethology: The biology of behavior.* New York: Holt, Rinehart, & Winston.

Ekman, P. (1973). Darwin and cross-cultural studies of facial expression. In P. Ekman (Ed.), *Darwin and facial expression: A century of research in review* (pp. 1–83). New York: Academic Press.

Ekman, P. (1980). *The face of man* New York: Garland Press.

Ekvall, R. B. (1968). *Fields on the hoof* New York: Holt, Rinehart & Winston.

Erikson, E. H. (1950). *Childhood and society* New York: Norton.

Erikson, E. H. (1985). *The life cycle completed* New York: Norton.

Eysenck, H. J. (1952). The effects of psychotherapy: An evaluation. *Journal of Consulting Psychology 16,* 319–324.

Fagot, B. I. (1973). Sex-related stereotyping of toddlers' behaviors. *Developmental Psychology 9,* 429.

False Memory Syndrome Foundation (1994). *Frequently asked questions.* Philadelphia, PA: FSM Foundation.

Fasteau, M. F. (1976). Men as parents. In D. S. David & R. Brannon (Eds.), *The forty-nine percent majority: The male sex role* (pp. 5–49). Reading, MA: Addison-Wesley.

Fawcett, J. (1983). Perceptions of the value of children: Satisfaction and costs. In *Determinants of fertility in developing countries* (pp. 429–444). R. A. Bulatao et al., (Eds.) New York: Academic Press.

Fein, R. (1978). Research on fathering: Social policy and an emergent perspective *Journal of Social Issues 34,* 122–135.

Festinger, L. (1964). *Conflict, decision, and dissonance* Stanford, CA: Stanford University Press.

Fisher, H. (1983). *The sex contract: The evolution of human behavior* New York: Quill.

Fisher, H. (1992). *Anatomy of love: The natural history of monogamy, adultery, and divorce* New York: Norton.

Foss, E. M. (1961–1969). *Determinants of infant behavior (Vol. I–IV).* London: Metheun.

Fox, R. (1978). *The Tory Islanders: A people of the Celtic fringe* New York: Cambridge University Press.

Fox, R. (1980). *The red lamp of incest.* New York: Dutton.

Fraser, S. (Ed.). (1995). *Bell curve wars: Race, intelligence and the future of America.* New York: Basic Books.

Freedman, D. G. (1974). *Human infancy: An evolutionary perspective.* Hillsdale, NJ: Erlbaum.

Freedman, D. G. (1979). *Human sociobiology: A holistic approach.* New York: The Free Press.

Freeman, D. (1983). *Margaret Mead and Samoa.* Cambridge, MA: Harvard University Press.

Freeman, R. B. (1975). Crime and unemployment. In J. Q. Wilson (Ed.), *Crime and public policy* (pp. 89–106). San Francisco: Institute for Contemporary Studies.

Freud, S. (1964). *The standard edition of the complete psychological works of Sigmund Freud* (James Strachey, trans. and Ed.). London: Hogarth.

Frontline (1995, April 12). *Divided Memories.* New York: Public Broadcasting Service.

Frontline (1995, May 15). Deadbeat Dads. *The Vanishing Father.* New York: Public Broadcasting Service.

Furstenberg, F. F. Jr. (1987). The new extended family: The experience of parents and children after remarriage. In K. Pasley & M. Ihinger-Tallman (Ed.) *Remarriage and stepparenting: Current research and theory* (pp. 42–62). New York: Guilford.

Furstenberg, F. F. Jr. (1988). Good dads–bad dads: Two faces of fatherhood. In A. Cherlin (Ed.), *The Changing American Family and Public Policy* (pp. 193–218). Washington, DC: The Urban Institute Press.

Furstenberg, F. F. Jr., Morgan, S. P., & Allison, P. D. (1987). Paternal participation and children's well-being after marital dissolution. *American Sociological Review 52,* 511–518.

Gangestad, S. W., & Simpson, J. A. (1990). Toward an evolutionary history of female sociosexual variation. *Journal of Personality 58,* 69–90.

Garbarino, J. (1986). Can American families afford the luxury of childhood? *Child Welfare 65,* 119–128.

Garbarino, J. (1993). Reinventing Fatherhood. *Families in Society: The Journal of Contemporary Human Services* (January), 51–54.

Garcia, J., & Koelling, R. A. (1966). Learning with prolonged delay of reinforcement. *Psychonomic Science 5*, 121–122.

Garfinkel, I., & McLanahan, S. S. (1986). *Single mothers and their children: A new American dilemma.* Washington, DC: The Urban Institute Press.

Geertz, C. (Ed.). (1974), *Myth, symbol, and culture* New York: Norton.

Gerstel, N., Riessman, C. K., & Rosenfeld, S. (1985). Explaining the symptomatology of separated and divorced women and men: The role of material conditions and social networks. *Social Forces 64*, 84–101.

Gil, D. G. (1970). *Violence against children.* Cambridge, MA: Harvard University Press.

Gilder, G. (1974). *Naked nomads: Unmarried men in American* New York: The New York Times Book Company.

Gilder, G. (1993). *Men and Marriage* Gretna, LA: Pelican.

Gillespie, R. W. (1975). *Economic factors in crime and delinquency: A critical review of the empirical evidence* Washington, DC: National Institute Law Enforcement and Criminal Justice.

Giveans, D. L., & Robinson, M. K. (1985). Fathers and the pre-school age child. In S.M.H. Hanson & F. W. Bozett (Ed.). Beverly Hills, CA: Sage.

Glenn, N. D., & Supancic, M. (1984). The social and demographic correlates of divorce and separation in the United States: An update and reconsideration. *Journal of Marriage and the Family 46*, 563–575.

Golinkoff, R. M., & Ames, G. H. (1979). A comparison of father's and mother's speech with their young children. *Child Development 50*, 28–52.

Goodall, J. (1986). *The Chimpanzees at Gombe* Cambridge, MA: Belknap.

Goode, W. J. (1970). *World revolution and family patterns* New York: The Free Press.

Gordon, M., & Creighton, S. J. (1988). Natal and non-natal fathers as sexual abusers in the United Kingdom: A comparative analysis. *Journal of Marriage and the Family 50*, 99–105.

Gray, J. (1994). *Men are from Mars; Women are from Venus* New York: HarperCollins.

Greenberg, M. (1985). *The birth of a father.* New York: Continuum.

Greene, B. (1984). *Good morning, merry sunshine: A father's journal of his child's first year* New York: Atheneum.

Greene, T. A. (1967). *Modern man in search of manhood* (pp. 9–23). New York: Association.

Greer, G. (1971). *The female eunuch* New York: McGraw-Hill.

Greer, G. (1990). *Daddy, we hardly knew you.* New York: Knopf.

Greif, G. L. (1985). Single fathers rearing children. *Journal of Marriage and the Family 47*, 185–191.

Griswold, R. L. (1993). *Fatherhood in America: A history* New York: Basic Books.

Gubernick, D. J., & Klopfer, P. H. (Eds.). (1981). *Parental care in mammals.* New York: Plenum.

Guggisberg, C.A.W. (1963). *Simba: The life of the lion.* Philadelphia: Chilton Books.

Gutman, L. T., & Wilfert, C. M. (1990). Gonococcal diseases in infants and children. In K. K. Holmes, P. Mardh, P. F. Sparling & P. J. Wiesner (Eds.). *Sexually Transmitted Diseases* (pp. 803–810). New York: McGraw-Hill.

Haas, L. (1990). Gender equality and social policy: Implications of a study of parental involvement in Sweden. *Journal of Family Issues 11*, 401–423.

Haldane, J. B. (1932). *The cause of evolution* New York: Longmans, Green & Co.

Hall, E. T. (1961). A system for the notation of proxemic behavior. *American Anthropologist 65*, 1003–1026.

Hall, E. T. (1969). *Hidden Dimension* New York: Doubleday.

Hall, E. T. (1973). *Silent Language* New York: Doubleday.

Hall, R. (Ed.). (1985). *Sexual dimorphism in Homo sapiens: A question of size.* New York: Praeger.

Hamburg, D. (1963). Emotions in perspective of human evolution evolution. In P. Knapp (Ed.), *Expression of emotions in man* (pp. 300–317). New York: International Universities Press.

Hames, R. B. (1988). The allocation of parental care among the Ye'kwana. In *Human reproductive behaviour: A Darwinian perspective.* L. Betzig, M. Borgerhoff-Mulder, & P. Turke (Eds.), New York: Cambridge University Press.

Hamilton, M. L. (1977). *Father's influence on children.* Chicago: Nelson.

Hamilton, W. D. (1964). The genetical evolution of social behaviour, Parts 1 and 2. *Journal of Theoretical Biology 7,* 1–52.

Handwerker, W. P. (1986). The modern demographic transition: An analysis of subsistence choices and reproductive consequences. *American Anthropologist 88,* 400–417.

Hanson, S.M.H., & Bozett, F. W. (Ed.) (1985). *Dimensions of fatherhood* Beverly Hills, CA: Sage.

Hanson, T. L., McLanahan, S., & Thomson, E. (1996). Double jeopardy: Parental conflict and stepfamily outcomes for children. *Journal of Marriage and the Family 58,* 141–154.

Hardin, G. (1968). The tragedy of the commons. *Science 162,* 1243–1248.

Harlow, H. (1971). *Learning to love* (pp. 63–64). San Francisco: Albion.

Harris, M. (1974a). *Cows, pigs, wars, and witches* New York: Random House.

Harris, M. (1974b). Why a perfect knowledge of all the rules one must know to act like a native cannot lead to the knowledge of how natives act. *Journal of Anthropological Research 30,* 242–251.

Harris, M. (1977). *Cannibals and kings: The origin of cultures* New York: Random House.

Harris, M. (1979). *Cultural materialism* New York: Random House.

Harris, M. (1981). *America now: The emergence of a changing culture.* New York: Simon and Schuster.

Harris, K. M., & Morgan, S. P. (1991). Fathers, sons, and daughters: Differential paternal involvement in parenting. *Journal of Marriage and the Family 53,* 531–544.

Hart, C.W.M., & Pilling, A. R. (1960). *The Tiwi of North Australia* New York: Holt, Rinehart & Winston.

Hartley, S. F. (1975). *Illegitimacy.* Berkeley, CA: University of California Press.

Hausfater, G., & Hrdy, S. B. (1984). *Infanticide: Comparative & evolutionary perspectives* Chicago: Aldine.

Healy, J. M., Jr., Malley, J. E., & Stewart, A. J. (1990). Children and their fathers after separation. *American Journal of Orthopsychiatry 60,* 531–543.

Heath, D. H. (1978). What meaning and effects does fatherhood have for the maturing of professional men? *Merrill-Palmer Quarterly 24,* 265–278.

Heaton, T. B. (1990). Marital stability throughout the child-rearing years. *Demography 27,* 55–63.

Heider, K. (1979). *Grand Valley Dani* New York: Holt, Rinehart, & Winston.

Herrnstein, R., & Murray, C. (1994). *The bell curve.* New York: The Free Press.

Hess, E. (1964). Imprinting in birds. *Science 146,* 1128–1139.

Hetherington, E. M. (1970). A developmental study of the effects of sex of the dominant parent on sex-role preference, and imitation in children. In T. D. Spencer & N. Kass (Eds.), *Perspectives in child psychology* (pp. 232–259). New York: McGraw-Hill.

Hetherington, M. E., Cox, M., & Cox, R. (1979). Divorced fathers. *The Family Coordinator 28,* 417–428.

Hewlett, B. S. (Ed.). (1992). *Father-child relations: Cultural and biosocial contexts* New York: Aldine de Gruyter.

Hinde R. A. (1982). *Ethology: Its nature and relations with other sciences* New York: Oxford University Press.

Hinde, R. A., & Stevenson-Hinde, H. (1973). *Constraints on learning* New York: Academic Press.

Hochschild, A. R. (1989). *The Second Shift: Working parents and the revolution at home.* New York: Viking.

Hoffman, C., & Teyber, E. C. (1985). Naturalistic observations of sex differences in adults and boys of different ages. *Merrill-Palmer Quarterly 31,* 93–97.

Hoffman, L. W., & Manis, J. D. (1979). The value of children in the United States: A new approach to the study of fertility. *Journal of Marriage and the Family 41,* 583–598.

Hoffman, S. (1977). Marital instability and the economic status of women. *Demography 14,* 67–77.

Hollingshead, A. B. (1949). *Elmtown's youth* New York: Wiley.

Hollingshead, A. B. (1975). *Elmtown revisited* New York: Wiley.

Hook, E. E., & Handsfield, H. H. (1990). Gonococcal infections in the adult. In K. K. Holmes, P. Mardh, P. F. Sparling, & P. J. Wiesner (Eds.). *Sexually Transmitted Diseases,* (pp. 821–842). New York: McGraw-Hill.

Hrdy, S. (1977). *Langurs of Abu: female and male strategies of reproduction* Cambridge, MA: Harvard University Press.

Hrdy, S. (1981). *The woman that never evolved* Cambridge, MA: Harvard University Press.

Huber, J. (1980). Will U.S. fertility decline toward zero? *The Sociological Quarterly 21,* 481–492.

Human Relations Area Files (1949). *HRAF.* New Haven, CT: HRAF Press.

Hunter, D. E., & Whitten, P. (Eds.), (1976). *Encyclopedia of anthropology.* New York: Harper and Row.

Hurlock, E. B. (1980). *Developmental psychology: A life-span approach* (5th ed.), New York: McGraw-Hill.

Immelmann, K., Barlow, G. W., Petrinovich, L., & Main, M. (Eds.). (1981). *Behavioral development* New York: Cambridge University Press.

Ingold, T., Riches, D., & Woodburn, J. (Eds.) (1988). *Hunters and gatherers, Vol. I: History, evolution and social change* New York: Berg.

International Labour Office (1986–1991). *Yearbook of Labour Statistics, (46th–50th ed.),* Geneva, Switzerland: International Labour Office.

Itani, I. (1963). Paternal care in the wild Japanese monkey (Macaca fuscata). In C. H. Southwich (Ed.), *Primate social behavior* (pp. 91–97). New York: Van Nostrand.

Jacobs, J. W. (1982). Effect of divorce on fathers: An overview of the literature. *American Journal of Psychiatry 139,* 1235–1241.

JAMA (1995). Ectopic pregnancy—United States, 1990–1992. *Journal of the American Medical Association 273,* 532.

Jankowiak, W. (1992). Father-child relations in urban China. In B. S. Hewlett (Ed.), *Father-child relations: Cultural and biosocial contexts* (pp. 345–363). New York: Aldine de Gruyter.

Jensen, A. R. (1972). *Genetics and education* (pp. 104–114). New York: Harpers & Row.

Johnson, C. L. (1974). *Child abuse in the Southeast* Athens, GA: Regional Institute of Social Welfare Research, University of Georgia.

Johanson, C. D., & White, T. (1980). A systematic assessment of early African hominids. *Science 203,* 321–329.

Jolly, A. (1972). *The evolution of primate behavior* New York: Macmillan.

Jung, C. G. (1955). *Modern man in search of a soul* New York: Harcourt Brace.

Jung, C. G. (1969). *Man and his symbols* New York: Doubleday.

Justice, B., & Justice, R. (1979). *The broken taboo* New York: Human Sciences Press.

Kahn, G., & Goldman, E. (1991). Munchausen syndrome by proxy: Mother fabricates infant hearing impairment. *Journal of Speech and Hearing research 34,* 957–959.

Kawai, M. (1958). On the system of social ranks in a natural troop of Japanese monkeys: Basic rank and dependent rank. *Primates 1,* 131–148.

Kellam, S. G., Ensminger, M. E., & Turner, J. (1977). Family structure and the mental health of children. *Archives of General Psychiatry 34,* 1012–1022.

Kimball, G. (1988). *50-50 parenting.* Lexington, MA: Lexington Books.

King, G. (1980). Alternative uses of primates and carnivores in the reconstruction of early hominid behavior. *Ethology and Sociobiology 1,* 99–110.

Kitson, G. C. (1982). Attachment to the spouse in divorce: A scale and its application. *Journal of Marriage and the Family 44,* 379–393.

Kleiman, D. G. (1977). Monogamy in mammals. *Quarterly Review of Biology 52,* 39–69.

Kleiman, D. G. (1981). The evolution of male parental investment in mammals. In D. J. Gubernick & P. H. Klopfer (Eds.) *Parental care in mammals* (pp. 232–265). New York: Plenum.

Koch, M.A.P., & Lowery, C. (1984). Visitation and the noncustodial father. *Journal of Divorce 68,* 47–65.

Koestner, R., Franz, C., & Weinberger, J. (1990). The family origins of empathic concern: a 26-year longitudinal study. *Journal of Personality and Social Psychology 58,* 709–717.

Kohlberg, L. (1981). *The philosophy of moral development* New York: Harper Row.

Kort, C., & R. Friedland (Eds.). (1986). *Father's book: shared experiences* Boston, MA: G. K. Hall.

Kruuk, H. (1972). *The spotted hyena: A study of predation and social behavior* Chicago: University of Chicago Press.

Kuhme, W. (1965). Communal food distribution and division of labour in African hunting dogs, *Nature 205,* 443–444.

Kummer, H. (1968). *Social organization of Hamadryas baboons* Chicago: University of Chicago Press.

Kurland, J. A. (1979). Paternity, mother's brother and human sociality. In *Evolutionary biology and human social behavior: An anthropological perspective* (pp. 145–180). North Scituate, MA: Duxbury Press.

Laing, R. D. (1967). *The politics of experience* New York: Ballantine.

Lamb, M. E. (Ed.). (1976). *The role of the father in child development* New York: Wiley.

Lamb, M. E. (Ed.). (1981). *The role of the father in child development (2nd ed),* New York: Wiley.

Lamb, M. E. (1982, October). Why Swedish fathers aren't liberated. *Psychology Today* 74–77.

Lamb, M. E. (1987). *The father's role: Cross-cultural perspectives.* Hillsdale, NJ: Erlbaum.

Lamb, M. E., & Levine, J. A. (1983). The Swedish parental insurance policy: An experiment in social engineering. In M. E. Lamb & A. Sagi (Eds.), *Fatherhood and family policy* (pp. 39–57). Hillsdale, NJ: Erlbaum.

Lamb, M. E., Pleck, J. H., & Levine, J. A. (1987). Effects of increased paternal involvement on fathers and mothers. In C. Lewis & M. O'Brien (Eds.), *Reassessing fatherhood: New observations on fathers and the modern family* (pp. 110–125). Beverly Hills, CA: Sage.

Landers, A. (1976, May). If you had it to do over again—would you have children? *Good Housekeeping,* 100–101.

LaRossa, R. (1988). Fatherhood and social change. *Family Relations 37*, 451–457.

LaRossa, R., & Reitzes, D. C. (1993). Continuity and change in middle class fatherhood, 1925–1939: The culture-conduct connection. *Journal of Marriage and the Family 55*, 455–468.

LaRossa, R., Gordon, B. A., Wilson, R. J., Bairan, A., & Jaret, C. (1991). The fluctuating image of the 20th century American father. *Journal of Marriage and the Family 53*, 987–997.

Lawick, H. van, & Lawick-Goodall, J. van (1971). *Innocent killers* Boston: Houghton Mifflin.

Leach, E. (1982). *Social Anthropology.* Glasgow: Fontana.

Leakey, R., & Lewin, R. (1992). *Origins reconsidered: In search of what makes us human* New York: Doubleday.

Lee, R. B., & DeVore, I. (Eds.). (1968). *Man in the hunter* Chicago: Aldine.

Lee, R. B. (1982). Eating Christmas in the Kalahari. In J. P. Spradley & D. W. McCurdy (Eds.). *Conformity and conflict* (pp. 14–21). Boston: Little Brown, and Co.

Lee-Peng, K., & Wing-Foo, T. (1995). Culture and mental illness in Singapore: A socio-cultural perspective. In I. Al-lssa (Ed.). *Handbook of culture and mental illness: An international perspective* (pp. 159–168). Madison, CT: International Universities Press.

Leland, K. N. (1994). On the evolutionary consequences of sexual imprinting. *Evolution 48*, 477–489.

LeMasters, E. E. (1974). *Parents in modern America* Homewood, IL: The Dorsey Press.

Lenington, S. (1981). Child abuse: The limits of sociobiology. *Ethology & Sociobiology 2*, 17–29.

Leon, A. C., Klerman, G. L., & Wickramaratne, P. (1993). Continuing female predominance in depressive illness. *American Journal of Public Health 83*, 754–757.

Levant, R., & Kelly, J. (1989). *Between father and child: How to become the kind of father you want to be* New York: Viking.

Levine, J. A. (1976). *Who will raise the children? New options for fathers (and Mothers)* New York: Lippincott.

Levinson, D., & Malone, M. J. (1980). *Toward explaining human culture: A critical review of the findings of worldwide cross-cultural research* New Haven, CT: HRAF Press.

Levi-Strauss, C. (1963). *Structural Anthropology* New York: Basic Books.

Levi-Strauss, C. (1979). *Myth & Meaning* New York: Schocken.

Levy-Shiff, R., & Israelashvili, R. (1988). Antecedents of fathering: Some further exploration. *Developmental Psychology 24*, 434–440.

Lewis, C., & O'Brien, M. (Eds). (1987). *Reassessing fatherhood: New observations on fathers and the modern family* Beverly Hills, CA: Sage.

Lewis, C. (1986). *Becoming a father.* Philadelphia: Open University Press.

Lindsey, D. (1994). *The welfare of children.* New York: Oxford University Press.

Low, B. S. (1994). Men in the demographic transition. *Human Nature 5*, 223–253.

Lorenz, K. (1958). The evolution of behavior. *Scientific American 199*, 67–78.

Lorenz, K. (1965). *Evolution and modification of behavior* Chicago: University of Chicago Press.

Louv, R. (1990). *Childhood's future: Listening to the American new hope for the next generation.* Boston, MA: Houghton Mifflin.

Louv, R. (1994, December). Remaking fatherhood. *Parents* 180–183.

Lovejoy, C. O. (1981). The origin of man. *Science 211*, 341–359.

Luepnitz, D. A. (1982). *Child Custody.* New York: Lexington.

Lurie, S. (1992). The history of the diagnosis and treatment of ectopic pregnancy: A medical adventure. *European Journal of Obstetrics & Gynecology and Reproductive Biology 43*, 1–7.

Lynn, D. B.(1974). *The father: His role in child development* Monterey, CA: Brooks/Cole.

Lynn, D. B., & Sawrey, W. L. (1959). The effects of father-absence on Norwegian boys and girls. *Journal of Abnormal and Social Psychology, 59*, 258–262.

Lyon, B. E., Montgomerie, R. D., & Hamilton, L. D. (1987). Male parental care and monogamy in snow buntings. *Behavioral Ecology Sociobiology, 20*, 377–382.

MacArthur, R. H., & Wilson, E. O. (1967). *The theory of island bio-geography* Princeton, NJ: Princeton University Press.

Maccoby, E. E., & Jacklin, C. N. (1974). *The psychology of sex differences* Stanford, CA: Stanford University Press.

Maccoby, E. E., & Mnookin, R. H. (1992). *Diving the child: Social and legal dilemmas of custody*. Cambridge, MA: Harvard University Press.

MacDermid, S. M., Huston, T. L., & Mchale, S. M. (1990). Changes in marriage associated with the transition to parenthood: Individual differences as a function of sex-role attitudes and changes in the division of household labor. *Journal of Marriage and the Family, 52*, 475–486.

Mackey, W. C. (1976). The adult male-child bond: An example of convergent evolution. *Journal of Anthropological Research, 32*, 58–73.

Mackey, W. C. (1980). A sociobiological perspective on divorce patterns of men in the United States. *Journal of Anthropological Research, 36*, 419–430.

Mackey, W. C. (1981). A cross-cultural analysis of adult–child proxemics in relation to the plowman-protector complex: A preliminary study. *Behavior Science Research, 16*, 187–223.

Mackey, W. C. (1985). *Fathering Behaviors: The dynamics of the man-child bond.* New York: Plenum.

Mackey, W. C. (1986). A facet of the man-child bond: The teeter-totter effect. *Ethology and Sociobiology, 7*, 117–135.

Mackey, W. C. (1988). Patterns of adult-child associations in 18 cultures: An index of the "nuclear family". *Journal of Contemporary Family Studies, 19*, 69–84.

Mackey, W. C. (1993). Marital dissolution by sex of the petitioner: A test of the man-child affiliative bond. *Journal of Genetic Psychology, 154*, 353–362.

Mackey, W. C. (1995). Oppression or protection? The "double standard" reconsidered. *Family in America, 9*, 5–8.

Mackey, W. C., & White, U. (1993). The abrading of the American father. *Family in America, 7*, 1–6.

Mackey, W. C., White, U., & Day, R. D. (1992). Reasons American men become fathers: Men's divulgences, women's perceptions. *Journal of Genetic Psychology, 153*, 435–446.

Maclachlan, M. D. (1983). *Why they did not starve*. Philadelphia: Ishi.

MacRoberts, M. (1970). The social organization of Barbary apes (*M. Sylvana*) on Gibraltar. *American Journal of Physical Anthropology, 33*, 83–95.

Main, M., & Weston, D. R. (1981). The quality of the toddler's relationship to mother and to father related to conflict behavior and the readiness to establish new relationships. *Child Development, 52*, 932–940.

Malinowski, B. (1927). *The father in primitive psychology* New York: Norton.

Margolis, M. (1984). *Mothers and Such* New York: Basic Books.

Maynard, J. (1979). Do fathers make good mothers? *Ladies Home Journal 96*, 152–154.

Maynard Smith, J. (1964). Group selection and kin selection. *Nature 20(4924)*, 1145–1147.

Maynard Smith (1975). *The theory of group evolution* (3rd ed.). New York: Harmondsworth, Penguin.

McCall, R. B. (1985, July). The importance of fathers: They're much more than breadwinners—their influence is unique. *Parent,* 120.

McCary, J. L. (1975). Freedom and growth in marriage (p. 289). Santa Barbara, CA: Hamilton.

McLanahan, S., & Booth, K. (1989). Mother-only families: Problems, prospects, and politics. *Journal of Marriage and the Family 51,* 557–580.

McLaughlin, B. (1978). Second look: The mother tongue. *Human Nature 1,* 89.

McLaughlin, B., White, D., McDevitt, T., & Raskin, R. (1983). Mothers' and fathers' speech to their young children: Similar or different? *Journal of Child Language 10,* 245–252.

McLoyd, B. C. (1989). Socialization and development in a changing economy: The effects of paternal job and income loss on children. *American Psychologist 44,* 293–302.

McMahan, P. (1976). The victorious coyote. *Natural history 41,* 42–51.

McNeill, W. H. (1976). *Plagues and peoples.* Garden City, New York: Anchor Press.

Mead, G. H. (1934). *Mind, self, and society* Chicago: University of Chicago Press.

Mead, M. (1963/orig. 1935). *Sex and temperament in three primitive societies.* New York: Morrow.

Mead, M. (1949). *Male and Female* (pp. 185–190). New York: Morrow.

Mead, S. L., & Rekers, G. A. (1979). Role of the father in normal psychosexual development. *Psychology Reports 45,* 923–931.

Mech, L. D. (1966). *The wolves of Isle Royale* Washington DC: Government Printing Office.

Mech, L. D. (1970). *The wolf* Garden City, New York: Natural History Press.

Merton, R. K. (1957). *Social theory and social structure* New York: Free Press.

Miller, E. M. (1993). Could r selection account for the African personality and life cycle? *Personality & Individual Differences 15,* 665–675.

Millett, K. (1978). *Sexual politics* New York: Ballantine.

Minorbrook, S. (1994). *U.S. News & World Report* 1/17, p.37.

Mischel, W. (1961a). Father-absence and delay of gratification: Cross-cultural comparisons. *Journal of Abnormal and Social Psychology 52,* 116–124.

Mischel, W. (1961b). Preference for delayed reinforcement and social responsibility. *Journal of Abnormal and Social Psychology 62,* 1–7.

Mock, D. W., & Fujioka, M. (1990). Monogamy and long-term pair bonding in vertebrates. *Trends in Ecology and Evolution 5,* 39–43.

Moehlman, P. D. (1980). Jackals of the Serengeti. *National Geographic 153,* 840–843.

Monahan, T. P. (1972). Family status and the delinquent child: A reappraisal and some new findings. *Social Forces 35,* 250–258.

Moore, D. E., & Cates, Jr., W. (1990). Sexually transmitted diseases and infertility. In K. K. Holmes, P. Mardh, P. F. Sparling, & P. J. Wiesner (Eds.). *Sexually transmitted diseases* (pp. 763–770). New York: McGraw-Hill.

Moore, F. (Ed.). (1961), *Readings in cross-cultural methodology* New Haven, CT: HRAF Press.

Mosher, L. R. (1969). Father absence and antisocial behavior in Negro and White males. *Acta Paedopsychiatrica 36,* 186–202.

Mosher, W. D., & Aral, S. O. (1985). Factors related to infertility in the United States 1965–1976. *Sexually Transmitted Diseases 12,* 117–125.

Mowat, F. (1963). *Never cry wolf* (pp. 96–108). Boston: Little, Brown, and Co.

Murdock, G. P. (1937). Comparative data on the division of labor by sex. *Social Forces 15,* 552.

Murdock, G. P. (1957). World ethnographic sample. *American Anthropologist 59,* 664–687.

Murdock, G. P. (1967). Ethnographic Atlas. *Ethnology 6*, 109–236.

Murdock, G. P., & Provost, C. (1973). Factors in the division of labor by sex: A cross-cultural analysis. *Ethnology 12*, 203–225.

Murie, A. (1944). *The wolves of Mount McKinley* Washington, DC: US Government Printing Office.

Murphy, J. M. (1976). Psychiatric labeling in cross-cultural perspective. *Science 191*, 1019–1028.

Murray, C. (1984). *Losing ground: American social policy, 1950–1980* New York: Basic Books.

Nag, M., White, B., & Peet, R. C. (1978). An anthropological approach to the study of the economic value of children in Java and Nepal. *Current Anthropology 19*, 293–306.

Nakhaie, M. R. (1995). Housework in Canada: The national picture. *Journal of Comparative Family Studies 26*, 417–422.

Nam, C. B. (1968). *Population and society* Boston: Houghton Mifflin Co.

Nash, J. (1965). The father in contemporary culture and current psychological literature. *Child Development 36*, 260–297.

Nash, J. (1976). Historical and social changes in the perception of the role of the father. In M. E. Lamb (Ed.). *The role of the father in child development* (pp. 62–68). New York: Wiley.

National Center for Health Statistics (1960–1991). *Vital statistics of the United States (marriage and divorce)*. Washington, DC: US Government Printing Office.

National Center for Health Statistics (1989). Children of divorce. *Vital and health statistics*. Series 21. #46. DHHS Pub. No. (PHS) 8901924. Public Health Service. Washington, DC: US Government Printing Office.

Neal, A. G., Groat, H. T., & Wicks, J. W. (1989). Attitudes about having children: A study of 600 couples in the early years of marriage. *Journal of Marriage and the Family 51*, 313–328.

Newman, P. L. (1982). When technology fails: Magic and religion in New Guinea. In J. P. Spradley & D. W. McCurdy, (Ed.), *Conformity and Conflict* (5th ed.) (pp. 300–309). Boston: Little, Brown, and Co.

Newsweek. (1989, July 31). Woman's work is never done: a stinging new study of two-career families, 65–67.

Newsweek (1993, August 30). A world without fathers: The struggle to save the black family, 18–28.

Nielsen, F. (1994). Sociobiology and sociology. *Annual Review of Sociology 20*, 267–303.

Ninio, A., & Rinott, N. (1988). Parents and their attributions of cognitive competence to infants. *Child Development 59*, 652–663.

Norbeck, E. (1976). *Changing Japan* (2nd. ed.). New York: Holt, Rinehart & Winston.

O'Campo, A., Gielen, C., Faden, R. R., Xue, X., Kass, N., & Want, M. (1995). Violence by male partners against women during the childbearing years: A contextual analysis. *American Journal of Public Health 85*, 1092–1097.

Osherson, S. (1986). *Finding our fathers: the unfinished business of manhood* New York: The Free Press.

Osofsky, J. D., & O'Connell, E. J. (1972). Parent-child interaction: Daughters' effects upon mothers' and fathers' behaviors. *Developmental Psychology 7*, 157–168.

Osofsky, J. D., & Osofsky, H. J. (1984). Psychological and developmental perspectives on expectant and new parenthood. In R. D. Parke (Ed.), *Review of child development research* (Vol. 7). Chicago: University of Chicago Press.

Packer, C., Collins, D. A., Sindimwo, A., & Goodall, J. (1995). Reproductive constraints on aggressive competition in female baboons. *Nature 373*, 60–63.

Page, C. (1994). *The McLaughlin Group*. 1/14/94.

Pakizegi, B. (1978). The interaction of mothers and fathers with their sons. *Child Development 49*, 479–482.

Palkovitz, R. J. (1987). Father-baby bonding. *Enquiry 7*, 6–9.

Papalia, D. E., & Olds, S. W. (1992). *Human Development* (5th ed.) New York: McGraw-Hill.

Parke, R. D. (1979a, April). The father of the child. *The Sciences 19*, 12–15.

Parke, R. D. (1979b). Perspectives on father-infant interaction. In J. D. Osofsky (Ed.), *The handbook of infant development* (pp. 549–590). New York: Wiley.

Parke, R. D. (1988). Foreword. P. Bronstein & C. P. Cowan (Eds.), In *Fatherhood today: Men's changing role in the family* (pp. ix–xii). New York: John Wiley.

Parke, R. D., & Sawin, D. B. (1977, November). Fathering: It's a major role. *Psychology Today.* 109–112.

Parsons, T., & Bales, R. F. (1955). *Family, socialization and interaction process* New York: The Free Press.

Patterson, G. R. (1980). Mothers: The unacknowledged victims. *Monographs of the Society for Research in Child Development* Chicago: University of Chicago Press.

Pearson-West, K. A. (1994). The last common bond. *The Washington Post* 1/9., p. C8.

Pedersen, F. A. (1976). Does research on children reared in father-absent families yield information on father influences? *The Family Coordinator 25*, 459–464.

Pedersen, F. A. (Ed.). (1980). *The father-infant relationship* New York: Praeger.

Pedersen, F. A., & Robson, K. S. (1969). Father participation in infancy. *American Journal of Orthopsychiatry 39:* 466–472.

Peters, D. L., & Stewart, Jr., R. B. (1981). Father-child interactions in a shopping mall: A naturalistic study of father role behavior. *The Journal of Genetic Psychology 138*, 269–278.

Piaget, J. (1966). *The psychology of intelligence.* Totowa, NJ: Littlefield.

Pierce, J. E. (1964). *Life in a Turkish village* New York: Holt, Rinehart & Winston.

Pirani, A. (1989). *The absent father: Crisis and creativity.* New York: Arkana.

Pittman, F. (1993, Sept/Oct). Fathers and sons: What it takes to be a man. *Psychology Today 26*, 52–54.

Playboy (1953–1995). Chicago, IL: Playboy Enterprises.

Pleck, J. H. (1985). *Working wives/working husbands.* Beverly Hills, CA: Sage.

Plomin, R. (1990). The role of inheritance in behavior. *Science 248*, 183–188.

Polatnick, M. (1973). Why men don't rear children: A power analysis. *Berkeley Journal of Sociology 18*, 45–86.

Popenoe, D. (1993). American family decline, 1960–1990: A review and appraisal. *Journal of Marriage and the Family 55*, 527–555.

Popenoe, D. (1996). *Life without father: Compelling new evidence that fatherhood and marriage are indispensable for the good of children and society.* New York: The Free Press.

Popper, K. R. (1959). *The logic of scientific discovery.* London: Hutchinson.

Popper, K. R. (1962). *Conjectures and refutations.* New York: Basic Books.

Potts, R. (1988). *Early hominid activities of human behavior.* New York: Aldine de Gruyter.

Price-Bonham, S., & Skeen, P. A. (1979). A comparison of black and white fathers with implications for parent education. *The Family Coordinator 289*, 53–59.

Pruett, K. D. (1987). *The nurturing father.* New York: Warner Books.

Radin, N. (1988). Primary caregiving fathers of long duration. In P. Bronstein & C. P. Cowan, (Eds.), *Fatherhood today: Men's changing role in the family* (pp. 127–141), New York: John Wiley.

Radin, N., & Goldsmith, R. (1985). Caregiving fathers of preschoolers: four years later. *Merrill-Palmer Quarterly 31*, 375–383.

Radin, N., & Harold-Goldsmith, R. (1989). The involvement of selected unemployed and employed men with their children. *Child Development 60*, 454–459.

Radloff, L. (1975). Sex difference in depression: The effects of occupation and marital status. *Sex Roles 1:* 249–265.

Rankin, R. P., & Maneker, J. S. (1985). The duration of marriage in a divorcing population: The impact of children. *The Journal of Marriage and the Family 47*, 43–52.

Rapoport, R., Rapoport, R. N., Strelitz, Z., & Kew, S. (1977). *Fathers, mothers, and society* New York: Basic Books.

Rasa, O.A.E. (1986). Parental care in carnivores. In W. Sluckin & M. Herbert (Eds.), *Parental Behavior* (pp. 117–151). Oxford, UK: Basil Blackwell Ltd.

Rebelsky, F., & Hanks, C. (1972). Fathers' verbal interactions with infants in the first three months of life. *Child Development 42*, 63.

Redican, W. K. (1976). Adult male-infant interactions in nonhuman primates. In M. E. Lamb (Ed.), *The role of the father in child development* (pp. 345–386). New York: Wiley.

Renne, K. S. (1976). Childlessness, health, and marital satisfaction. *Social Biology 23*, 183–197.

Richards, C. E. (1977). *People in perspective: An introduction to cultural anthropology* (2nd. ed.). New York: Random House.

Ridley, M. (1993). *The red queen: Sex and the evolution of human nature.* New York: Macmillan.

Risman, B. J. (1986). Can men "mother"? Life as a single father. *Family relations 35*, 95–102.

Ritner, G. (1992). *Fathers' liberation ethics: A holistic ethical advocacy for active nurturant fathering* New York: University Press of America.

Robins, L. N., & Hill, S. Y. (1966). Assessing the contributions of family structure, class, and peer groups to juvenile delinquency. *Journal of Criminal law, Criminology, and Police Science 57*, 325–334.

Rogers, J. R. (1990). Female suicide: The trend toward increased lethality in method of choice and its implications. *Journal of Counseling & Development 69*, 37–38.

Rohner, R. P. (1975). *They love me, they love me not* New Haven, CT: HRAF Press.

Rohner, R. P., & Rohner, E. C. (1982). Enculturative continuity and the importance of caretakers: Cross-cultural codes. *Behavior Science Research 17*, 91–114.

Rohner, R. P., Naroll, R., Barry, H., Divale, W. T., Erickson, E. E., Schaefer, J. M., & Sipes, R. G. (1978). Guidelines to holocultural research. *Cultural Anthropology 19*, 128–129.

Roopnarine, J. L., Talukder, E., Jain, D., Joshi, P., & Srivastav, P. (1992). Personal wellbeing, kinship tie, and mother-infant and father-infant interactions in single-wage and dual-wage families in New Delhi, India. *Journal of Marriage and the Family 54*, 293–301.

Rosenblatt, P. C., Peterson, P., Portner, H., Cleveland, M., Mykkanen, A., Foster, R., Holm, G., Joel, B., Reisch, H., Kreuscher, C., & Phillips, R. (1973). A cross-cultural study of responses to childlessness. *Behavior Science Notes 3*, 221–231.

Rosenthal, N. E. (1993). Diagnosis and treatment of seasonal affective disorder. *JAMA 270*, 2717–2719.

Rosenthal, R., & Jacobson, L. (1968). *Pygmalion in the Classroom: Teacher expectation and pupils' intellectual development* New York: Holt, Rinehart & Winston.

Rosnow, R. L. (1974). When he lends a helping hand, bite it. In J. B. Maas (Ed.), *Readings in psychology* (3rd ed.) (pp. 22–24). Del Mar, CA: CRM Books.

Ross, E. B., & Harris, M. (1987). *Death, Sex, and Fertility: Population regulation in Preindustrial and developing societies* New York: Columbia University Press.

Rossi, A. S. (1977). A biosocial perspective on parenting. *Daedalus 106*, 1–31.

Rothman, B. K. (1989). *Recreating motherhood: Ideology and technology in a patriarchal society* New York: Norton.

Rowe, D. C. (1994). *The limits of family influence: Genes, experience, and behavior* New York: Guilford Press.

Rubin, L. B. (1976). *Worlds of pain: Life in the working class.* New York: Basic Books.

Rubin, Z. (1974). Jokers wild in the lab. In J. B. Maas (Ed.), *Readings in psychology* (3rd. ed.) (pp. 25–27). Del Mar, CA: CRM Books.

Rudnai, J. A. (1973). *The social life of the lion* Wallingford, PA: Washington Square.

Rushton, J. P. (1985). Differential K theory: The sociobiology of individual and group differences. *Personality and Individual Differences 6*, 441–452.

Rushton, J. P. (1995). *Race, evolution, and behavior: A life history perspective* New Brunswick, NY: Transaction.

Russell, D.E.H. (1986). *The secret trauma: Incest in the lives of girls and women.* New York: Basic Books.

Russell, G. (1983). *Are fathers really changing?* New York: Queensland Press.

Ryden, H. (1974). The lone coyote likes family life. *National Geographic 146*, 279–292.

Sack, S. M. (1987). *The complete legal guide to marriage, divorce, custody and living together* New York: McGraw-Hill.

Santrock, J. W. (1995). *Life span development* (5th ed.). Madison, Wisconsin: Brown & Benchmark.

Scarr, S., & McCartney, K. (1983). How people make their own environments: A theory of genotype → environment effects. *Child Development 54*, 424–435.

Schaffer, H. R., & Emerson, P. (1964). The development of social attachments in infancy. *Monographs of the society for research in child development 29*, #3.

Schaller, G. B. (1972). *The Serengeti lion* Chicago: University of Chicago Press.

Schaller, G. B., & Lowther, G. R. (1969). The relevance of carnivore behavior to the study of early hominids. *Southwestern Journal of Anthropology 25*, 307–336.

Scherer, K. R., & Wallbott, H. G. (1994). Evidence for universality and cultural variation of differential emotion response patterning. *Journal of Personality & Social Psychology 66*, 310–328.

Schlegel, A. (1972). *Male dominance and female autonomy* New Haven, CT: HRAF Press.

Schultz, K. F., Murphy, F. K., Patamasucon, P., & Meheus, A. Z. (1990). Congenital syphilis. In K. K. Holmes, P. Mardh, P. F. Sparling, & P. J. Wiesner (Eds.), *Sexually Transmitted Diseases* (pp. 821–842). New York: McGraw-Hill.

Sears, W. (1991). *Keys to becoming a father* New York: Barrons.

Seccombe, K., & Lee, G. R. (1986). Female status, wives' autonomy, and divorce: A cross-cultural study. *Family Perspective 20*, 241–250.

Seemanova, E. (1971). A study of children of incestuous matings. *Human Heredity 21*, 108–128.

Seligman, M.E.P., & Hager, J. L. (1972). *Biological boundaries of learning* (pp. 1–6). New York: Appleton-Century Crofts.

Seltzer, J. A. (1991). Relationships between fathers and children who live apart: The father's role after separation. *Journal of Marriage and the Family 53*, 79–101.

Seva, A., & Fernandez-Doctor, A. (1995). Culture and mental illness in the Iberian Peninsula. In I. Al.-lssa (Ed.), *Handbook of culture and mental illness: An international perspective* (pp. 281–290). Madison, CT: International Universities Press, Inc.

Sexton, P. (1969). *The feminized male* New York: Random House.

Sexton, P. (1970). How the American boy is feminized. *Psychology Today 3*, 23–29.

Sexton, P. (1973). Personal communication.

Shakespeare, W. (1936). *Macbeth.* In G. L. Kittredge (Ed.), *Complete Works of William Shakespeare* New York: Grolier.

Shakespeare, W. (1936). *Romeo and Juliet.* In G. L. Kittredge (Ed.), *Complete Works of William Shakespeare* New York: Grolier.

Shapiro, J. L. (1987, January). The expectant father. *Psychology Today* 36–42.

Shelton, B. A. (1992). *Women, men, and time: Gender differences in paid work, housework, and leisure* New York: Greenwood Press.

Shipman, P. (1986). Scavenging or hunting in early hominids. *American Anthropologist 88,* 27–43.

Sigelmann, C. K., & Adams, R. M. (1990). Family interactions in public: Parent-child distance and touching. *Journal of Nonverbal Behavior 14,* 63–75.

Sitarz, D. (1990). *Divorce yourself: The national no-fault no-lawyer divorce handbook.* Carbondale, IL: Nova.

Skinner, B. F. (1938). *The behavior of organisms.* New York: Appleton.

Skinner, B. F. (1953). *Science of human behavior* New York: Macmillan.

Skinner, B. F. (1971). *Beyond freedom and dignity* New York: Knopf.

Small, M. F. (Ed.). (1984). *Female Primates* New York: Alan R. Liss.

Smith, H. L., & Morgan, S. P. (1994). Children's closeness to father as reported by mothers, sons and daughters: Evaluating subjective assessments with the Rasch model. *Journal of Family Issues 15,* 3–29.

Smith-Morris, M. (Ed.). (1990). *The economist book of vital world statistics* New York: Times Bks.

Smuts, B. (1995). The evolutionary origins of patriarchy. *Human Nature 6,* 1–32.

Smuts, B. B., Cheney, D. L., Seyfarth, R. M., Wrangham, R. W., & Struhsaker, T. T. (Eds.). (1986). *Primate Societies.* Chicago: University of Chicago Press.

Smuts, B. B., & Guberhick, D. J. (1992). Male-infant relationships in nonhuman primates: Paternal investment or mating effort? In B. S. Hewlett (Ed.), *Father-child relations: Cultural and biosocial contexts* (pp. 1–30). New York: Aldine de Gruyter.

Snyder, M., Tanke, E. D., & Bersheid, E. (1995). Social perception and interpersonal behavior: On the self-fulfilling nature of social stereotypes. In E. Aronson (Ed.), *Readings about the social animal* (pp. 486–500) (7th ed.) New York: H. W. Freeman & Co.

Somervell, P. D., Manson, S. M., & Shore, J. H. (1995). Mental illness among American Indians and Alaska natives. In I. Al-lssa (Ed.) *Handbook of culture and mental illness: An international perspective* (pp. 315–330). Madison, CT: International Universities Press, Inc.

Sorenson, S. B., Rutter, C. M., & Aneshensel, C. S. (1991). Depression in the community: An investigation into age of onset. *Journal of Consulting and Clinical Psychology 59,* 541–546.

Spanier, G. B., & Casto, R. F. (1979). Adjustment to separation and divorce: An analysis of 50 case studies. *Journal of Divorce 2,* 241–253.

Spelke, E. P., Zelazo, J., Kagan, & Kotelchuck, M. (1973). Father interaction and separation protect. *Developmental Psychology 9,* 83–90.

Spitz, R. A. (1968). *First year of life.* New York: International Universities Press.

Stearman, A. M. (1989). *Yuqui: Forest nomads in a changing world* New York: Holt, Rinehart, & Winston.

Stein, J. A., Golding, J. M., Siegel, J. M., Burnam, M. A., & Sorenson, S. B. (1988). Long-term psychological sequelae of child sexual abuse: The Los Angeles epidemiologic catchment area study. In G. E. Wyatt and G. J. Powell (Eds.), *Lasting effects of child sexual abuse* (pp. 135–148). Beverly Hills, CA: Sage.

Stephens, W. N. (1963). *The family in cross-cultural perspective* New York: Holt, Rinehart & Winston.

Stevenson, M. R., & Black, K. N. (1988). Paternal absence and sex-role development: A meta analysis. *Child Development 59,* 793–814.

Stewart, F. H. (1977). *Fundamentals of age-group systems* New York: Academic Press.

Stewart, R. B., Jr. (1990). *The second child: family transitions and adjustments.* Newbury Park, CA: Sage.

Stolberg, S. (1994). Scientific studies are generating controversy. *Austin American-Statesman.* 1/16, E1.

Stoneman, Z., & Brody, G. H. (1981). Two's company, three makes a differences: an examination of mother's and father's speech to their young children. *Child Development 52,* 705–707.

Streiker, L. D. (1989). *Fathering: Old game, new rules: A look at the changing roles of fathers* Nashville, TN: Abingdon Press.

Suiter, J. J. (1991). Marital quality and satisfaction with the division of household labor across the family life cycle. *Journal of Marriage and the Family 53,* 221–230.

Symons, D. (1979). *The evolution of human sexuality* New York: Oxford University Press.

Szasz, T. S. (1961). *The myth of mental illness* New York: Dell.

Tannen, D. (1990). *You just don't understand* New York: Ballantine.

Tasch, R. J. (1952). The role of the father in the family. *Journal of Experimental Education 20,* 319–361.

Taub, D. M. (1984). *Primate paternalism* New York: Van Nostrand Reinhold.

Teleki, G. (1973). The omnivorous chimpanzee. *Scientific American 228,* 33–42.

Thompson, P. R. (1978). The evolution of territoriality and society of top carnivores. *Social Science Information 17,* 949–992.

Thomson, E. (1983). Individual and couple utility of children. *Demography 20,* 507–518.

Tiger, L., & Fox, R. (1971). *The Imperial Animal* New York: Delta.

Tinbergen, N. (1951). *The Study of Instinct* Oxford: Clarendon Press.

Tronick, E. G., Morilli, A., & Winn, S. (1987). Multiple caretaking of Efe (Pygmy) infants. *American Anthropologist 89,* 96–106.

Tuncer, C. (1995). Mental illness in an Islamic-Mediterranean culture: Turkey. In I. Al-Issa (Ed.), *Handbook of culture and mental illness: An international perspective* (pp. 169–184). Madison, CT: International Universities Press, Inc.

Turnbull, C. (1972). *The Mountain People.* New York: Simon & Schuster.

Turner, V. (1969). *The ritual process* Chicago: Aldine.

Tyler, A. H. (1986). The abusing father. In M. E. Lamb (Ed.), *The father's role: applied perspectives* (pp. 256–275). New York: Wiley.

United Nations (1985–1992). *United Nations: Demographic Yearbook* New York: Times Books.

United Nations (1973). *Demographic yearbook* New York: Author.

United Nations (1982). *Demographic yearbook* New York: Author.

United Nations (1992). *Demographic yearbook* New York: Author.

United Nations (1993). *Demographic yearbook* New York: Author.

U.S. Bureau of the Census (1975). *Historical Statistics of the United States: Colonial Times to 1970 Part I* Washington, DC: US Government Printing Office.

U.S. Bureau of the Census (1976). *Statistical abstract of the United States: 1977.* (97th ed.). Washington, DC: US Government Printing Office.

U.S. Bureau of the Census (1987). *Statistical abstract of the United States: 1988* (108th edition). Washington, DC: US Government Printing Office.

U.S. Bureau of the Census (1989). *Statistical abstract of the United States: 1990* (110th edition). Washington DC: US Government Printing Office.

U.S. Bureau of the Census (1990). *Statistical abstract of the United States: 1991* (111th ed.). Washington, DC: U.S. Government Printing Office.

U.S. Bureau of the Census (1992). *Statistical abstract of the United States: 1993* (113th ed.). Washington, DC: US Government Printing Office.

U.S. Bureau of the Census (1993). *Statistical abstract of the United States: 1994* (114th ed.) Washington, DC: US Government Printing Office.

U.S. Bureau of the Census (1994). *Statistical abstract of the United States: 1995* (115th ed.). Washington, DC: US Government Printing Office.

U.S. Department of Justice (1993). *Uniform Crime Reports* Washington, DC: US Government Printing Office.

Van den Berghe, P. L. (1979). *Human family systems* New York: Elsevier.

Varma, V. K., & Chakrabarti, S. (1995). Social correlates and cultural dynamics of mental illness in traditional society: India. In I. Al-Issa (Ed.), *Handbook of culture and mental illness: An international perspective* (pp. 115–128). Madison, CT: International Universities Press, Inc.

Waco Tribune Herald (The) (1994). "Jesse's right, wrong". 1/16, p. 14A.

Waddington, C. H. (1975). *The evolution of an evolutionist* Ithaca, NY: Cornell University Press.

Waite, L. J., Haggstrom, G. W., & Kanouse, D. E. (1985). The consequences of parenthood for the marital stability of young adults. *American Sociological Review 50,* 850–857.

Wallace, P., & Gotlib, I. (1990). Marital adjustment during the transition to parenthood: stability and predictors of change. *Journal of Marriage and the Family 52,* 21–29.

Wallerstein, J. S., & Blakeslee, S. (1989). *Second chances: Men, women & children: A decade after divorce who wins, who loses* New York: Ticknor & Fields.

Wallerstein, J. S., & Kelly, J. B. (1980). *Surviving the breakup: How children and parents cope with divorce* New York: Basic Bks.

Washburn, S. L., & Devore, I. (1961). Social behavior of baboons and early man. In S. L. Washburn (Ed.), *Social life of early man* Chicago: Aldine Pub. Co.

Wattenberg, B. J. (1987). *The birth dearth* New York: Pharos Bks.

Wedenoja, W. (1995). Social and cultural psychiatry of Jamaicans, at home and abroad. In I. Al-Issa (Ed.), *Handbook of culture and mental illness: An international perspective* (pp. 215–230). Madison CT: International Universities Press, Inc.

Weinberg, S. K. (1955). *Incest Behavior* New York: Citadel.

Weisner, T. S., & Gallimore, R. (1977). My brother's keeper: Child and sibling caretaking. *Current Anthropology 18,* 169–190.

Weissman, M.M.R., Bland, G., Canino, C., Faravelli, S., Greenwald, H. G., Hwu, P. R., Joyce, E. G., Karam, C. K., Lee, J., Lellouch, J. P., Lepine, S., Newman, M., Rubio-Stipec, J. E., Wells, P., Wickramaratne, H. U., Wittchen, E. K., & Yeh. (1994). *World Psychiatric Association Teaching Bulletin on Depression 2,* 1–3.

Weissman, M. M., & Klerman, G. L. (1995). Depression's double standard: Clues emerge as to why women have higher rates of depression. *Scientific American 272,* 23.

Weitzman, L. J. (1985).*The divorce revolution: The unexpected social and economic consequences for women and children in America* New York: The Free Press.

Westrom, L. (1991). Pelvic inflammatory disease. *Journal of the American Medical Association 266,* 2612.

Westrom, L., & Mardh, P. (1990). Acute pelvic inflammatory disease (PID) in sexually transmitted disease. In K. K. Holmes, P. Mardh, P. F. Sparling, & P. J. Wiesner *Sexually Transmitted Diseases* (pp. 593–614). New York: McGraw-Hill.

Westrom, L., Riduan, J., Reynolds, G., Alula, H., & Thompson, S. E. (1992). Pelvic inflammatory disease and fertility. *Sexually Transmitted Disease 19,* 185–192.

White, D., Burton, M. L., & Brudner, L. A. (1977). Entailment theory and method: A cross-cultural analysis of the sexual division of labor. *Behavior Science Research 12,* 1–24.

White, D. R., Burton, M. L., & Dow, M. M. (1981). Sexual division of labor in African agriculture: A network autocorrelation analysis. *American Anthropologist 83*, 824-847.

White, L. K., & Kim, H. (1987). The family-building process: child-bearing choices by parity. *Journal of Marriage and the Family 49*, 271–280.

White, S. W., & Bloom, B. L. (1981). Factors related to the adjustment of divorcing men. *Family Relations 30*, 349–360.

Whitehead, B. D. (1993, April). Dan Quayle was right. *Atlantic Monthly* (pp. 55–60).

Whiting, J.W.M. (1964). Effects of climate on certain cultural practices. In W. H. Goodenough (Ed.), *Explorations in cultural anthropology* (pp. 511–514). New York: McGraw-Hill.

Whiting, B. B., & Whiting, J.W.M. (1975). *Children of six cultures: A psycho-cultural analysis* Cambridge, MA: Harvard University Press.

Whyte, M. K. (1978). Cross-cultural codes dealing with the relative status of women. *Ethnology 12*, 211–237.

Williams, E., & Radin, N. (1993). Paternal involvement, maternal employment and adolescents' academic achievement: an 11 year follow-up. *American Journal of Orthopsychiatry 63*, 306–312.

Willner, D. (1975). *Sexual appropriation and social space.* Paper presented at the 74th annual meeting of the American Anthropological Association.

Wilson, J. Q., & Herrnstein, R. (1985). *Crime and human nature* New York: Simon & Schuster.

Winnicott, D. W. (1965). *The maturational process and the facilitating environment.* New York: International Universities Press.

Yarrow, L. (1982, May). How to get your husband to help. *Parents* 55–59.

Yogman, M. W. (1982). Development of the father-infant relationship *Theory and Research in Behavioral Pediatrics 1*, 221–279.

Young, S. P., & Jackson, H. T. (1951). *The clever coyote* (pp. 82–88). Washington, DC: Wildlife Management Institute.

Zelizer, V. A. (1985). *Pricing the Priceless child: The changing social value of children* New York: Basic Books.

Zihlman, A., & Tanner, N. (1978). Gathering and the hominid adaptation. In L. Tiger & H. T. Fowler (Eds.), *Female hierarchies* (pp. 163–194). Chicago: Beresford Book Service.

Author Index

Subject Index